Antæus

EDITED BY

DANIEL HALPERN

NO. 71/72, AUTUMN, 1993

Special co-editor for
Antæus 71/72
JEANNE WILMOT CARTER

Founding Editor
PAUL BOWLES

Founding Publisher
DRUE HEINZ

Associate Publisher
JEANNE WILMOT CARTER

Publicity & Marketing Manager
WILLIAM CRAGER

Production Manager
VINCENT JANOSKI

Business Manager
ELAINA KOCHIS

Administrative Assistant
DONNA LAWDER

Assistant Editor
TOM THOMPSON

Editorial Assistants
KAREN GAFFNEY
ERICA SMITH

Special thanks to William Bratton, Brian Cullman, Rachel Felder, and Quincy Troupe
for their help in preparing this issue of ANTÆUS.

Contributing Editors
ANDREAS BROWN   JOHN HAWKES
JOHN FOWLES   STANLEY KUNITZ
DONALD HALL   W.S. MERWIN
MARK STRAND

ANTÆUS *is published semiannually by The Ecco Press, 100 West Broad Street, Hopewell, NJ 08525.*
Distributed by W. W. Norton & Company, Inc., 500 Fifth Avenue, New York, NY 10110, Ingram
Periodicals, 347 Reedwood Drive, Nashville, TN 37217, and B. DeBoer, Inc., 113 East Centre St.,
Nutley, NJ 07110. Distributed in England & Europe by W. W. Norton & Company, Inc.

Contributions and Communications: ANTÆUS
100 West Broad Street, Hopewell, NJ 08525.
Back issues available—write for a complete listing.

ISSN 0003-5319
Printed by Quinn-Woodbine, Inc.
ISBN 0-88001-326-5
Library of Congress Card Number: 70-612646
Copyright © 1993 by ANTÆUS, *Hopewell, NJ*
Cover art: Tina Turner. Illustrated by Guy Peellaert. Copyright by Guy Peellaert.
Publication of this magazine has been made possible in part by a grant
from the National Endowment for the Arts.
Logo: Ahmed Yacoubi

The reason people make lyric poems and blues songs is because our life is short, sweet and fleeting.

—CHARLES SIMIC

Many people think that the world should speak the same language . . . But I don't agree. If that was the way the earth was two hundred years ago, we would have no jazz. We would have no folk music to listen to from anywhere else. We would have only one thing, it would be like New Age music forever.

—KEITH JARRETT

Myth and music [are] languages which, in their different ways, transcend articulate expression, while at the same time—like articulate speech, but unlike painting—requiring a temporal dimension in which to unfold. But this relation to time is of a rather special nature: it is as if music and mythology needed time only in order to deny it. Both, indeed, are instruments for the obliteration of time. Below the level of sounds and rhythms, music acts upon a primitive terrain, which is the physiological time of the listener; this time is irreversible and therefore irredeemably diachronic, yet music transmutes the segment devoted to listening to it into a synchronic totality, enclosed with itself. Because of the internal organization of the musical work, the act of listening to it immobilizes passing time; it catches and enfolds it as one catches and enfolds a cloth flapping in the wind. It follows that by listening to music, and while we are listening to it, we enter into a kind of immortality.

—CLAUDE LEVI-STRAUSS

It's an education that unless you are a part of it, no one can understand. You see, this is something you just don't write down in books and learn to manipulate from technical angles or anything. It's inspiration.

—JIMMY SCOTT

Music heard so deeply
That it is not heard at all, but you are the music
While the music lasts.

—T.S. ELIOT

All art aspires towards the condition of music.

—WALTER PATER

CONTENTS

I

II

III

IV

V

DOC POMUS: A SPECIAL FEATURE

VI

VII

I

ARISTOTLE

Theory of Music

Concerning music there are some questions which we have already raised; these we may now resume and carry further; and our remarks will serve as a prelude to this or any other discussion of the subject. It is not easy to determine the nature of music, or why any one should have a knowledge of it. Shall we say, for the sake of amusement and relaxation, like sleep or drinking, which are not good in themselves, but are pleasant, and at the same time "make care to cease," as Euripides says? And for this end men also appoint music, and make use of all three alike—sleep, drinking, music—to which some add dancing. Or shall we argue that music conduces to virtue, on the ground that it can form our minds and habituate us to true pleasures as our bodies are made by gymnastic to be of a certain character? Or shall we say that it contributes to the enjoyment of leisure and mental cultivation, which is a third alternative? Now obviously youths are not to be instructed with a view to their amusement, for learning is no amusement, but is accompanied with pain. Neither is intellectual enjoyment suitable to boys of that age, for it is the end, and that which is imperfect cannot attain the perfect or end. But perhaps it may be said that boys learn music for the sake of the amusement which they will have when they are grown up. If so, why should they learn themselves, and not, like the Persian and Median kings, enjoy the pleasure and instruction which is derived from hearing others? (for surely persons who have made music the business and profession of their lives will be better performers than those who practice only long enough to learn). If they must learn music, on the same principle they should learn cookery, which is absurd. And even granting that music may form the character, the objection still holds: why should we learn ourselves? Why cannot we attain true pleasure and form a correct judgment from hearing others, like the Lacedaemonians?—for they, without learning music, nevertheless can correctly judge, as they say, of good and bad melodies. Or again, if music should be used to promote cheerfulness and refined intellectual enjoyment, the objection still remains—why should we learn ourselves instead of enjoying the performances of others? We may illustrate what we are saying by our conception of the Gods; for in the poets Zeus does not himself sing or play on the lyre. Nay, we call professional performers vulgar; no freeman would play or sing unless he were intoxicated or in jest. But these matters may be left for the present.

The first question is whether music is or is not to be a part of education. Of the three things mentioned in our discussion, which does it produce?—education or amusement or intellectual enjoyment, for it may be reckoned under all three, and seems to share in the nature of all of them. Amusement is for the sake of relaxation, and relaxation is of necessity sweet, for it is the remedy of pain caused by toil: and intellectual enjoyment is universally acknowledged to contain an element not only of the noble but of the pleasant, for happiness is made up of both. All men agree that music is one of the pleasantest things, whether with or without song; as Musaeus says,

"Song is to mortals of all things the sweetest."

Hence and with good reason it is introduced into social gatherings and entertainments, because it makes the hearts of men glad: so that on this ground alone we may assume that the young ought to be trained in it. For innocent pleasures are not only in harmony with the perfect end of life, but they also provide relaxation. And whereas men rarely attain the end, but often rest by the way and amuse themselves, not only with a view to a further end, but also for the pleasure's sake, it may be well at times to let them find a refreshment in music. It sometimes happens that men make amusement the end, for the end probably contains some element of pleasure, though not any ordinary or lower pleasure; but they mistake the lower for the higher, and in seeking for the one find the other, since every pleasure has a likeness to the end of action. For the end is not eligible for the sake of any future good, nor do the pleasures which we have described exist for the sake of any future good but of the past, that is to say, they are the alleviation of past toils and pains. And we may infer this to be the reason why men seek happiness from these pleasures.

But music is pursued, not only as an alleviation of past toil, but also as providing recreation. And who can say whether, having this use, it may not also have a nobler one? In addition to this common pleasure, felt and shared in by all (for the pleasure given by music is natural, and therefore adapted to all ages and characters), may it not have also some influence over the character and the soul? It must have such an influence if characters are affected by it. And that they are so affected is proved in many ways, and not least by the power which the songs of Olympus exercise; for beyond question they inspire enthusiasm, and enthusiasm is an emotion of the ethical part of the soul. Besides, when men hear imitations, even apart from the rhythms and tunes themselves, their feelings move in sympathy. Since then music is a pleasure, and virtue consists in rejoicing and loving and hating aright, there is clearly nothing which we are so much concerned to acquire and to cultivate as the power of forming right judgments, and of taking delight in good dispositions and noble actions. Rhythm and melody supply imitations of anger and gentleness, and also of courage and temperance, and of all the qualities contrary to these and of the other qualities of character, which hardly fall short of the actual affections, as we know from our own experience, for in listening to such strains our souls undergo a change. The habit of feeling pleasure or pain at mere representations is not far removed from the same feeling about realities; for example, if any one delights in the sight of a statue for its beauty only, it necessarily follows that the sight of the original will be pleasant to him. The objects of no other sense, such as taste or touch, have any resemblance to moral qualities; in visible objects there is only a little, for there are figures which are of a moral character, but only to a slight extent, and all do not participate in the feeling about them. Again, figures and colors are not imitations, but signs, of moral habits, indications which the body gives of states of feeling. The connection of them with morals is slight, but in so far as there is any, young men should be taught to look, not at the works of Pauson, but at those of Polygnotus, or any other painter or sculptor who expresses moral ideas. On the other hand, even in mere melodies there is an imitation of character, for the musical modes differ essentially from one another, and those who hear them are differently affected by each. Some of them make men sad and grave, like the so-called Mixolydian, others enfeeble the mind, like the relaxed modes, another, again, produces a moderate and settled temper, which appears to be the peculiar effect of the Dorian; the Phrygian inspires enthusiasm. The whole subject has been well treated by philosophical writers on this branch of education, and they confirm their arguments by facts. The same principles apply to rhythms; some have a character of rest, others of motion, and of these latter again, some have a more vulgar, others a nobler movement. Enough has been said to show that music has a power of forming the character, and should therefore be introduced into the education of the young. The study is suited to the stage of youth, for young persons will not, if they can help, endure anything which is not sweetened by pleasure, and music has a natural sweetness. There seems to be in us a sort of affinity to musical modes and rhythms, which makes some philosophers say that the soul is a tuning, others, that it possesses tuning.

And now we have to determine the question which has been already raised, whether children should be themselves taught to sing and play or not. Clearly there is a considerable difference made in the character by the actual practice of the art. It is difficult, if not impossible, for those who do not perform to be good judges of the performance of others. Besides, children should have something to do, and the rattle of Archytas, which people give to their children in order to amuse them and prevent them from breaking anything in the house, was a capital invention, for a young thing cannot be quiet. The rattle is a toy suited to the infant mind, and education is a rattle or toy for children of a larger growth. We conclude then that they should be taught music in such a way as to become not only critics but performers.

The question what is or is not suitable for different ages may be easily answered; nor is there any difficulty in meeting the objection of those who say that the study of music is vulgar. We reply (1) in the first place, that they who are to be judges must also be performers, and that they should begin to practice early, although when they are older they may be spared the execution; they must have learned to appreciate what is good and to delight in it, thanks to the knowledge which they acquired in their youth. As to (2) the vulgarizing effect which music is supposed to exercise, this is a question which we shall have no difficulty in determining, when we have considered to what extent freemen who are being trained to political virtue should pursue the art, what melodies and what rhythms they should be allowed to use, and what instruments should be employed in teaching them to play; for even the instrument makes a difference. The answer to the objection turns upon these distinctions; for it is quite possible that certain methods of teaching and learning music do really have a degrading effect. It is evident then that the learning of music ought not to impede the business of riper years, or to degrade the body or render it unfit for civil or military training, whether for bodily exercises at the time or for later studies.

The right measure will be attained if students of music stop short of the arts which are practiced in professional contests, and do not seek to acquire those fantastic marvels of execution which are now the fashion in such contests, and from these have passed into education. Let the young practice even such music as we have prescribed, only until they are able to feel delight in noble melodies and rhythms, and not merely in that common part of music in which every slave or child and even some animals find pleasure.

From these principles we may also infer what instruments should be used. The flute, or any other instrument which requires great skill, as for example the harp, ought not to be admitted into education, but only such as will make intelligent students of music or of the other parts of education. Besides, the flute is not an instrument which is expressive of moral character; it is too exciting. The proper time for using it is when the performance aims not at instruction, but at the relief of the passions. And there is a further objection; the impediment which the flute presents to the use of the voice detracts from its educational value. The ancients therefore were right in forbidding the flute to youths and freemen, although they had once allowed it. For when their wealth gave them a greater inclination to leisure, and they had loftier notions of excellence, being also elated with their success, both before and after the Persian War, with more zeal than discernment they pursued every kind of knowledge, and so they introduced the flute into education. At Lacedaemon there was a choragus who led the chorus with a flute, and at Athens the instrument became so popular that most freemen could play upon it. The popularity is shown by the tablet which Thrasippus dedicated when he furnished the chorus to Ecphantides. Later experience enabled men to judge what was or was not really conducive to virtue, and they rejected both the flute and several other old-fashioned instruments, such as the Lydian harp, the many-stringed lyre, the "heptagon," "triangle," "sambuca," and the like—which are intended only to give pleasure to the hearer, and require extraordinary skill of hand. There is a meaning also in the myth of the ancients, which tells how Athene invented the flute and then threw it away. It was not a bad idea of theirs, that the Goddess disliked the instrument because it made the face ugly; but with still more reason may we say that she rejected it because the acquirement of flute-playing contributes nothing to the mind, since to Athene we ascribe both knowledge and art.

Thus then we reject the professional instruments and also the professional mode of education in music (and by professional we mean that which is adopted in contests), for in this the performer practices the art, not for the sake of his own improvement, but in order to give pleasure, and that of a vulgar sort, to his hearers. For this reason the execution of such music is not the part of a freeman but of a paid performer, and the result is that the performers are vulgarized, for the end at which they aim is bad. The vulgarity of the spectator tends to lower the character of the music and therefore of the performers; they look to him—he makes them what they are, and fashions even their bodies by the movements which he expects them to exhibit.

We have also to consider rhythms and modes, and their use in education. Shall we use them all or make a distinction? and shall the same distinction be made for those who practice music with a view to education, or shall it be some other? Now we see that music is produced by melody and rhythm, and we ought to know what influence these have respectively on education, and whether we should prefer excellence in melody or excellence in rhythm. But as the subject has been very well treated by many musicians of the present day, and also by philosophers who have had considerable experience of musical education, to these we would refer the more exact student of the subject; we shall only speak of it now after the manner of the legislator, stating the general principles.

We accept the division of melodies proposed by certain philosophers into ethical melodies, melodies of action, and passionate or inspiring melodies, each having, as they say, a mode corresponding to it. But we maintain further that music should be studied, not for the sake of one, but of many benefits, that is to say, with a view to (1) education, (2) purgation (the word "purgation" we use at present without explanation, but when hereafter we speak of poetry, we will treat the subject with more precision); music may also serve (3) for intellectual enjoyment, for relaxation and for recreation after exertion. It is clear, therefore, that all the modes must be employed by us, but not all of them in the same manner. In education the most ethical modes are to be preferred, but in listening to the performances of others we may admit the modes of action and passion also. For feelings such as pity and fear, or, again, enthusiasm, exist very strongly in some souls, and have more or less influence over all. Some persons fall into a religious frenzy, whom we see as a result of the sacred melodies—when they have used the melodies that excite the soul to mystic frenzy—restored as though they had found healing and purgation. Those who are influenced by pity or fear, and every emotional nature, must have a like experience, and others in so far as each is susceptible to such emotions, and all are in a manner purged and their souls lightened and delighted. The purgative melodies likewise give an innocent pleasure to mankind. Such are the modes and the melodies in which those who perform music at the theater should be invited to compete. But since the spectators are of two kinds—the one free and educated, and the other a vulgar crowd composed of mechanics, laborers, and the like—there ought to be contests and exhibitions instituted for the relaxation of the second class also. And the music will correspond to their minds; for as their minds are perverted from the natural state, so there are perverted modes and highly strung and unnaturally colored melodies. A man receives pleasure from what is natural to him, and therefore professional musicians may be allowed to practice this lower sort of music before an audience of a lower type. But, for the purposes of education, as I have already said, those modes and melodies should be employed which are ethical, such as the Dorian, as we said before; though we may include any others which are approved by philosophers who have had a musical education. The Socrates of the *Republic* is wrong in retaining only the Phrygian mode along with the Dorian, and the more so because he rejects the flute; for the Phrygian is to the modes what the flute is to musical instruments—both of them are exciting and emotional. Poetry proves this, for Bacchic frenzy and all similar emotions are more suitably expressed by the flute, and are better set to the Phrygian than to any other mode. The dithyramb, for example, is acknowledged to be Phrygian, a fact of which the connoisseurs of music offer many proofs, saying, among other things, that Philoxenus, having attempted to compose his *Mysians* as a dithyramb in the Dorian mode, found it impossible, and fell back by the very nature of things into the more appropriate Phrygian. All men agree that the Dorian music is the gravest and manliest. And whereas we say that the extremes should be avoided and the mean followed, and whereas the Dorian is a mean between the other modes, it is evident that our youth should be taught the Dorian music.

WILLIAM H. GASS

The Music of Prose

To speak of the music of prose is to speak in metaphor. It is to speak in metaphor because prose cannot make any actual music. The music of prose has the most modest of inscriptions. Its notes, if we could imagine sounding them, do not have any preassigned place in an aural system. Hence they do not automatically find themselves pinned to the lines of a staff, or confined in a sequence of pitches. Nor is prose's music made of sounds set aside and protected from ordinary use as ancient kings conserved the virginity of their daughters. In the first place, prose often has difficulty in getting itself pronounced at all. In addition, any tongue can try out any line; any accent is apparently okay; any intonation is allowed; almost any pace is put up with. For prose, there are no violins fashioned with love and care and played by persons devoted to the artful rubbing of their strings. There are no tubes to transform the breath more magically than the loon can by calling out across a lake. The producers of prose do not play scales or improve their skills by repeating passages of De Quincey or Sir Thomas Browne, although that might be a good idea. They do not work at *Miss iss ip pi* until they get it right. The sound of a word may be arbitrary and irrelevant to its meaning, but the associations created by incessant use are strong, so that you cannot make the sound, *m o o n,* without seeming to mean *moon*. By the time the noun has become a verb, its pronunciation will feel perfectly appropriate to the mood one is in when one moons, say, over a girl, and the *moo* in the mooning will add all its features without feeling the least discomfort. In music, however, the notes are allowed to have their own way and fill the listener's attention with themselves and their progress. Nonmusical associations (thinking of money when you hear *do re mi* played) are considered irrelevant and dispensable.

In sum, prose has no notes, no scale, no consistency or purity of sound, and only actors roll its Rs, prolong its vowels, or pop its Ps with any sense of purpose.

Yet no prose can pretend to greatness if its music is not also great; if it does not, indeed, construct a surround of sound to house its meaning the way flesh was once felt to embody the soul, at least till the dismal day of the soul's eviction and the flesh's decay.

For prose has a pace; it is dotted with stops and pauses, frequent rests; inflections rise and fall like a low range of hills; certain tones are prolonged; there are patterns of stress and harmonious measures; there is a proper method of pronunciation, even if it is rarely observed; alliteration will trouble the tongue, consonance ease its sounds out, so that any mouth making that music will feel its performance even to the back of the teeth and to the glottal's stop; mellifluousness is not impossible, and harshness is easy, drum roll and clangor can be confidently called for—lisp, slur, and growl; so there will be a syllabic beat in imitation of the heart, while rhyme will recall a word we passed perhaps too indifferently; vowels will open and consonants close like blooming plants; repetitive schemes will act as refrains, and there will be phrases—little motifs—to return to like the tonic; clauses will be balanced by other clauses the way a waiter carries trays; parallel lines will nevertheless meet in their common subject; clots of concepts will dissolve and then recombine, so we shall find endless variations on the same theme; a central idea, along with its many modifications, like soloist and chorus, will take their turns, until, suddenly, all sing at once the same sound.

Since the music of prose depends upon its performance by a voice, and since, when we read, we have been taught to maintain a library's silence, so that not even the lips are allowed to move, most of the music of the word will be that heard only by the head, and, dampened by decorum, will be timorous and hesitant. That is the hall, though, the hall of the head, where, if at all, prose (and poetry, too, now) is given its little oral due. There we may say, without allowing its noise to go out of doors, a sentence of Robert South's, for instance: "This is the doom of fallen man, to labour in the fire, to seek truth *in profundo,* to exhaust his time and impair his health and perhaps to spin out his days, and himself, into one pitiful, controverted conclusion"; holding it all in the hush of our inner life, where every imagined sound we make is gray and no more material than smoke, and where the syllables are shaped so deeply in our throats nothing but a figment emerges, an *eidolon,* a shadow, the secondhand substance of speech.

Nevertheless, we can still follow the form of South's sentence as we say it to ourselves: "This is the doom of fallen man..." What is?

> ... to labour in the fire
> ... to seek truth *in profundo*

	. . . to exhaust his time
and	. . . [to] impair his health
and perhaps	. . . to spin out his days
and	. . . [to spin out] himself

" . . . into one pitiful, controverted conclusion." That is, we return again and again to the infinitive—"to"—as well as to the pile up of "his" and "him," and if we straighten the prepositions out, all the hidden repeats become evident:

> . . . to labour into one pitiful, controverted conclusion
> . . . to seek truth in one pitiful, controverted conclusion
> . . . to exhaust his time in one pitiful, controverted conclusion
> . . . to impair his health [obtaining] one pitiful, controverted conclusion
> . . . to spin out his days into one pitiful, controverted conclusion
> . . . [to spin out] himself into one pitiful, controverted conclusion

To labour, seek, exhaust, impair, spin out . . . what? Work, truth, time, health, days, himself. Much of this tune, said soto voce in any case, doesn't even get played on any instrument, but lies inside the shadow of the sentence's sound like still another shadow.

So South's prose has a shape which its enunciation allows us to perceive. That shape is an imitation of its sense, for the forepart is like the handle of a ladle, the midsections comprise the losses the ladle pours, and its ending is like a splashdown.

> This is the doom of fallen man, to labour in the fire,
> > to seek truth *in profundo,*
> > to exhaust his time
> > and impair his health,
> > and perhaps to spin out his days,
> > and himself,
> into one pitiful, controverted conclusion.

In short, one wants South to say: "pour out his days . . . *in two one pit eee full, conn trow verr ted conn clue zeeunn . . .*" so as to emphasize the filling of the pit. However, "spin" does anticipate the shroud which will wrap around and signify "the doom of fallen man."

In short, in this case, and in a manner which Handel, his contemporary, would approve, the sound (by revealing the spindle ["to"] around which the sentence turns, and the action which it represents is wound), certainly enhances the sense.

However, South will not disappoint us, for he plays all the right cards, following our sample with this development: "There was then no pouring, no struggling with memory, no straining for invention..." We get "pour" after all, and "straining" in addition. The pit is more than full, it runneth over.

Often a little diction and a lot of form will achieve the decided lilt and accent of a nation or a race. Joyce writes "Irish" throughout *Finnegans Wake,* and Flann O'Brien's musical arrangements also dance a jig. Here Mr. Shanahan is extolling the virtues of his favorite poet, that man of the pick and people, Jem Casey:

> Yes, I've seen his pomes and read them and...do you know what I'm going to tell you, I have loved them. I'm not ashamed to sit here and say it, Mr. Furriskey. I've known the man and I've known his pomes and by God I have loved the two of them and loved them well, too. Do you understand what I'm saying, Mr. Lamont? You, Mr. Furriskey?
>
> Oh that's right.
>
> Do you know what it is, I've met the others, the whole lot of them. I've met them all and know them all. I have seen them and I have read their pomes. I have heard them recited by men that know how to use their tongues, men that couldn't be beaten at their own game. I have seen whole books filled up with their stuff, books as thick as that table there and I'm telling you no lie. But by God, at the heel of the hunt, there was only one poet for me.

Although any "Jem" has to sparkle if we're to believe in it, and even though his initials, JC, are suspicious, I am not going to suggest that "Casey" is a pun on the Knights of Columbus.

> No 'Sir,' no 'Mister,' no nothing. Jem Casey, Poet of the Pick, that's all. A labouring man, Mr. Lamont, but as sweet a singer in his own way as you'll find in the bloody trees there of a spring day, and that's a fact. Jem Casey, an ignorant God-fearing upstanding labouring man, a bloody navvy. Do you know what I'm going to tell you, I don't believe he ever lifted the latch of a school door. Would you believe that now?

The first paragraph rings the changes on "known" and "loved," while the second proceeds from "know" and "met" to "seen" and "heard," in a shuffle of sentences of the simplest kind, full of doubled vowels, repeated phrases, plain talk and far-from-subtle rhyme; characteristics which lead it to resemble the medieval preacher's rhythmic prose of persuasion. It is the speech, of course, of the barroom bore and alcoholic hyperbolist, a bit bullyish and know-it-all, even if as empty of idea as a washed glass, out of which O'Brien forms an amusing though powerful song of cultural resentment.

It is sometimes said that just as you cannot walk without stepping on wood, earth, or stone, you cannot write without symbolizing, willy-nilly, a series of clicks, trills, and moans; so there will be music wherever prose goes. This expresses an attitude both too generous and too indifferent to be appropriate. The sentence with which Dreiser begins his novel *The Financier*, "The Philadelphia into which Frank Algernon Cowperwood was born was at his very birth already a city of two hundred and fifty thousand and more," certainly makes noise enough, and, in addition to the lovely "Philadelphia," there is "Algernon" and "Cowperwood," which most people might feel make a mouthful; but the words, here, merely stumble through their recital of facts, happy, their job done, to reach an end, however lame it is. Under different circumstances, the doubling of "was" around "born" might have promised much (as in Joyce's paradisal phrase, "when all that was was fair"); however, here it is simply awkward, and followed unnecessarily by another "birth," the reason, no doubt, for Dreiser's mumpering on about the population. After another sentence distinguished only by the ineptness of its enumeration ("It was set with handsome parks, notable buildings, and crowded with historic memories"), the author adds fatuousness to his list of achievements: "Many of the things that we and he knew later were not then in existence—the telegraph, telephone, express company, ocean steamer, or city delivery of mails." "We and he" do ding dong all right, but rather tinnily. Then Dreiser suffers a moment of expansiveness ("There were no postage-stamps or registered letters"), before plunging us into a tepid bath of banality whose humor escapes even his unconscious: "The street-car had not arrived, and in its place were hosts of omnibuses, and for longer travel, the slowly developing railroad system still largely connected with canals." It makes for a surreal image, though: those stretches of track bridged by boats; an image whose contemplation we may enjoy while waiting for the streetcar to arrive.

"Bath of banality" is a bit sheepish itself, and brings to mind all the complaints about the artificiality of alliteration, the inappropriateness of rhyme in prose, the unpleasant result of pronounced regular rhythms in that workaday place, the lack of high seriousness to be found in all such effects: in short, the belief that "grand" if not "good" writing undercuts its serious and sober message when it plays around with shape and the shape of its sounds; because, while poetry may be permitted to break wind and allow its leaves to waltz upon an anal breeze, prose should never suggest it had eaten beans, but retain the serious, no-nonsense demeanor of the laboring man in *At Swim-two-birds*.

Some tunes are rinky-dink indeed, and confined to the carnival, but I get the impression that most of these complaints about the music of prose are simply the fears of lead-eared moralists and message gatherers, who want us to believe that a man like Dreiser, who can't get through three minutes of High Tea without blowing his nose on his sleeve, ought to model our manners for us, and tell us truths as blunt and insensitive, but honest and used, as worn shoes.

What they wish us to forget is another kind of truth, that language is not the low-born gawky servant of thought and feeling, it is need, thought, feeling, and perception itself. The shape of the sentence, the song in its syllables, the rhythm of its movement, is the movement of the imagination too; it is the allocation of the things of the world to their place in the world of the word; it is the configuration of its concepts— not to neglect them—like the stars which are alleged to determine the fate of we poor creatures who bear their names, suffer their severities, enjoy their presence of mind, and the sight of their light in our night . . . all right . . . all right . . . okay: the glow of their light in our darkness.

Let's remind ourselves of the moment in *Orlando* when the Queen (who has, old as she is, taken Orlando up as if he were a perfumed hanky, held him close to her cleavage, and made plans to house him between the hills of her hope) sees something other than her own ancient figure in her household mirror:

> Meanwhile, the long winter months drew on. Every tree in the Park was lined with frost. The river ran sluggishly. One day when the snow was on the ground and the dark paneled rooms were full of shadows and the stags were barking in the Park, she saw in the mirror, which she kept for fear of spies always by her, through the door, which she kept for fear of murderers always open, a boy—could it be Orlando?—kissing a girl—who in the Devil's name was the brazen

hussy? Snatching at her golden-hilted sword she struck violently at the mirror. The glass crashed; people came running; she was lifted and set in her chair again; but she was stricken after that and groaned much, as her days wore to an end, of man's treachery.

Where shall we begin our praise of this passage, which, in *Orlando*, is merely its norm? And what shall we observe first among its beauties? perhaps, in that simple opening sentence, the way the heavy stresses which fall on "mean," "while" (and equally on the comma's strong pause), "long," "win," "months," "drew," and finally "on" again, make those months do just that (the three "ons," the many m's and n's don't hurt, nor does the vowel modulation: een, ile, ong, in, on, ou, on), or the way the river, whose flow was rapid enough reaching "run," turns sluggish suddenly in the middle of the guggle in that word. Or maybe we should admire the three "ands" which breathlessly connect a cold snowy ground with shadowy rooms and barking stags; and then, with confidently contrasting symmetry, how the three semicolons trepidate crashing, running, lifting, in response. Or should we examine, instead, the complex central image of the figure in the glass, and the way the two clauses beginning with "which" are diabolically placed? or the consequent vibration of the sentence from the public scene of Orlando in embrace to the Queen's personal shock at what she's seen out the open door, thanks to her "magic" mirror. Nor should the subtle way, through word order mainly, that Virginia Woolf salts her prose with a sense of the era—her intention quite serious but her touch kept light in order to recall the Elizabethan period without parody—be neglected by our applause.

It is precisely the Queen's fear of spies and murderers that places the mirror where it can peer down the corridor to the cause of her dismay—that is the irony—but it is the placement of the reasons ("which she kept for fear of spies always by her," etc.) between the fragments of the perceptions ("through the door," "a boy," and so on) which convince the reader of the reality of it. It is not enough to have a handful of ideas, a few perceptions, a metaphor of some originality on your stove, the writer must also know when to release these meanings; against what they shall lean their newly arrived weight; how, in retrospect, their influence shall be felt; how the lonely trope will combine with some distant noun to create a new flavor.

What is said, what is sounded, what is put in print like a full plate in front of the reader's hungry eye, must be weighed against what is kept back, out of view, suggested, implied. The Queen, in her disappointed rage, has fallen to the floor, but we are told only that she was lifted and put back in her chair again. And nothing will henceforth be the same in the last morose moments of her life. On account of a kiss caught by a mirror through a door kept ajar out of fear of another sort of assault.

In music, sounds form phrases; in prose, phrases form sounds. The sentence almost immediately above was written to demonstrate this, for it naturally breaks into units: "On account of a kiss/ caught by a mirror/ through a door kept ajar/ out of fear of another/ sort of assault." These fragments, in turn, can be subdivided further: "On account/of a kiss . . ." Certain pieces of the pattern act like hinges: "kiss/caught," "door/kept," for instance, while possessives play their part, and the form, article-noun ("a count/a kiss/a mirror/a door/a jar/an other/ a ssault,"), stamps on the sentence its special rhythm.

Words have their own auditory character. We all know this, but the writer must revel in it. Some open and close with vowels whose prolongation can give them expressive possibilities (*Ohio*, for instance), others are simply vowel-heavy (like *aeolian*), still others open wide but then close sharply (*ought*), or are as tight-lipped as *tip*, as unending as *too*, or as fully middled as *balloon*. Some words look long but are said short (such as *rough* and *sleight*), some seem small enough but are actually huge (*otiose* and *nay*). A few words *whisper*, *tintinnabulate*, or *murmur*, as if they were made of their meanings, while *Philadelphia* (already admired) is like a low range of hills. Some words rock, and are jokey, like *okeydokey*. Or they clump, like *lump* and *hump* and *rump* and *stump*, or dash noisily away in a rash of *ash/mash/bash* or *brash/crash/smash* or *lash/hash/ stash* or *clash/trash/splash/succotash*. Vowel changes are equally significant, whether between *ring, rang*, and *rung; scat* and *scoot; pet* and *pat; pit* and *pot;* or *squish* and *squooze*.

The Latinate measures of the great organist, Henry James, find an additional function for the music of prose. Here all it takes is a parade of the past tense ("he had") down a street paved with negations.

> He had not been a man of numerous passions, and even in all these years no sense had grown stronger with him than the sense of being bereft. He had needed no priest and no altar to make him for ever widowed. He had done many things in the world—he had done al-

most all but one: he had never, never forgotten. He had tried to put into his existence whatever else might take up room in it, but had failed to make it more than a house of which the mistress was eternally absent.

If some men are has-beens, poor Stransom (in James's judgment) is a had-not-been. The passage is crammed with loss: "bereft," "widowed," "failed," "absent," in addition to the doubling of "sense," "no," "never," in succeeding sentences, and the gloomy repetition of the past tense, particularly "been" and "done." Our hero, we cannot help but hear, is a "transom." He only looks on. But the music of the passage ties terms together more firmly than its syntax: "being," for instance, with "bereft," "done" with "one," "ever" with "never" and "what-" with "ever" as well. Each sentence, all clauses, commence with poor Stransom's pronoun, or imply its presence: "he had . . . he had . . . he had," trochee along like a mourning gong.

Musical form creates another syntax which overlaps the grammatical and reinforces that set of directions sometimes, or adds another dimension by suggesting that two words, when they alliterate or rhyme, thereby modify one another, even if they are not in any normally modifying position. Everything a sentence is is made manifest by its music. As Gertrude Stein writes:

Papa dozes mamma blows her noses.
We cannot say this the other way.

Music makes the space it takes place in. I do not mean the baroque chamber where a quartet once competed against the slide of satin, the sniff of snuff, or the rustle of lace cuffs, or the long symphonic hall full of coughing, whispered asides and program rattle, or the opera house where the plot unfolding on the stage plays poorly against the ogling in the boxes and the distractions in the stalls, or even the family's music room where heavy metal will one day leave its scratches like chalk screech on the window panes—none of these former or future pollutions of our pleasure; but again in that hall of the head (it holds so much!) where, when the first note sounds behind the lids, and no late arrivals are allowed to enter . . . when the first note sounds as if the piano were putting a single star down in a dark sky, and then, over there, in that common darkness, another, the way, for instance, the *1926* Sonata of Bartok begins, or a nocturne of Chopin's, slowly, so we can observe its creation, its establishment of relation; because we do see what we hear, and the music rises and falls or feels far away or comes from close by like the lobe of the ear, and is bright or dim, wide or thin, or forms chains or cascades, sometimes as obvious as a cartoon of Disney's, splashy and catchy, and sometimes as continuous and broad and full as an ocean; while at other times there is only a *ding* here and a *ping* there in a dense pitchlike lack, and one waits for the sounds to come back, and fill the abyss with clangor, as if life were all that is.

And when we hear, *we* hear; when we see, and say: "ah! Sport!," *we* see; our consciousness of objects is *ours*, don't philosophers love to say? and though we share a world it is, from the point of view of consciousness, an overlapping one: I see the dog with delight, you with fear; I see its deep moist eyes, you see its cruel wet mouth; I hear its happy panting, you hear its threatening growl; and I remember my own loyal pooch, and you the time a pug pursued you down the street; so we say the same word *dog,* yet I to welcome and you to warn, I to greet and you to cringe; and even when we think of what our experience means, and ponder the place of pets in the human scheme, thus sharing a subject as we have our encounter, we will pursue our problem differently, organize it in dissimilar ways, and doubtless arrive at opposite ends.

But I can shape and sound a sentence in such a way my sight of things, my feeling for what I've seen, my thoughts about it all, are as fully present as the ideas and objects my words by themselves bear. D. H. Lawrence, for instance, in that great chapter of *Sea and Sardinia* called "The Spinner and the Monks," does not simply tell us he saw two monks walking in a garden.

> And then, just below me, I saw two monks walking in their garden
> between the naked, bony vines, walking in their wintry garden of
> bony vines and olive trees, their brown cassocks passing between the
> brown vine-stocks, their heads bare to the sunshine, sometimes a
> glint of light as their feet strode from under their skirts.

Anyone can put a pair of monks in a garden and even observe their no-doubt-sandalled feet flash, but Lawrence is a whole person when he perceives, when he repeats, when he plans his patterns; so that, just as he himself says, it is as if he hears them speaking to one another.

> They marched with the peculiar march of monks, a long, loping
> stride, their heads together, their skirts swaying slowly, two brown

monks with hidden hands, sliding under the bony vines and beside the cabbages, their heads always together in hidden converse. It was as if I were attending with my dark soul to their inaudible undertone. All the time I sat still in silence, I was one with them, a partaker, though I could hear no sound of their voices. I went with the long stride of their skirted feet, that slid springless and noiseless from end to end of the garden, and back again. Their hands were kept down at their sides, hidden in the long sleeves and the skirts of their robes. They did not touch each other, nor gesticulate as they walked. There was no motion save the long, furtive stride and the heads leaning together. Yet there was an eagerness in their conversation. Almost like shadow-creatures ventured out of their cold, obscure element, they went backward and forwards in their wintry garden, thinking nobody could see them.

And we go to and fro here, too, as the sentences do, passing between vowel and idea, perception and measure, moving as the syllables move in our mouth, admiring the moment, realizing how well the world has been realized through Lawrence's richly sensuous point-of-view.

They clothe a consciousness, these sounds and patterns do, the consciousness the words refer to, with its monks and vines, its stilled observant soul, its sense of hearing them speak as well as seeing them striding along together, the quality of mystery and community the passage presents by putting them in the light of a late winter afternoon.

And I noticed that up above the snow, frail in the bluish sky, a frail moon had put forth, like a thin, scalloped film of ice floated out on the slow current of the coming night. And a bell sounded.

A beautiful precise image, translucent itself, is carried forward by an arrangement of f's and l's, o's and u's with such security their reader has to feel he's heard that bell even before it sounds.

Suddenly the mind and its view have a body, because such sentences breathe, and the writer's blood runs through them, too, and they are virile or comely, promising sweetness or cruelty, as bodies do, and they allow the mind they contain to move, and the scene it sees to have an eye.

The soul, when it loves, has a body it must use. Consequently, neither must neglect the other, for the hand which holds your hand must belong to a feeling being, else you are caressing a corpse; and that loving self, unless it can fill a few fingers with its admiration and concern, will pass no more of its passion to another than might a dead dry stick.

The music of prose, as elementary as it is, as limited as it is in its effects, is nonetheless far from frivolous decoration; it embodies Being; consequently, it is essential that that body be in eloquent shape: to watch the mimsy paddle and the fat picnic, the snoozers burn and crybabies bellow . . . well, we didn't go to the beach for that.

II

W.H. AUDEN

Notes on Music and Opera

*Opera consists of significant situations in
artificially arranged sequence.*

—GOETHE

*Singing is near miraculous because it is the
mastering of what is otherwise a pure instrument
of egotism: the human voice.*

—HUGO VON HOFMANNSTHAL

What is music about? What, as Plato would say, does it imitate? Our
experience of Time in its twofold aspect, natural or organic repetition,
and historical novelty created by choice. And the full development of
music as an art depends upon a recognition that these two aspects are
different and that choice, being an experience confined to man, is more
significant than repetition. A succession of two musical notes is an act of
choice; the first causes the second, not in the scientific sense of making it
occur necessarily, but in the historical sense of provoking it, of providing it with a motive for occurring. A successful melody is a self-
determined history; it is freely what it intends to be, yet is a meaningful
whole, not an arbitrary succession of notes.

Music as an art, i.e., music that has come to a conscious realization of
its true nature, is confined to Western civilization alone and only to the
last four or five hundred years at that. The music of all other cultures
and epochs bears the same relation to Western music that magical verbal formulas bear to the art of poetry. A primitive magic spell may be
poetry but it does not know that it is, nor intend to be. So, in all but
Western music, history is only implicit; what it thinks it is doing is fur-
nishing verses or movements with a repetitive accompaniment. Only in
the West has chant become song.

Lacking a historical consciousness, the Greeks, in their theories of music, tried to relate it to Pure Being, but the becoming implicit in music betrays itself in their theories of harmony in which mathematics becomes numerology and one chord is intrinsically "better" than another.

Western music declared its consciousness of itself when it adopted time signatures, barring and the metronome beat. Without a strictly natural or cyclical time, purified from every trace of historical singularity, as a framework within which to occur, the irreversible historicity of the notes themselves would be impossible.

In primitive proto-music, the percussion instruments which best imitate recurrent rhythms and, being incapable of melody, can least imitate novelty, play the greatest role.

The most exciting rhythms seem unexpected and complex, the most beautiful melodies simple and inevitable.

Music cannot imitate nature: a musical storm always sounds like the wrath of Zeus.

A verbal art like poetry is reflective; it stops to think. Music is immediate, it goes on to become. But both are active, both insist on stopping or going on. The medium of passive reflection is painting, of passive immediacy the cinema, for the visual world is an immediately given world where Fate is mistress and it is impossible to tell the difference between a chosen movement and an involuntary reflex. Freedom of choice lies, not in the world we see, but in our freedom to turn our eyes in this direction, or that, or to close them altogether.

Because music expresses the opposite experience of pure volition and subjectivity (the fact that we cannot shut our ears at will allows music to assert that we cannot *not* choose), film music is not music but a technique for preventing us from using our ears to hear extraneous noises and it is bad film music if we become consciously aware of its existence.

Man's musical imagination seems to be derived almost exclusively from his primary experiences—his direct experience of his own body, its tensions and rhythms, and his direct experience of desiring and choosing—and to have very little to do with the experiences of the outside world brought to him through his senses. The possibility of making music, that is, depends primarily, not upon man's possession of an auditory organ, the ear, but upon his possession of a sound-producing instrument, the vocal cords. If the ear were primary, music would have begun as program pastoral symphonies. In the case of visual arts, on the other hand, it is a visual organ, the eye, which is primary for, without it, the experiences which stimulate the hand into becoming an expressive instrument could not exist.

The difference is demonstrated by the difference in our sensation of motion in musical space and visual space.

An increase in the tension of the vocal chords is conceived in musical space as a going "up," a relaxation as a going "down." But in visual space it is the bottom of the picture (which is also the foreground) which is felt as the region of greatest pressure and, as the eye rises up the picture, it feels an increasing sense of lightness and freedom.

The association of tension in hearing with up and seeing with down seems to correspond to the difference between our experience of the force of gravity in our own bodies and our experience of it in other bodies. The weight of our own bodies is felt as inherent in us, as a personal wish to fall down, so that rising upward is an effort to overcome the desire for rest in ourselves. But the weight (and proximity) of other objects is felt as weighing down on us; they are "on top" of us and rising means getting away from their restrictive pressure.

All of us have learned to talk, most of us, even, could be taught to speak verse tolerably well, but very few have learned or could ever be taught to sing. In any village twenty people could get together and give a performance of *Hamlet* which, however imperfect, would convey enough of the play's greatness to be worth attending, but if they were to attempt a similar performance of *Don Giovanni,* they would soon discover that there was no question of a good or a bad performance because they could not sing the notes at all. Of an actor, even in a poetic drama, when we say that his performance is good, we mean that he simulates by art, that is, consciously, the way in which the character he is playing would, in real life, behave by nature, that is, unconsciously. But for a singer, as for a ballet dancer, there is no question of simulation, of singing the composer's notes "naturally"; his behavior is unabashedly and triumphantly art from beginning to end. The paradox implicit in all drama, namely, that emotions and situations which in real life would be sad or painful are on the stage a source of pleasure becomes, in opera, quite explicit. The singer may be playing the role of a deserted bride who is about to kill herself, but we feel quite certain as we listen that not only we, but also she, is having a wonderful time. In a sense, there can be no tragic opera because whatever errors the characters make and whatever they suffer, they are doing exactly what they wish. Hence the feeling that *opera seria* should not employ a contemporary subject, but confine itself to mythical situations, that is, situations which, as human beings, we are all of us necessarily in and must, therefore, accept, however tragic they may be. A contemporary tragic situation like that in Menotti's *The Consul* is too actual, that is, too clearly a situation some people are in and others, including the audience, are not in, for the latter to forget this and see it as a symbol of, say, man's existential estrangement. Consequently the pleasure we and the singers are obviously enjoying strikes the conscience as frivolous.

On the other hand, its pure artifice renders opera the ideal dramatic medium for a tragic myth. I once went in the same week to a performance of *Tristan und Isolde* and a showing of *L'Eternal Retour,* Jean Cocteau's movie version of the same story. During the former, two souls, weighing over two hundred pounds apiece, were transfigured by a transcendent power; in the latter, a handsome boy met a beautiful girl and they had an affair. This loss of value was due not to any lack of skill on Cocteau's part but to the nature of the cinema as a medium. Had he used a fat middle-aged couple the effect would have been ridiculous because the snatches of language which are all the movie permits have not sufficient power to transcend their physical appearance. Yet if the lovers are young and beautiful, the cause of their love looks "natural," a consequence of their beauty, and the whole meaning of the myth is gone.

> The man who wrote the Eighth Symphony has a right to rebuke the man who put his rapture of elation, tenderness, and nobility into the mouths of a drunken libertine, a silly peasant girl, and a conven-

tional fine lady, instead of confessing them to himself, glorying in them, and uttering them without motley as the universal inheritance.

—Bernard Shaw

Shaw, and Beethoven, are both wrong, I believe, and Mozart right. Feelings of joy, tenderness and nobility are not confined to "noble" characters but are experienced by everybody, by the most conventional, most stupid, most depraved. It is one of the glories of opera that it can demonstrate this and to the shame of the spoken drama that it cannot. Because we use language in everyday life, our style and vocabulary become identified with our social character as others see us, and in a play, even a verse play, there are narrow limits to the range in speech possible for any character beyond which the playwright cannot go without making the character incredible. But precisely because we do not communicate by singing, a song can be out of place but not out of character; it is just as credible that a stupid person should sing beautifully as that a clever person should do so.

If music in general is an imitation of history, opera in particular is an imitation of human willfulness; it is rooted in the fact that we not only have feelings but insist upon having them at whatever cost to ourselves. Opera, therefore, cannot present character in the novelist's sense of the word, namely, people who are potentially good *and* bad, active *and* passive, for music is immediate actuality and neither potentiality nor passivity can live in its presence. This is something a librettist must never forget. Mozart is a greater composer than Rossini but the Figaro of the *Marriage* is less satisfying, to my mind, than the Figaro of the *Barber* and the fault, is, I think, Da Ponte's. His Figaro is too interesting a character to be completely translatable into music, so that co-present with the Figaro who is singing, one is conscious of a Figaro who is not singing but thinking to himself. The barber of Seville, on the other hand, who is not a person but a musical busybody, goes into song exactly with nothing over.

Again, I find *La Bohème* inferior to *Tosca,* not because its music is inferior, but because the characters, Mimi in particular, are too passive; there is an awkward gap between the resolution with which they sing and the irresolution with which they act.

The quality common to all the great operatic roles, e.g., Don

Giovanni, Norma, Lucia, Tristan, Isolde, Brünnhilde, is that each of them is a passionate and willful state of being. In real life they would all be bores, even Don Giovanni.

In recompense for this lack of psychological complexity, however, music can do what words cannot, present the immediate and simultaneous relation of these states to each other. The crowning glory of opera is the big ensemble.

The chorus can play two roles in opera and two only, that of the mob and that of the faithful, sorrowing or rejoicing community. A little of this goes a long way. Opera is not oratorio.

Drama is based on the Mistake. I think someone is my friend when he really is my enemy, that I am free to marry a woman when in fact she is my mother, that this person is a chambermaid when it is a young nobleman in disguise, that this well-dressed young man is rich when he is really a penniless adventurer, or that if I do this such and such a result will follow when in fact it results in something very different. All good drama has two movements, first the making of the mistake, then the discovery that it was a mistake.

In composing his plot, the librettist has to conform to this law but, in comparison to the dramatist, he is more limited in the kinds of mistake he can use. The dramatist, for instance, procures some of his finest effects from showing how people deceive themselves. Self-deception is impossible in opera because music is immediate, not reflective; whatever is sung is the case. At most, self-deception can be suggested by having the orchestral accompaniment at variance with the singer, e.g., the jolly tripping notes which accompany Germont's approach to Violetta's deathbed in *La Traviata*, but unless employed very sparingly such devices cause confusion rather than insight.

Again, while in the spoken drama the discovery of the mistake can be a slow process and often, indeed, the more gradual it is the greater the dramatic interest, in a libretto the drama of recognition must be tropically abrupt, for music cannot exist in an atmosphere of uncertainty; song cannot walk, it can only jump.

On the other hand, the librettist need never bother his head, as the dramatist must, about probability. A credible situation in opera means a situation in which it is credible that someone should sing. A good libretto plot is a melodrama in both the strict and the conventional sense of the word; it offers as many opportunities as possible for the characters to be swept off their feet by placing them in situations which are too tragic or too fantastic for "words." No good opera plot can be sensible for people do not sing when they are feeling sensible.

The theory of "music-drama" presupposes a libretto in which there is not one sensible moment or one sensible remark: this is not only very difficult to manage, though Wagner managed it, but also extremely exhausting on both singers and the audience, neither of whom may relax for an instant.

In a libretto where there are any sensible passages, i.e., conversation not song, the theory becomes absurd. If, for furthering the action, it becomes necessary for one character to say to another "Run upstairs and fetch me a handkerchief," then there is nothing in the words, apart from their rhythm, to make one musical setting more apt than another. Wherever the choice of notes is arbitrary, the only solution is a convention, e.g., *recitativo secco.*

In opera the orchestra is addressed to the singers, not to the audience. An opera-lover will put up with and even enjoy an orchestral interlude on condition that he knows the singers cannot sing just now because they are tired or the scene-shifters are at work, but any use of the orchestra by itself which is not filling in time is, for him, wasting it. "Leonora" III is a fine piece to listen to in the concert hall, but in the opera house, when it is played between scenes one and two of the second act of *Fidelio,* it becomes twelve minutes of acute boredom.

If the librettist is a practicing poet, the most difficult problem, the place where he is most likely to go astray, is the composition of the verse. Poetry is in its essence an act of reflection, of refusing to be content with the interjections of immediate emotion in order to understand the nature of what is felt. Since music is in essence immediate, it follows that the words of a song cannot be poetry. Here one should draw a distinction between lyric and song proper. A lyric is a poem intended to be chanted. In a chant the music is subordinate to the words which limit the range and tempo of the notes. In song, the notes must be free to be whatever they choose and the words must be able to do what they are told.

The verses of *Ah non credea* in *La Sonnambula*, though of little interest to read, do exactly what they should: suggest to Bellini one of the most beautiful melodies ever written and then leave him completely free to write it. The verses which the librettist writes are not addressed to the public but are really a private letter to the composer. They have their moment of glory, the moment in which they suggest to him a certain melody; once that is over, they are as expendable as infantry to a Chinese general: they must efface themselves and cease to care what happens to them.

There have been several composers, Campion, Hugo Wolf, Benjamin Britten, for example, whose musical imagination has been stimulated by poetry of a high order. The question remains, however, whether the listener hears the sung words as words in a poem, or, as I am inclined to believe, only as sung syllables. A Cambridge psychologist, P. E. Vernon, once performed the experiment of having a Campion song sung with nonsense verses of equivalent syllabic value substituted for the original; only six per cent of his test audience noticed that something was wrong. It is precisely because I believe that, in listening to song (as distinct from chant), we hear, not words, but syllables, that I am not generally in favor of the performances of operas in translation. Wagner or Strauss in English sounds intolerable, and would still sound so if the poetic merits of the translation were greater than those of the original, because the new syllables have no apt relation to the pitch and tempo of the notes with which they are associated. The poetic value of the words may provoke a composer's imagination, but it is their syllabic values which determine the kind of vocal line he writes. In song, poetry is expendable, syllables are not.

"History," said Stephen Dedalus, "is the nightmare from which I must awake." The rapidity of historical change and the apparent powerlessness of the individual to affect Collective History has led in literature to a retreat from history. Instead of tracing the history of an individual who is born, grows old and dies, many modern novelists and short story writers, beginning with Poe, have devoted their attention to timeless passionate moments in life, to states of being. It seems to me that, in some modern music, I can detect the same trend, a trend towards composing a static kind of music in which there is no marked difference between its beginning, its middle and its end, a music which sounds remarkably like primitive proto-music. It is not for me to criticize a composer who writes such music. One can say, however, that he will never be able to write an opera. But, probably, he won't want to.

The golden age of opera, from Mozart to Verdi, coincided with the golden age of liberal humanism, of unquestioning belief in freedom and progress. If good operas are rarer today, this may be because, not only have we learned that we are less free than nineteenth-century humanism imagined, but also have become less certain that freedom is an unequivocal blessing, that the free are necessarily the good. To say that operas are more difficult to write does not mean that they are impossible. That would only follow if we should cease to believe in free will and personality altogether. Every high C accurately struck demolishes the theory that we are the irresponsible puppets of fate or chance.

WILLIAM MATTHEWS

The Precisions of Passion

"The vocal instrument is the most difficult of all because it does not exist," says the legendary operatic tenor Alfredo Kraus. He has just come from teaching a master class at Juilliard, and the voice is on his mind. But first there are amenities; Kraus is a courtly man. "Would you like a coffee?" he asks me.

His wife, Rosa, brings the coffee, and Kraus apologizes that it may be too strong. It's delicious. "You must hate American coffee," I suggest. Kraus laughs; he's too polite to say so. "We are not used to it."

When he talks about singing, he puts his natural reticence aside. In what sense does he mean that the voice doesn't exist?

An unplayed piano is a piece of furniture, but a singer's voice has no location until it's in use. And even then the voice a singer hears is not the one an audience hears: a singer hears his or her own voice primarily from inside the cave of the body, and the audience hears the freed voice. "You don't hear your voice as it really is, because there are two sounds mixed—the inside and the outside."

Also, "your voice changes from day to day. You don't know why."

Kraus looks out the window of the apartment, near Lincoln Center, that he and Rosa inhabit for the month they will be in New York. First dusk sifts the air. "The light was very beautiful today," he says; "why, then, do you suppose they would color the glass like that?" A closer look reveals the window glass is faintly tinted. Something has been done the wrong way.

Kraus's study of the voice, his sense of how best to preserve his voice, and his carefully structured annual schedule are all part of the central paradox of his professional life: to be fastidious, thorough and careful is the best way to release the ardent romanticism, intensity and passion of the youthful characters he portrays. It is like the slow work of preparing a firework, painstakingly assembled so that a beautiful bravura rush of grace and light comes forth with all the illusion of effortlessness.

"Singing is the only career in music you can have and not be a good musician," Kraus has often said. But a voice is not enough. "To sing you need [two-beat pause] also a voice."

You need, also, Kraus would say, to know your voice and its limits. Speaking of his youth, Kraus has said, "My voice was never splendid, and I knew it. My voice is not of tremendous quality, so wonderful in beauty. But it was a material, and you have to know how to manage it."

Asked how he would describe his voice now, he calls it "not tremendously beautiful, but recognizable and characteristic. It's a light, lyric tenor with a lot of metal in the voice and great facility in the high register." At the word "facility" a phenomenon occurs that happens often in talking with Kraus about the voice: a word appears which refers not only to the voice but also to the technique by which it is deployed. Each thing is a part of the other.

Some part of a singer's dynamic range is part of the voice, but learning to expand and use the range is a matter of technique. "If you're always *forte*, you don't make colors."

Even the management of the voice is part of the voice. Kraus sings about fifty performances a year and works with a comparatively small repertoire. His light, clear voice and technical mastery make him especially at home in the bel canto repertory: *La Favorita, L'Elisir d'Amore, Don Pasquale, Lucrezia Borgia, Lucia di Lammermoor, I Puritani, La Sonnambula, The Barber of Seville*. In the French repertory, he sings *Manon, Werther, Faust, Tales of Hoffman, The Pearl Fishers*. Kraus sings some roles in the Italian-language Mozart operas; he has sung Ferrando in *Cosi fan Tutti* and Ottavio in *Don Giovanni*. He has sung Faust in Boito's *Mefistofele*, and frequently sings his two famous Verdi roles, Alfredo in *La Traviata* and the Duke of Mantua in *Rigoletto*.

"It's a risk to sing Puccini, because the orchestra is heavy, and you try to push your voice." Kraus has occasionally sung Rinuccio in the one-act *Gianni Schicci*, but has otherwise left Puccini alone after singing *Tosca, La Bohème* and *Madama Butterfly* a couple times each when he was young. By the time he was in his mid-thirties, Kraus was an acclaimed artist and could decline roles with impunity. "As an artist," he says, "you have to have the vanity to say no."

Or, as Leonie Rysanek, at sixty-six one year Kraus's senior and still a formidable singer, put it: "The first word to learn is *no*, if you want a career."

Such willfulness one must cultivate, Kraus thinks. He had a few days earlier watched the young American tennis star Pete Sampras lose a televised Davis Cup match before a partisan and very vocal French crowd in Lyons. "That was hard," Kraus says, "and not really fair. He had to play against almost everyone in the building. He will have to learn to be fierce."

"The voice is like a tube or a channel," Kraus says. The metaphor is ballistic: the voice takes its shape from the throat that expels it.

"To put every sound in the right position is difficult." The notion that sounds have a place should make sense to anyone who has looked at a score, whether or not the onlooker can read music. In the notation of an ascending octave, let's say, each note is one step higher than its predecessors; together they form a kind of staircase. So a score is not just a convenient way to write down musical instructions; it's also a map of the relative *positions* of the sounds. "Map" reminds us of the limitations of a score—it's two-dimensional, and thus a score has a similar relationship to the sounds it encodes (they come from a three-dimensional tube or channel), as a map has to a globe or to the earth.

There are three further complications to understanding the process Kraus describes.

One is that the voice is moving. It passes through the sounds. We could say it moves by means of them, the way one might pick a path across a streambed by stepping on exposed stones.

The second is that in singing opera you are not just producing sounds; each sound is also part of a word, and the words drive the plot—the intrigues, the probable or improbable twists of fate, and ultimately the emotional lives of the characters, their very destinies. "You have to transmit the word," Kraus insists. It's possible to make glorious sound with slack attention to the words you're singing. Joan Sutherland did it for much of her career, hitting the notes accurately and singing with feeling, but the words were drowned in the long, blurred, never-breaking wave of her melisma.

The third is that the proper position for each sound is partially determined by the sound that came before it and the sound toward which it will travel next. You want to make this voyage by the most technically economical and least arduous path possible. The situation could be compared to the difference between expert and inept billiards players. The expert plans each shot to leave the cue ball in the best position for the next several shots. The tyro blasts away and waits to see where the cue ball will stall, and only then plots his next move.

Plots seems the right verb, since singing opera is a narrative, a story of what it feels like to be under great emotional pressure. Thus his life-long fascination with technique. "Emotion," Kraus likes to say, "is a part of our intelligence."

The circumstances under which an international star like Kraus performs are largely influenced by market conditions, and thus have changed considerably during his career.

"In Europe we used to have *maestro concertante* and *direttore d'orchestra*—two different things," Kraus recalled in an *Opera News* interview with Edwin Newman. "*Concertare* means 'to put together' . . . all the people who participate in an opera." Sometimes this would entail as much as a week of rehearsal using only the piano. "How to do the recitatives, how to go to a high note and make it *piano,* how to do a *diminuendo,* the feeling, the meaning—they tried to explain everything to us."

Competition for big names that will guarantee a full house and continuous improvement in the technology of air travel have combined to tempt star singers to vault from opera house to opera house. But if you sing in two different cities on successive nights, Kraus warns, "your subconscious is working in two places, and it's too busy."

There are other dangers to this practice. There's never a single way to do an opera. There need to be many, depending on the conductor, the cast, the qualities and limitations of their voices, which of the singers are also actors, etc. If the principals have too little time together, what results can be professional but superficial.

Operagoers who heard both Kraus and Luciano Pavarotti sing Nemorino in the Metropolitan Opera's production of *L'Elisir d'Amore* in late 1991 had a chance to see how casting choices change an opera to produce quite different and equally credible experiences of it.

Pavarotti is both a charismatic superstar and an extravert. He doesn't immerse himself in a character so much as he inhabits one. It's not only the beautiful bloom of his voice that reminds us that he's in there. Even his stage business suggests not only that he's enjoying playing Nemorino, but also that he's enjoying being Luciano Pavarotti. Nemorino is a credulous bumpkin, greatly the world's fool. Pavarotti's aggressive charm underlines the gap between the character's view of the world and the world's view of him.

Kraus's is an aristocratic temperament, and would not permit him the little sob that Pavarotti built into "Una furtiva lagrima," Nemorino's tender second-act aria. Kraus's reticence and tastefulness predispose him to play well characters whose emotions are implied; his Nemorino suggests by a credulous manner his reserve of clear-hearted dignity. So Kraus's Nemorino is a little nobler than the world he moves in, and when he sings the role, the force and persistence of his love for Adina seems the central engine of the plot. Kraus's more restrained portrayal makes the opera more romantic.

When Pavarotti sings the role, the social comedy of the opera, the gap between how the characters understand themselves and how we see them, is more central. The love potion is self-delusion, not so much a failing as a social lubrication.

Kraus greatly prefers live performance to recordings. It's not only that studio recordings are often made out of sequence and then cobbled together in the editing room, like a movie. It's also that a performance is a conspiracy, the creation of an atmosphere between performers and audience. "A record is something dead," Kraus says, leaning forward in his chair for emphasis, "because it's repeatable."

Kraus may be right that the audience doesn't always realize when it has been given a superficial performance, but audiences have a subconscious, just as singers do. Sometimes the quality of attention an audience pays to a performance is an eloquent instance of how alert that subconscious can be.

Performers know that there are different kinds of silence from an audience. There is a kind of rapt intensity, like a stretched rope, that only great performances can compel. There are of course varying degrees of attention in the middle range, and at the bottom of this scale there is an inert and inattentive torpor, a kind of mental slouching and bad posture, that all performers dread: it means you might as well be addressing a stableful of dead horses.

The roles to which Kraus has limited himself, in careful stewardship of his voice, are often light, lyrical, and uncomplicated emotionally. He has spoken with admiration, and a faint undertow of melancholy, of roles like Otello that must be sung by heavier-voiced and more "heroic" tenors (Placido Domingo and Jon Vickers are the recent prototypes).

But Kraus's career is heroic. He has treated himself as a diligent musician rather than a *divo*. He has treated his audience as an accomplice. He has treated the music he sings as a river which, thank God, it is not possible to cross the same way twice. He continues to teach because he continues to be a student.

"Everything came together," he said once after a particularly soulful and intelligent performance of *La Traviata*. "Everyone came together, and that doesn't often happen." A near-grin, a kind of deliberate false start, rippled across his mouth at "often." Understatement was at work. The perfectionist was almost happy.

ELIZABETH HARDWICK

The Eternal Heartbreak

Billy Budd, Foretopman, Herman Melville's mysterious, lyrical tragedy, is a contemplation of the unaccountable extremes of human character—of goodness appearing as naturally as a sunrise, and of evil inhabiting a human soul also naturally, we might say, or at least without necessity or even clear advantage. Into this curious and immensely affecting reflection on the human condition, Melville has imagined details of great and challenging singularity. He also, as a story-teller, has provided a miraculous plot that will tie the characters together on the level of action, without which the tale would be a philosophical daydream, an assertion rather than a drama. Billy Budd, a young sailor of remarkable beauty, good nature and loyalty, is accused by the master-at-arms, a sort of naval MP, of intention to mutiny. The sailor, who under stress suffers from a stutter or speech pause, is unable to express his innocence and outrage and strikes out at the accuser, killing him by a blow. According to maritime law, he must be hanged and his body consigned to the sea.

Ah, but who is Billy Budd? He is a curiosity indeed, almost defying credible description. He is the Handsome Sailor, he is Apollo with a portmanteau, he is Baby Budd, Beauty—all of these things as he comes swinging onto the English ship *Indomitable,* wearing a silk handkerchief, a Scotch tam with a tartan band, aged twenty-one, an able-bodied seaman, fit to climb the great sails, as if ready to fly. Billy is also from the first a creature of inborn moral sweetness. He is free and innocent, a beautiful changeling from nowhere. In fact he is an orphan, an illiterate, reminding one of a freshly hatched, brilliantly colored bird. His only flaw is the one mentioned, the Englishman's stutter or pause when under stress. For the rest, he brings a glow of peace and physical perfection by his presence.

Melville gives evidence of a compositional strain to bring credibility to his extraordinary youth, to the extremity of his perfection accompanied by the purest naturalness. The pictorial Billy: "a lingering adolescent expression in the as yet smooth face, all but feminine in purity of natural complexion." And again: "Cast in the mould peculiar to the finest physical examples of those Englishmen on whom the Saxon strain would seem not at all to partake of any Norman or other admixture, he showed in his face that humane look of reposeful good nature which the Greek sculptor in some instances gave to the heroic strong man, Hercules."

John Claggart, the master-at-arms, is a mirror opposite to Billy Budd. His unaccountable but concentrated hostility to the universally loved Billy is again a conundrum, an exceptional circumstance. Claggart exhibits the strange and troubling "motiveless malignity" that Coleridge in a sort of psychological resignation falls back on as the explanation for Shakespeare's Iago. Like Billy, Claggart has no known past, no baggage of previous circumstance traveling with him. He has entered the navy at thirty-five, causing his shipmates to imagine some cloud of disrepute driving him. Once aboard, Claggart reveals a calculated adaptability that serves him well. "His constitutional sobriety, his ingratiating deference to superiors, together with a particular ferreting genius ... capped by a certain austere patriotism, abruptly advanced him to the position of master-at-arms." His nature, the appalling traps he sets for Billy by the use of weak and corrupted conspirators, his sniveling denunciation of the young sailor to Captain Vere—none of this can be seen as useful to Claggart, since he has nothing to fear from Billy and nothing to gain from his destruction. In the end, Melville will need, in the absence of plausible causality, to rely upon assertion as the source of Claggart's deformation. The master-at-arms' character is said to be "not engendered by vicious training or corrupting books, or licentious living, but born with him and innate, in short, 'a depravity according to nature.'"

The third character, Captain Vere, sometimes called Starry Vere, is a rare being, but not one of as extreme definition as are the other two principals. Vere is fair-minded, bookish, decent, thoughtful, reserved. In the end he is bound by marine law, the letter and the precedent of it, to allow Billy's execution, even though the circumstances violate his sense of justice. Billy, in striking Claggart, his superior officer, has fallen into the rigorous jurisdiction of the law of the sea. That the blow should have killed Claggart is a circumstance beyond reprieve.

The Britten opera opens with a brief flash-forward of Vere as an old man lamenting with sorrow the happenings on the ship *Indomitable* in the year 1797, during the French Wars and "in the difficult and dangerous days after the Mutiny at the Nore." The mutiny referred to took place at Spithead when the crew seized the ship and sent the officers ashore in protest against the brutal conditions prevailing in the British Navy. The Great Mutiny, as it was called, was a threat to Britain's sea power and also was felt to connect with the tide of revolutionary feeling spreading from France and from Napoleon's conquests. After the prologue, the opening scene of Britten's opera is a picture of the gross and cruel servitude practiced on British ships. The *Indomitable* has been called to shift from mercantile seagoing to serve as a man-o'-war in the naval battles with the French. For this purpose, men are dragged off the street or from merchant vessels and impressed into service. A novice, frightened and inexperienced, is forced on board and brutally flogged for merely slipping on the deck.

Billy Budd, not a recruit but an able-bodied seaman by choice, is sent to the *Indomitable* from a homeward-bound ship named *Rights o' Man*, referring to Tom Paine's famous radical work. Billy is willing to serve, and as he boards his new berth he cheerfully waves goodbye to his departing vessel, calling out, "Farewell, *Rights o' Man*," a harmless salutation that Claggart chooses to regard with suspicion, as if the goodbye signified a mutinous, rebellious nature.

The tragedy, the tale of dark treachery, annihilating the bright innocent, Billy Budd, takes place entirely on the ship. A ship afloat is by its very structure a profoundly resonant dramatic device. It is, first of all, a man-made intruder that sets against the elements, the winds, the storms, the calms, the uncertainty of its human and mechanical equipment. The great age of ocean explorations, centuries before the *Indomitable*—the age of, for instance, Columbus, now undergoing a vulgar and provincial downgrading—is scarcely imaginable to us today. Even the eighteenth-century vessel of Melville's fiction is under sail, without power, demanding every sort of daring and perseverance. Billy Budd, manning the great topsail, is therefore a romantic vision of strength and the spirit of adventure.

A ship against the elements is one thing, but it also contains the dangerous human drama of beings brought together in a random way, strangers of no previous acquaintance, each trapped in a void, with no exit possible until the voyage is completed. A ship at sea is, then, a prison, and as in land-locked prisons there will be a hierarchy of fixed positions, men in power over others, tempting to tyranny on the part of the powerful and to baseness as the lower orders struggle to survive. Such a base one is Squeak, a ship's corporal, a miserable creature who does Claggart's bidding.

Billy Budd is the final representation on Melville's genius. The manuscript was left in a trunk at the time of his death in 1891 and did not see publication until 1924. The early success of his seafaring novels had not prepared the public for the immense rhetorical and imaginative complexities of *Moby-Dick,* and indeed he ceased to have a public. Twenty years near the end of his life were spent as an inspector in the Customs House in New York City. Melville knew neglect and despair, and it is fitting to look at his last work of fiction as somehow a summation of the state of mind to which his experience of life had brought him. The conflict between simple, unaffected beauty and goodness and chaotic, willful destructiveness does appear to find a promising resolution that is not overwhelmed by Billy's death. His purity seems to live on and is given a transcendent force in the description of his last moments, moments that recall Christ's crucifixion. "At the same time it chanced that the vapoury fleece hanging low in the East, was shot through with a soft glory as of the fleece of the Lamb of God seen in mystical vision; and simultaneously therewith, watched by the wedged mass of upturned faces, Billy ascended; and ascending, took the full rose of dawn."

The libretto used by Benjamin Britten for the powerful opera he created out of Melville's story bears the name of Eric Crozier, a frequent collaborator of the composer's, and also the name of the distinguished novelist E.M. Forster. It is difficult to find the Forster voice in the libretto, although the novelist's attraction to this story of male beauty and innocence is easy to grant. In the original tale there is very little dialogue, and its formal dimensions are largely discursive and reflective. A libretto, with its violent condensations, its transposal of the dilatory expansiveness of prose fiction, must meet the demands of the stage and, most perplexing of all, the demands of the singing voice as the vessel of plot action, feeling, interpretation, poetry and character. Sometimes the dialogue of the *Billy Budd* libretto is a bit more "matey" than would be true of Melville, even though here the setting is an English ship. Melville's wonderful "God bless Captain Vere!" is fixed in the mind of generations of readers and the change in the libretto to "Starry Vere, God bless you!" is a bit of a jar to the student of literature. But that is a trifle.

It must be said that the *Billy Budd* libretto works. The story is told, the tragedy unfolds, the ship is used as a powerful visual enclosure, and the work is a triumph of musical theater in the highest sense. We may note the practical dilemma of having as a hero a baritone whose outstanding feature is a striking, dominating physical beauty. Heroines in opera are offered as beautiful, fascinating and seductive, and to achieve this, much use is made of blond wigs and flowing, concealing garments—a transformation is at hand, often quite imperfect. But a beautiful young man is something else—a beautiful young man with a superior singing voice. That we must leave to chance.

The opera is set in two acts, and the musical and dramatic tension is unrelenting, broken only by a few rhymed sea chanteys of what might be called a mixed national character, since they pair "Genoa" and "Shenandoah," "Nantucket" and "bucket"—that sort of thing. And there is a break from the dilemma of character when the ship suddenly has a chance to engage the French in battle. Due to a mist and an unsteady breeze, the chase is lost, but the scene is an interesting diversion in itself. It reveals the contrary nature of the sailors, surly and discontent at one moment but patriots eager to uphold the honor of the British navy at the next moment.

The ending of the opera is somber, as the voices of the crew rise in an ominous grumble of revulsion at the fate of Billy. But the angry, threatening voices die away, as they must, and we move to Vere's final despairing epilogue. In Melville's story, the captain is wounded in battle and dies murmuring, "Billy Budd, Billy Budd." Still, the flash-forwards to Vere as an old man, reflecting upon the curious drama on board the *Indomitable*, finally seem a proper addition. Vere is the moral center of the tragedy, an Englishman of the finest stripe, his whole being illuminated by a flame of conscience and culture. In that way he is a contrast to Billy and to Claggart, who are what they are, helplessly.

At one point Melville makes an interesting conjecture, saying that only Claggart and Captain Vere truly understand the challenge represented by Billy's nature. To Claggart the amazement of the young, handsome sailor is to "be nothing more than innocent!"—just that and nothing more, an unimaginable condition to a complex and devious soul. The violent happenings on the *Indomitable* are part of the eternal heartbreak of human experience. Out of a difficult and profound moral dilemma, Benjamin Britten in *Billy Budd* created a work of great beauty and immense emotional power. A grand opera in every sense.

MAY SARTON

Without Regret

Has there ever been in music or theater a part as seductive for a great prima donna as the Marschallin of *Der Rosenkavalier*? Always there in the distance when the singer is young, the Marschallin is the beautiful reward of growing older, when the ingenue roles she used to sing with joy and still could manage seem a little tame, a little obvious, beside this fascinating woman, created for her by a great poet married to a great composer. It is the romantic theme carried high, almost to the sublime.

That is possibly why *Der Rosenkavalier* has a sacred place in the hearts and minds of devout operagoers, as well as a special appeal to the androgynous, since Octavian, the Marschallin's lover, is written for a woman's voice. I have sometimes wondered how it would sound with a countertenor, but at once I sense, no, that would damage the extraordinary purity of the duets and something unearthly that makes the listener shiver with the intense pleasure, a pleasure not entirely sensual, that they provide.

Why is the Marschallin such a great creation? I know of no other play or opera that makes so clear what it is to be an aristocrat—not to be pretentious or high and mighty but perfectly natural, so she can accept a passionate night with Octavian without mannerism, and without regret, as part of what she calls the mystery of life. She always keeps her balance, even under stress. Here she is a contrast to Octavian, who is a little raw, a little lacking in taste at certain moments. He is, after all, an adolescent, intoxicated by his conquest. Nevertheless, he is written and given music to express immense erotic joy.

It is for the Marschallin to come back from the night's passion to a philosophical mood, the onset of melancholy that is her signature and has given the singer transcendentally beautiful soliloquies on the themes of time, aging and life itself—always changing, as she foresees will happen in her love affair with Quinquin, her name for Octavian.

Her freshness of approach is dazzling as she admits to herself what most women would choose to bury or push aside as too painful. She is at the same time a realist, quite unsentimental, and a believer in the essential mystery life must keep, through the relentless passage of time. The latter haunts her. She confesses to getting up at night to stop all the clocks in the castle. Aristocratic, impulsive, honest, philosophical, she is always aware. While Octavian protests that they must live in the present and enjoy it without thinking of the future, she sees quite clearly and is brave enough to face what she sees—his inevitable falling in love with a young woman.

What makes the Marschallin so fascinating? That at the very moment when she foretells the future and accepts what time will take from her, she is able to smile and say, "One must take things lightly, with a light heart and light hands hold and take, hold and let go"—*halten und nehmen, halten und lassen.* This is where the height of romanticism comes close to the sublime. The moment could be melodramatic and self-pitying. Instead we are shown a radiant acceptance: "Leicht muss man sein."

The whole opera seems to me Rilkean. Rilke's thirteenth *Sonnet to Orpheus,* Part II, might be the text for an aria by the Marschallin:

> Sei allem Abschied voran, als wäre er hinter dir,
>> wie der Winter, der eben geht.
> (Anticipate parting as though you had left it
>> behind you, like the long winter, going at last.)

After an Act II that is close to farce, Act III brings Marie Therese back onstage. It is a new princess who can be coldly furious as she forces Baron Ochs to give up his fiancée and get out. She can ridicule men and their brutality with a harsh, commanding laugh.

But are we prepared for the change in her attitude toward Octavian, caught in nervous suspense between her and Sophie? She has changed sides, as she remembers that she too was forced into a marriage, as Sophie is about to be. She identifies with the girl and is curt with Octavian when he hesitates to go and comfort Sophie, demands even that he woo her rival.

Is it because she realizes that a short time ago their passionate night was for him, so young, chiefly an intoxicating conquest, that he was perhaps more in love with himself than with her? Does she see, as he takes Sophie so tenderly in his arms, that he has grown up a little, and this love may be true love?

What makes the Marschallin so fascinating? In the end, having been able to take quite simply a passionate love affair, without regret, she can with infinite grace accept its end and her lover's marriage.

Is it excruciatingly painful, as one might imagine? No, what makes the Marschallin so fascinating is that within her own journey into the mystery of life she has celebrated so poignantly in Act I, she now reaches a new peak of understanding. She does not blame Octavian, the childlike Quinquin who could give her pleasure but nothing more; she sees him as shallow in the way most men are. She is through with amorous play and will now explore not others but herself and the meditative joys of solitude. She too has grown.

At this crucial place in the opera it is astonishing to remember that Marie Therese is not a middle-aged woman but exactly thirty-two.

ALFRED CORN

French Baroque Music

A decade ago, anyone mentioning the name of the composer Marin Marais would have drawn a blank from all but musicologists, and probably from the majority of them as well. No more: last year's surprise hit film *Tous les matins du monde*, directed by French director Alain Corneau, has made this obscure baroque master something of a celebrity three hundred years after the fact. People with no special education in French music now speak enthusiastically about Marais and have made the Jordi Savall CD recordings of his pieces for *viole* (viola de gamba) relative best-sellers in an industry noted for small profit margins. Instead of historical accuracy, *Tous les matins du monde* has a good story to offer, artful cinematography, and an interesting performance by Gérard Depardieu, not to mention some beautiful excerpts of French baroque music. That music seems to have taken most of the audience by surprise, even though the past two decades have had excellent accounts of it under the brilliant conducting of William Christie, John Eliot Gardiner, Nikolaus Harnoncourt, and Marc Minkowski. Revival of French Baroque coincides with the movement to return to "original instruments," and it's hard to say which came first, an enthusiasm for the sound of early woodwinds and brass or exploration of the neglected repertory once played on them. Music connoisseurs were already aware of the variety and depth of seventeenth- and eighteenth-century French music, but Corneau's film, despite or because of its cavalier approach to history, has now brought in a larger public, eager to learn first about Marais, but then eventually about Couperin, Lully, Charpentier, and Rameau as well.

The Baroque was the first period of classical music I got to know in any depth, without, even so, ever stopping to ask why its celebrated composers—Vivaldi, Bach, Scarlatti, Handel—seemed to be Italian and German only. Still, Bach had written "French" suites for keyboard, and his *Ouvertüren* were described as being in "Französich" style, so the French, too, had evidently composed Baroque music. For whatever reason, though, none was ever programmed at major concert halls; so there was no stimulus for tracking down the obscure labels of the few companies that recorded it. Later, because of an admiration for Debussy and Ravel, I followed up on *their* esteem for French keyboard composers of the eighteenth century and found recordings of Couperin and Rameau. The latter's *Pièces de clavecin en concert* was agreeable music and so was a budget anthology of Couperin's harpsichord pieces, but nothing in them compelled me to seek further. French baroque continued in its curious habit of never being programmed and so was never written about at length outside musicological journals.

The neglect of this music is unfortunately symptomatic of a widespread contemporary failure to understand French culture at large, perhaps because its special characteristics set it rather apart. The French have produced one of the great European traditions, and a bit of almost everything can be found in the vast storehouse of their cultural history. Yet they have consciously willed to cultivate some traits more than others, with the result that generalizations about French thought and art have more-than-usual validity. A former province of the Roman Empire, *la douce France* shares with Italy an axiomatic belief in the value of pleasure. From that follows a devotion to art—art, which, though it may instruct, must always "please." Along with an overriding concern for sensuous appeal, French art has returned again and again to the rapture and attendant problems of romantic love. In a famous mythological contest, the Trojan prince Paris accorded first place to the goddess of Love and Beauty, and the French capital city has never seen drawbacks in his choice serious enough to justify crowning any other candidate. Being the country of art has meant being the domain, above all, of earthly love—for which suitable contexts and personnel must be provided. Hence the central place of women and the feminine sensibility in French culture, so different, to take one example, from the gruff, "masculine" common sense of England. Starting with the medieval period (Christine de Pisan) to the seventeenth century (Mme. de La Fayette) to the twentieth (Colette and Yourcenar), women have been taken seriously in France as writers and shapers of "goût," a word with larger resonances in French than its approximate English equivalent "taste." Even at the most incandescent moment of the Enlightenment, a time when purely rational and impersonal categories were the rule, Diderot, composing a philosophical treatise like the *Rêve d'Alembert*, would cast it as a "Platonic" dialogue with a fictionalized Mlle. de L'Espinasse as one of the participants. Diderot implies that no argument is considered well expressed until a female interlocutor has understood and approved it.

A paradox in the history of French baroque music is that its founder was Italian, an Italian who was something of an aesthetic turncoat. The cultivated minority among privileged patrons of art in France had professed admiration for Italian baroque music from its earliest phase. When she came to France in 1600, Henri IV's bride Maria de' Medici imported music and performers along with the Florentine cooking methods that are said to be the foundation of French cuisine. Importation of *italianitá*, at varying degrees of intensity, continued during the following decades. Once installed as prime minister in the first part of Louis XIV's reign, Cardinal Mazarin, Italian and also a passionate opera lover, summoned composers, musicians, and designers of stage "machines" to Paris to foster French acceptance of Italian artistic taste, and, by extension, the appropriateness of his governmental position.

    Dislike of Italian music usually went along with political opposition to Mazarin and his centralizing policies—though, of course, detractors could find purely aesthetic arguments against compositional practice in the other tradition. Italian music was held to be unduly complicated, absurdly dissonant, and, when coupled with words, destructive to ready comprehension of a foreign-language text few could have followed anyway. Writing operas in French would solve part of the problem, yet a public that found nothing ridiculous in hearing Phèdre's delirium expressed in highly polished couplets still objected to the idea that a dramatic work should be sung. Why obscure a poet's words with florid melismas and an arsenal of distorting ornaments? What the Italians considered passionate singing style, one French critic described as a "musique de gouttières," a music of rain-gutters, in other words, the nocturnal wailing of cats. French composers had for a long time provided music for the adored *ballet de cour* (court ballet) and written short arias with the simplicity of folk song, but the complex form of Italian opera was alien to them. An idiomatic French music-drama did not become possible until a poorly educated Italian resident in the king's service, known mainly as a ballet master and fiddler, found a way to fuse Italian opera and the French court ballet into a form that foregrounded dramatic and textual values, allowed for the French audience's love of dance and visual spectacle, and, at the same time, incorporated musical scores of distinct interest and beauty.

How this composer, his origins so little resembling anything at the French court and his training in music so sketchy, managed to found French opera and become its dictator is one of the absorbing chapters in the history of self-made men. Giovanni Battista Lulli was born the son of a Florentine miller in 1623 and was brought to France in his fourteenth year by Roger de Lorraine, Chevalier de Guise, as a sort of present for his niece, Mlle. de Montpensier, Princesse d'Orléans. She had asked her uncle to find someone to practice Italian with, but, once Lully was installed and dressed in her livery, it seems she never actually found time for it, satisfied with an occasional *buon giorno* tossed to him in passing, probably in the manner of the speaker in Ruth Draper's famous monologue "The Italian Lesson." The princess was firmly anti-Mazarin, and it may be that taking on the young, uneducated, odd-looking, and none-too-clean Italian was a factional equivalent to the princely habit of keeping a stable of dwarves and fools to confront court visitors with. Her young charge never learned French perfectly but changed his first name to Jean-Baptiste and the spelling of his surname to Lully.

As a boy he had developed a considerable knack for mime, dancing, singing, and violin playing, and, once in Paris, attended every theatrical performance he could manage to slip into. Informed of his special talents, the princess subsidized music lessons that enabled him to perform and compose "according to the rules." He was soon arranging little concerts for Mlle. de Montpensier in modest imitation of the famous "Vingt-quatre violons du roi." During the Fronde, the princess was among the most active against Louis, with the result that she was banished to her medieval castle in the provinces. Lully begged to be dismissed, returned to Paris, and, shortly after, entered the king's service—as a ballet master at first, since the ballet was Louis's special passion (not merely as a spectator but also as a tireless participant).

The king's favor arose partly because of his enthusiasm for ballet but also because of Lully's particular charm, subservience mixed with a certain directorial brusqueness that made him seem something more than a vacuous courtier. One story tells of how the king grew tired of waiting for the curtain to rise on the ballet *Alcidiane* while last-minute adjustments were being made and sent word of his royal impatience to Lully—who simply brushed it aside. Thinking that he hadn't been understood, Louis dispatched a high-ranking noble to tell the ballet master that his sovereign was still waiting for the performance to begin. Without hesitation, Lully said, "The king is the master. He can wait as long as it suits him." The baffled nobleman reported back to Louis, who for the length of a whole-note rest considered his alternatives, then laughed and said that it was best to bear with his busy friend. In France, *esprit* is also the master. When Lully was ready, the curtain rose.

By a series of adroit maneuvers impossible to present in a short essay, Lully eventually managed to have himself appointed director of the Académie Royale de Musique in 1672, with the right to permit or forbid staged musical performance anywhere in the realm. Louis was absolute monarch of France, and Lully of French music, which his Machiavellian skills were able to defend against the partisans of Italian style. This would not have mattered so much if it weren't also true that Lully went on to create the French opera, or *tragédie lyrique*, the first of which was his *Cadmus et Hermione*, performed in 1673. It took features from Italian opera and combined these with the old *ballet de cour*, the result a mixed genre with sung recitative, arias, choruses, and dance, but always with an insistence that music would enhance rather than obscure the libretto. As for strictly instrumental passages, Lully forged a style that set itself apart by certain rhythmic and harmonic earmarks, in particular, the *notes inégales*, or dotted rhythm, which had begun as a kind of optional ornament but later became the standard treatment of an unbroken run of same-value notes. All Lully's operas begin with an overture that has a slow opening passage in dotted rhythm, followed by a fast-tempo section with canonic or fugal texture, and then a return to the slow-tempo opening. At last opera had found an idiomatic form in France, and Lully's innovations began to influence other kinds of composition as well, sometimes beyond the borders of France. The Bach *Ouvertüren*, composed in "French" style, all have first movements that follow the dotted-rhythm slow-fast-slow form of the Lullian overture, although, by the time Bach wrote them, Lully's influence was beginning to wane even in France. For this North German composer to write in "French" style was, paradoxically, only to underline his provinciality, showing that he was not quite up to date; yet his abilities were of a kind to transcend temporary stylistic shifts, in works of greatness beyond the limits of a particular place or time.

Pivotal developments in music history do not always guarantee that the works incorporating them will appeal to a later era. Audiences in France and the United States have had, however, a chance to judge the stageworthiness of Lullian opera in the first-rate revival of *Atys* conducted by William Christie, and the verdict is in: Lully belongs to the ranks of great opera composers. Aside from a clear and sensitive setting of the text, what looked like rather simple music on the page turned out to be compelling when heard in the theater. The choruses seem to drive all resistance before them with an *ostinato*-style vehemence that resembles some of our contemporary minimalists. A mood of dark mystery emanates from the Act III ensemble "Dormons, dormons tous" where allegorical representatives of sleep urge the opera's hero to make an Orphic descent into the realm of dreams. An accompaniment of recorders in a lulling minor-key melody set against a string background makes for memorable music, inducing not sleep but the rapt hypnosis of effective theater. A plaintive dialogue between Cybèle and a chorus of nature divinities at the conclusion of Act V anticipates scenes composed with a similar structure in Gluck's *Orfeo,* or the passionate interchange between Elettra and the chorus in Mozart's *Idomeneo* more than a century later.

Continuing in the mode of paradox, music history brings us next a great French composer who became the leading exponent of *Italian* taste in his native land. Almost nothing is known about the early life of Marc-Antoine Charpentier, but tradition says that he went to Rome in the 1670s and studied under Carissimi, so that aspects of Italian music were always afterward part of his compositional practice. Partisans of the domestic product complained in particular of his dissonances, moderate compared to what you find on every page, for example, of Monteverdi, but nevertheless outside French harmonic conventions of the day. At this distance we can see that Charpentier's critics were mistaken and cite harmonic richness as one of his principal strengths. His dissonances are most often the result of chordal suspensions and resolve in a perfectly regular way. One of the most beautiful examples is found in the setting of the phrase "et unam sanctam catholicam at apostolicam ecclesiam" in the Credo of Charpentier's *Missa* "Assumpta est Maria" (1699), where suspensions in the tenor line make for ravishing discords essential to the effect of awestruck celebration. The work as a whole is one of the high points in Charpentier's oeuvre and is also the first instance of a mass using orchestral accompaniment. To Charpentier goes the honor as well of having composed the first cantata in French, and the first sonata. Doing so was one more bid for the Italian style in music, but even without these innovations Charpentier made that influence felt. For one thing, the majority of his work is church music, composed on Latin texts. Italian is much closer to church Latin than French is, and so Italian compositional habits don't distort Latin as they do French. In any case, the worshiper was supposed to have liturgical texts more or less by heart, so the insistence on textual clarity was less urgent. It's no surprise, then, to see that Charpentier used melisma freely in his church compositions, without perhaps relying on it as much as Italian opera does.

Despite his gifts, Charpentier did not achieve a fame at all comparable to Lully's, whether because of the reigning prejudice against Italian style or because of Charpentier's less energetic efforts at self-advancement. Even the composition of *Médée,* an opera in conformity with Lullian rather than Italian practice, brought him only moderate recognition. He had a few patrons who saw his genius, and he was eventually appointed choirmaster of the Sainte Chapelle, but he remained in a relative obscurity that has only begun to be dispelled in the twentieth century. And high time: his music repays close study, as several conductors have seen—among them William Christie, who acknowledged Charpentier's special status by naming his performing ensemble "Les Arts Florissants," after one of the composer's early cantatas.

Tous les matins du monde (the film mentioned earlier) includes, along with Marais's music, an excerpt from François Couperin's *Leçons des Ténèbres,* a setting of passages from Lamentations used during the Tenebrae services of Holy Week. Written for solo and duo women's voices, it was commissioned by the Convent of Longchamp, a religious community for women of noble rank, known for excellent musical performances. I first heard the work in Alfred Deller's performance, which was authentic enough for the standards of his time and, beyond that, abounded in musical finesse. In any case, the notes were Couperin's, and it was apparent from the first that he was a composer out of the ordinary. Especially striking in the *Leçons* is Couperin's setting of the letters of the Hebrew alphabet, which mark divisions in Jeremiah's prophecy. Here the argument that melisma obscured the text applied less than ever, and the composer was free to exercise ornamental invention to the fullest extent. The section written for two voices achieves heartrending intensity, where voices intertwine like tendrils in a vineyard, straining toward heaven as the light begins to fail and shadows of the Passion approach. Each section concludes with a solemn exhortation that Jerusalem return to the Lord, the setting of the holy city's name shaken by musical sobs somewhat in the manner of Jewish cantorial singing. Hearing this powerfully original work sent me on a quest to find other recordings of Couperin back in the early seventies, and so I was led to the *Concerts royaux, L'Apothéose de Lully,* and *Les Nations.*

Couperin's development is yet another installment in the story of Italian influences on French music. Because he was born in France and came from a family of musicians, Couperin imbibed the French style like mother's milk, but his strongest early enthusiasm was the music of Corelli. He published his first trio sonatas under an Italian pseudonym (but, encouraged by their reception, signed all later compositions with his own name). *Le Parnasse ou L'Apothéose de Corelli,* written in 1724, is a musical "deification" or at least a canonization of Arcangelo Corelli, a programmatic work whose successive movements depict the deceased Italian composer petitioning the Muses on Mount Parnassus to admit him to their company. He drinks the waters of the Hippocrene fountain, is seized by "enthusiasm," falls asleep, is wakened by the Muses, and taken to his place at the side of Apollo, after which he offers thanks for the favor.

Program music was not at all typical for the time, but we can see that Couperin judged his experiment a success, for he composed a companion piece the following year, his *L'Apothéose composé à la mémoire immortelle de l'incomparable Monsieur Lully,* intended as an aesthetic counterweight to the Corelli homage. That had been written in Couperin's approximation of Italian style, with bravura passages for strings, imitative part-writing, and pungent dissonances. The Lully apotheosis, more than twice as long, keeps to French restraint and elegance, with a greater attention to melody and a less complex musical texture. To the strings-and-harpsichord continuo of the first, Couperin adds flutes and oboes, a significant expansion of sonic options, certainly, but also a confirmation of the intention to write in the French style. For, if the characteristic instrument of the Italian Baroque is a string, and of the German, a "clavier," for the French Baroque, it is a woodwind. The string can produce an almost vocal expression of intense feeling, and, like the keyboard, can handle rapid sequences of notes of equal value. The woodwind is a bit less agile and never sounds good when pushed beyond mezzo-forte, but it has a haunting sonority and suits the soft plaintiveness of French melody. Besides that, woodwinds are associated with the pastoral world, civilized counterparts to the pipes played by shepherds during long hours of keeping watch over their flocks.

In the *L'Apothéose de Lully*, woodwinds seem entirely appropriate in the opening scene, where Couperin wants us to imagine the earlier master at ease in the Elysian Fields making music with other "lyric shades." In a series of movements similar to those in the Corelli apotheosis, Lully is invited by Apollo to come up to Parnassus, and his departure is mourned by the shades of his contemporaries in a *"plainte"* scored for lulling flutes, which we can now hear played on the early instruments they were written for, wooden flutes with a much softer, more "pastoral" timbre than the modern version in silver. What Couperin envisioned overall was a fusion of Italian and French style, "les goûts réunis," as he termed it, and the remainder of the Lully apotheosis is an enactment of that reunion under Apollo's supervision. The same will is apparent in *Les Nations*, a symphonic work in four parts, one titled *La française*, one *L'espagnole*, one *La piémontaise*, and the last *L'impériale*. There was of course no Italian "nation" in the seventeenth century; we have to see *all* these pieces as partaking in the project of aesthetic reunification, epitomized in *L'impériale*, which is Couperin's maturest adaptation of Corelli to his purposes. A political dimension is apparent here, since, although neither the Piedmont nor Spain was notable for its musical style, they had both become allied to France, so that a certain plausibility inheres in Louis's Augustan vision of empire, conceived by Couperin in aesthetic as well as political terms. All of eighteenth-century Europe followed the French, just as the twentieth century has been swayed, in developed countries at least, by "the American way of life." It's worth noting, though, that whereas French taste in literature, painting, dress, architecture, and the decorative arts prevailed in the eighteenth century, its influence in music never outdistanced the Italian.

It was a work of Marais's, though not the viola da gamba pieces, that made me resolve, back in the early seventies, to hear all the French Baroque music available. Because of the Couperin *Leçons des Ténèbres*, I bought a Cardinal LP titled "Music at the Court of Louis XIV," with one of the *Concerts royaux*, which were composed for Louis during his retirement at Marly. There was also a suite of music taken from the opera *Alcyone* by someone named Marin Marais. When I played it, the special sonorities of the original instruments, combined with a music at times piercingly sweet, at times elegantly melancholy, made a deep impression on me. After Lully, it was customary for French operas to conclude with a grand *chaconne*, a slow dance movement in three-quarter time, based on a repeated harmonic progression (very often a stepwise descent from tonic to dominant—the subtonic sometimes flatted—and back to the tonic for the repeat). Within this narrow frame, French composers exercised enormous melodic and rhythmic invention to provide variety and interest for a movement of six or seven minutes of uninterrupted repetition. The chaconne is always one of the high points in French Baroque music, and Marais's weighs in as one of the most beautiful ever written, with surprising *concertato* effects between strings and the gorgeous original woodwinds. I looked for other works of Marais, but there were none to be found, and so the wide range of the viola da gamba pieces were unknown to me until Corneau's film. We now have a CD of the complete *Alcyone* conducted by Marc Minkowski, and I've discovered that one of the instrumental pieces in the Harnoncourt recording was in the opera actually a chorus; standards of "authenticity" have tightened in the interim.

The film of Marais's life takes several liberties with history, beginning with the account of his teacher Sainte-Colombe, who is presented as a fierce recluse, spurning the opportunity to join the king's service in order to be left alone with his art. In fact, Sainte-Colombe was employed by the king and still managed to write his very reckonable works for *viole*. The romance between his daughter and Marais is a fiction, but the film could not do without it, and the association of Marais's extremely beautiful piece "La Rêveuse" with the jilted young woman was an effective touch, so that I'm no longer able to hear it without thinking of the wrenching story presented in the film. Marais's compositions for viola da gamba, vast in number, are some of the great discoveries in the current revival. They combine the folklike quality of French vocal music with, on the one hand, a bent toward melancholy of a very deep dye, and, on the other, a drive toward virtuoso writing that bespeaks an Italian influence. Listening to the haunting minor-key melodies of these pieces I think of Nerval's poem, "Fantaisie," which begins:

> Il est un air pour qui je donnerais
> Tout Rossini, tout Mozart et tout Weber,
> Un air très vieux, languissant et funèbre,
> Qui pour moi seul a des charmes secrets!

(There is a song for which I would give/All of Rossini, Mozart, and Weber,/An old song, languishing and funereal,/Which, for me alone, has secret charms.) He goes on to place the song in the reign of Louis

XIII, and it seems to me that a feature of Marais's *pièces de viole* is an archaizing penchant for the French music of the early seventeenth century. Perhaps that is how to account, allegorically, for the apocryphal romance in Corneau's film: Marais's attachment to, and never-quite-total abandonment of, Sainte-Colombe's daughter may stand for his relationship to the native tradition. Some traces of that melancholy profundity were passed on to J.S. Bach and given a Lutheran coloration in his unsurpassable suites for cello solo. Otherwise, Marais's works for viola da gamba stand apart, not of the same order as works by those (like Forqueray or even Sainte-Colombe) to whom he was compared in his day.

Marais' opera *Alcyone* (1706), Lullian in its organization but more advanced in its harmonic language, is rightly viewed as a work that partly prefigures the opera of Jean-Philippe Rameau. The truth is that the early eighteenth century produced a rich mulch of operas and cantatas from which Rameau's overshadowing achievement sprang. Without the example of Campra, Montéclair, and Clérambault, as well as Marais, Rameau's operas would not have taken the form they did, but it is also true that he goes well beyond his models and is in fact an indispensable stepping stone in the history of the genre. The lobby of the Palais Garnier, formerly the Opéra de Paris, has a series of monumental statues representing the great operatic composers. Of these, only two are French, Lully and Rameau. But no works by Lully were in the operatic repertory after the eighteenth century and none by Rameau after the nineteenth, until the recent interest in original instruments and early performance practice led to their revival.

Rameau was born in Dijon in 1683 and spent his early years as an active musician in the provinces, playing organ for churches and composing sacred works. He came to Paris a number of times in his youth and settled there permanently in 1722, the year he published his *Traité de l'harmonie*. With the dawn of the century of Enlightenment it was inevitable that musical theorists would eventually try to bring the spirit of classification and *lumière* to the art of music. Rameau's *Traité* was the first of a number of revised and expanded treatises on the origin and significance of harmony, and it was these that established him as an important figure even before his compositions were widely known. Putting his theories into practice, Rameau developed an arresting harmonic vocabulary it is beyond the scope of this essay to analyze. Nevertheless, we can locate the beginning of French music's special preoccupation with harmony (for Berlioz, Fauré, Debussy, Ravel, Poulenc, and Messiaen, for example) in Rameau's writings. The theoretical grounds for them have inevitably been challenged although residual traces of his ideas remain in comments on harmony even so recent as Virgil Thomson's. In music history, Rameau counts as a theorist as well as a composer, then, and we have some interesting cantatas and motets by him and some effective chamber music; but his main importance for us is as a composer of opera (both the *tragédie lyrique* and *opéra-ballet* styles).

Not, however, until 1732, when Michel Pignolet de Montéclair staged his *Jepthé* at the Académie Royale de la Musique, did Rameau, at the age of fifty, turn to opera. There had been dramatic compositions on religious subjects before (Charpentier's *David et Jonathas,* for example, which was commissioned by a Jesuit college), but none had ever been produced at the Académie. Montéclair's originality went beyond the choice of subject matter; he used the orchestra to accompany recitatives, and he concerned himself with instrumental color as an expressive resource. Rameau (none of whose completed operas use religious stories for their librettos) adapted these innovations for his first opera, *Hippolyte et Aricie* (1733), a recasting of the Phèdre story that French audiences had held in special regard ever since its treatment by Racine. This opera doesn't embody the perfection and suavity of later works, but its occasional roughness is inseparable from the fierce passions he brought to what is, after all, a gruesome fable. Rameau and his librettist Pellegrin are able to draw on the strengths of their Euripidean, Senecan, and Racinian models to produce a work of tragedy in the grand style. Perhaps this is the last echo in music of the *grand siècle,* soon to be replaced by the softer pastoral mode in vogue during the reign of Louis XV, used even in the later works of Rameau. I can only take the "highlight" approach here, singling out Phèdre's defiantly tragic aria "Cruelle mère des amours" for special notice, as well as mentioning the extraordinary *Trio des Parques,* where the three Fates foresee Theseus's destiny and express their horror in a long, slow chant composed in descending enharmonic chords over an agitated orchestral accompaniment. This number had to be dropped from the first performance: singers were unable to manage their parts. The even-temperament tuning required for this startling bit of *Effektmusik* was still new to contemporary ears, and, in operas that came after, Rameau never again resorted to enharmonic chords so glaringly exposed. Some of the strangeness remains even for us, but then the destiny foreseen by Rameau's Fates is more than strange: a father's calling down destruction on his son demands music out of the ordinary.

Few of Rameau's operas have ever been staged in America, and none by major opera companies (although James Richman and the Concert Royal's production of *Le Temple de la gloire* was not at all amateurish). James Levine has been unyielding on the question of doing Rameau at the Met, perhaps because he thinks tickets would be hard to sell or that the house is too big for music on this scale. There have been some concert performances, the most notable William Christie's near-perfect account of *Castor et Pollux* and *Les Indes galantes* at the Brooklyn Academy of Music earlier this year, for which we must be grateful. *Castor et Pollux*, Rameau's second tragedy, represents his characteristic strengths very well. The libretto by Danchet keeps some of the tragic grandeur of *Hippolyte et Aricie* even though the story is less gripping than that of the earlier opera. *Castor et Pollux* was mounted in 1736, and by this date all of Rameau's musical strengths were in place. Far from husbanding his creative energies, the composer lavishes musical invention in number after number, varying the melodic, rhythmic, and harmonic approaches and applying a wide range of orchestral color. "Tristes apprêts," the Act I soprano solo for the character Télaïre, in its marble-like simplicity and nobility anticipates Gluck, which is another way to say that it sounds timeless. Prominent in the orchestral accompaniment is the bassoon, a signature instrument for Rameau and associated with some of his most ravishing inventions. At the purely theoretical level, the aria explores the potential of subdominant harmony and the effect of adding a sixth to it, all in the interest of deepening musical expression of the text. Though it is very short, I can't resist mentioning the orchestral interlude that accompanies Jupiter's Act V descent in a "machine": over a soft cloud of string harmonies, a solo flute repeats a rising and falling motif on different degrees of the scale, with an effect of profound depth and sweetness, now dissonant to, now consonant with, the strings. The remainder of the act untangles the story's quasi-tragic complications to achieve a happy ending, but the interlude has already shown, in purely musical terms, that Jupiter's tender mercies are going to do precisely that. During the Christie concert performance, this was one of the moments when the audience held its breath.

Les Indes galantes is the high point in an alternative genre, the *opéra-ballet*, which in the later eighteenth century rivaled and perhaps even supplanted Lullian opera in public favor. Dramatic works where dance predominated in the form of a series of *entrées* loosely integrated into the plot had been written and performed throughout the seventeenth century but were overshadowed by the novelty of Lully's *tragédie lyrique* until Rameau took them up. We can think of their resurgence of popularity as being of a piece with the disfavor into which grandeur and seriousness fell after the reign of Louis XIV. In *opéra-ballet,* the libretto is deemphasized and is more often based on pastoral or comic subjects than tragic or dramatic ones. The lion's share of the music is for dance and has therefore a rhythmic energy difficult or impossible to achieve in vocal settings of French poetry. Not that moments of high seriousness are excluded: in "Les Incas," the ballet's second *entrée,* the Inca Huascar, confronted with the destruction of his culture by Spanish invaders, sings a noble and moving aria to the sun-god, "Soleil, on a détruit tes superbes asiles," the spirit of which anticipates last year's anti-Columbus discussion during the quincentenary of his voyage. Anyone considering the rich subject of the use that European art has made of contact with the New World must look at this *opéra-ballet.* For the French, "les Indes" included all countries outside Europe, just as "le désert" was anywhere outside Paris. Hence the settings for the three other *entrées* comprising this work (after the Prologue in Hébé's garden) are Turkey, Persia, and Louisiana, as well as Peru. The Louisiana section, titled "Les Sauvages," includes the dance of the same name, based on an early keyboard work Rameau composed after attending a performance by American Indians at a theater in one of the popular fairs of the day. The thumping rhythms and elementary minor-key melody of this *entrée* provided the one note of exoticism in a score otherwise written in the composer's own French style. The storm scene in "Le Turc généreux" and the volcanic eruption in "Les Incas" are exciting early examples of tone-painting in music, but they are not representative of Rameau's essential genius. That is unmistakable, though, in the quartet "Tendre amour," which comes in the third *entrée* ("Les Fleurs") and must be the most beautiful ensemble writing in opera between Monteverdi and Mozart. Genius is also resplendently apparent in the concluding chaconne, perhaps the grandest example of the genre ever composed. It was quite clear to the audience at the Brooklyn Academy performance that they had just heard a work unsurpassed in variety and brilliance of invention, expertly conducted and thrillingly sung.

Only a few French operas that I would like to see have I actually seen. Most of them I know by recordings, but even at-home listening can be powerful. Those times when I want to forget everything cheap, boring, and ugly in experience, an unfailing remedy is to play the

"Entrée d'Abaris" from *Les Boréades*. *Les Boréades* was Rameau's last opera and never performed in his lifetime (in fact, not until 1975, in John Eliot Gardiner's realization). The music for this short ballet number is scored for flute, strings, and, yes, the bassoon—a ravishing and also moving use of Rameau's signature instrument. The melody played by flute is imitated half a bar later by the bassoon in a lower register, producing a series of motivic overlaps at once simple and rich. The harmony and part-leading collaborate in an effect of graceful sophistication joined to the tender, reconciled melancholy of advanced years, the blend heart-catching in a way no other works I can think of are—well, perhaps the later Haydn string quartets. Listening to the soft downward flow of the theme alternating with upward climbing strings, you think: This music itself is the "machine" that raises the listener above the stage, up to the divine realm, where Love and Beauty reign, supported by the virtues of Clarity and Restraint; where the language spoken, when it is not pure music, is French, and everyone understands all that is said *à demi-mot*.

French music did not become the norm in the eighteenth century, and, considering the achievements of Handel, Gluck, Haydn, and Mozart, we cannot regret that fact. Even in France, the balance tipped in favor of the Italian style after the Paris première and enormous popular success of Pergolesi's *La serva padrona* in the 1750s. That so small a challenger should topple the immense prestige of the official tradition is surprising only if we ignore competing strains that had been active in French music since the mid-seventeenth century. The aesthetic battle has long since ended. There's no need, then, to depreciate French music in order to insure the survival of other styles. The stance to take now is to think of French Baroque music as a threatened species, deserving of as much performance and study as possible. Conductors, planners of repertory, moguls of the recording industry, and musicologists, the responsibility is yours: musical Jupiters, board *la machine*, descend, and continue to perform your deeds of justice and mercy.

The author would like to offer special thanks to Christopher Corwin for his expertise and assistance in writing this essay, and to acknowledge a debt to the work of Cuthbert Girdlestone and H. Wiley Hitchcock for information and particular judgments.

NED ROREM

Virgil (1944)

Manhattan during the war and up through the early 1950s was governed by Aaron Copland and Virgil Thomson, the father and mother of American music. Young composers joined one faction or the other, there was no third. Both were from France through Nadia Boulanger, but Copland's camp was Stravinsky-French and contained a now-vanished breed of neo-classicist like Alexie Haieff and Harold Shapero, while Thomson's camp was Satie-French and contained a still-vital breed of neo-catholic like Lou Harrison and John Cage. (The Teutonisms of Wolpe-via-Schoenberg were as yet quiescent.) A few lone wolves like me were still socially partial to one or the other. I saw less of Aaron than of Virgil, simply because the latter was my employer for a while.

With the hard lens of hindsight it's clear that, beyond an occasional letter of reference or a pat on the back, neither musician, during decades of fraternizing, ever lifted a finger toward my music, be it by performance, verbal recommendation, or through their copious prosifying. Naturally they were more important to me than I to them—they were older; to this day I recall every word that each ever said, and realize how their professional behavior stamped mine. Yet such awareness stems from tenacity: instruction is taken, not given, and they set an example just by being. Beyond those elements of themselves that were at the disposal of anyone, I owe nothing to either man. Still, with the soft lens of hindsight I cannot today recall either man without my eyes welling at the accumulation of affection that comes only from patience and the years.

On the face of it, entry to the Empire City through Virgil Thomson's door would seem the ideal route for a twenty-year-old, half Julien Sorel, half Alice Adams, anxious about a solid career in the shifting sands of musical composition. Thomson at forty-eight was the best English-language critic in the world; by extension he was one of our most-played composers. His daily reviews and Sunday sermons in the

Herald Tribune, although of smaller readership than Olin Downes at the *Times,* had larger cachet, and that cachet—the power to put a musician on the map and keep him there—had much to do with his own music being commissioned and performed. Virgil was shrewd as they come about everything but Virgil. When in 1953 he retired from the paper, the performance frequency of his music plummeted overnight to the surprise of no one but himself.

Meanwhile, at the start of the new year 1944, he was at his peak, writing words and music non-stop, socializing too, and with a presumably satisfactory sex life. There are three conditions of success to which we all aspire—success in work, in society, and in love—but nobody can juggle more than two simultaneously; to succeed in all three at once means that one of them is collapsing—we're dancing on a volcano's brink. For now he seemed blessed, at least from where I sat.

I sat at a long table in the end of the dining room between parlor and bedroom. The European tone of the Chelsea, which smelled of camphor and lavender in the old-maidish lobby and of cinnamon and citronella in Virgil's apartment, set me more or less at ease: it reeked of childhood. My duties as in-house copyist were to work under the master's guiding eye from 10 till noon and from 1 till 3 five days a week. For these twenty hours I received twenty dollars of which five went to Morris for rent, five to a savings account, and ten to concert tickets, music, books, groceries, subways and beer. During the first week I had lunch with Virgil (I didn't yet call him that) while he taught me the ropes. After that at midday Morris would meet me at a Riker's hash-house on Eighth Avenue, or I'd eat alone somewhere or maybe nowhere.

The copying tasks began with short pieces, graduating eventually to big ones, rendering everything in Virgil's oeuvre that had not hitherto been printed into legible fair-copy. The problem lay less in making a readable facsimile than in deciphering the original. Virgil's pencilled calligraphy, like the manuscript of Pierre Boulez—a man whose music was as fancy as Virgil's was plain, and who was in all ways except keenness remote from Thomson (the two would nevertheless become, a decade later, staunch friends for reasons of expedience)—was slapdash, almost as though he didn't want to be deciphered. (Gide: "Don't be too quick to understand me.")

Every week my script improved. Re-examining the script today, it appears overly ornate, with scrolls and curlicues formed by the special music fountain pens that could write thick and thin in India ink, but it was a marked contrast to the original. Virgil, of course, showed me examples by his previous secretaries to use as models, and once sent me uptown to the atelier of Arnold Arnstein, dean of copyists, where five young people were bent over the scribblings of the Current Great (Schuman, Moore, Menotti, Barber) and transferring, by means of slide rules and compasses, rough drafts onto transparent paper—onion skin, as it was called—for photo-reproduction. After a month or so of clarifying early works of Virgil—whimsical settings of Georges Hugnet or Jean Racine or King Solomon, for example, or the dumb sonata for solo flute, or the truly touching 1928 *Stabat Mater* on a text of Max Jacob (the only beautiful piece he ever penned), or sonic one-page portraits of friends that had never been inked—I graduated to bigger things. I did the score and parts of the Third Symphony (subtitled the "Hymn Tune"), scheduled for performance by the Philharmonic the next season. The responsibility was intimidating: Rozinski would be conducting from my score, eighty men would be playing from my parts, and if someone sounded a false note, the error would not only be traceable to humble me, but expensive rehearsal time would be spent in correcting the error.

More than the responsibility, though, was the instructive value. Yes, I was skeptical about, even contemptuous of, and mostly bemused by, what I felt to be Virgil's sappy stuff (and jealous that big-time performers should be hoodwinked), for I hadn't yet perceived sophistication in the simplemindedness. But the experience, for a young composer, of being answerable to every one of the myriad notes in this or that score was more vital than theory. The best way to learn how a piece of music is confected—be it Monteverdi or Charles Mingus—is to copy it. Not impersonate but reproduce literally, like Borges's mad (sane) anti-hero, Pierre Menard, who "translated"—from Spanish into Spanish, so to speak—all of *Don Quixote* word for word, then called it his own.

Among my chores as apprentice was to accompany the boss to rehearsals. Virgil-as-performer was insecure, hence feisty. In private his lucidity was exemplary since as a critic he could do the impossible—put into words that which can't be put into words, by describing one art in terms of another. When playing a Mozart sonata, for example, for friends in his living room, he would raise both hands high then let them fall with great authority onto all the wrong keys; yet he would accompany this action with such explicatory eloquence about how all of Mozart's instrumental slow movements are really subliminal love duets that he gave an illusion of virtuosity. But in public he could offend. Once when he was engaged to guest-conduct one of his affairs—I think it was *The Mayor La Guardia Waltzes*—with Stokowski's Youth Orchestra, his insecurity grew apparent not through reticence but through bullying. During the rehearsal he shrieked at the kids to play softer. He was hissed. Stokowski meanwhile, as was his wont, strolled coolly among the instrumentalists while Virgil ranted on the podium. "Leopold," cried Virgil, "how do I make them play softer?" Stokowski, all aplomb, turned toward his adoring orchestra, put a finger to his lips, and simply whispered: "Softer."

Another time, before the live Wednesday night performance on WOR of the master's recently orchestrated *Five Portraits*, I became embarrassed more for me than for him. During the previous weeks, while copying the score and parts of this new piece and weary of Virgil's endless series of moronic tonic-dominant progressions, I spiced up a couple of chords with added sevenths. Hearing this at the rehearsal, Virgil had a fit. I realized my miscalculation (the "improvements" diminished the music, if possible) and it was my lot to go into the orchestra and correct each part while the conductor, Alfred Wallenstein, and players expensively waited.

After the performance Virgil took me to Bleeck's Tavern, better known as the Artists and Writers Restaurant, a hangout of *Herald Tribune* employees on West 40th. With us were Edward James and Yvonne de Casa Fuerte, both of Virgil's generation. Yvonne, a marquise, French and poor despite her rich Spanish title, was sweating out the war as a violinist in American pick-up orchestras. Plain, even gross-featured, she exuded nevertheless a whiff of strong glamour with her copper hair and ostrich plumes, her gruff gallic authority which does not exist in American females, and her inability, despite long residence here, to speak English. (André Breton, asked why he never learned our language while living in New York, replied *"Pour ne pas ternir mon français."* And Gertrude Stein, whose French was said to be rocky and accented despite the bulk of her seventy-two years on foreign soil, could have said as much, in reverse. Indeed, might not her clarity in English—in *American*—have been dimmed had she stayed home?) In the 1920s Yvonne had founded the Sérénade Concerts in Paris which promoted Darius Milhaud, the young Igor Markevich, Henri Sauguet, Vittorio Rieti (whose mistress she was), Francis Poulenc and Nicolas

Nabokov. Now in New York she was active in the League of Composers, a cousin of the French organization. In fact, besides Yvonne, there were four powerful women who, in this pre-feminist era, ran the bureaucratic side of New Music: Claire Reis, who had invented the League in 1923; Minna Lederman, who started the dazzling *Modern Music* magazine, verbal artery of "the cause" until its demise in 1946, and who as I write remains vital in her late nineties; Louis Varèse, wife and biographer of Edgard the innovator, excellent translator of Rimbaud, and parental figure to all; and Alma Morgenthau, sister of Henry Jr. and mother of Barbara Tuchman, who gave money. What these women said went. Claire, Minna, and Alma were each touchingly, because hopelessly, in love with Aaron Copland. Yvonne and Louise were not (they were also not Jewish). Yvonne, my first brush with the dynamic of a continental lady, remained a staunch ally, especially during my Paris years when she became cultural attaché at the American embassy. As for Edward James, natural son of Edward the Seventh, he was shortish and thin and married to Tilly Losch, but queer, very, and a patron of the arts beginning with the late Diaghilev ballets. He had written the text and paid for Poulenc's first big choral piece with orchestra, *Sècheresses*, and otherwise sought the company of the highborn and of rough trade. I never saw him again after this Wednesday, but Gavin Lambert eventually wrote a novel about him called *Norman's Letter*.

Virgil invited me for a weekend to the New Jersey house of his Harvard chum, art historian Briggs Buchanan (whose portrait I'd copied). Of this outing I recall the half-dozen taffy apples we bought at the bus station for the Buchanan children, a shimmering garden with dahlias, the room shared with Mr. Thomson, and, most crucially, Erik Satie's *Socrate*. Virgil sang me this little cantata in his composer's voice (i.e., his non-voice of definitive expressivity), and during that half hour I felt my notion of the world's musical repertory change shape, swell, shrink, as the cantata ensconced itself in my ken where it would permanently lodge, along with *The Rite of Spring*, as one of those three or four artistic experiences against which I would judge all others in the coming years.

What can be said of *Socrate*? On that special morning I was most struck by the second movement wherein teacher strolls with pupil by the river; the intonations are continual non-developmental iterations of adjacent couplets, as in the line *Est-il rien de plus suave et de plus délicieux?* Such contagious monotone chutzpah, honest and respectful. But when I later bought the score and rehashed it on my own piano, the three scenes bloomed differently beneath my fingers. *Socrate* is, in a sense, without style—without immediate location in time. Oddly, when you talk to confirmed Satie freaks who think of the composer as "minimal," they've usually heard his every work except the masterpiece, *Socrate*. (Although "master" is the one thing Satie was not; it's what Germans are.) I've sung it to myself every week of my life without getting bored, the joy of expectation remaining always fresh. Satie's philosophy, in relating the conventionally unrelated—equating wit with sorrow as a qualitative expression, for instance—was not far from yesterday's pop culture which made the ordinary extraordinary by removing it from context. Elsewhere, conversely, like the surrealists, he treated his eccentric subject matter straightforwardly. In the margins of his compositions he inserted little verbal jokes, whimsical advice to the performer or "impossible" directions not unlike those Ives was employing at the same time in America. *Socrate* itself is fairly long as pieces go; as a program in itself, fairly short. Nothing "goes" with it, least of all other works by Satie since, in a way, they are all contained within *Socrate*. The texts from Plato's *Dialogues*, highly truncated in the French translation, are set to music without romantic gyration, even without vocal embellishment, almost as they would be spoken. They are set literally, so to speak, with respect. Respect—that is, humility—is not a quality one quite associates with greatness. Yet humility is precisely the genius of *Socrate:* Plato is not illustrated, not interpreted, by the music: he is encased by the music, and the case is not a period piece; rather, it is from all periods. Which is what makes the music so difficult to identify. Is it from modern France? ancient Greece? or from Pope Gregory's fourth century? Why the music seems never static I do not know, for in the academic sense *Socrate* has no development beyond the normal evolution imposed by the words. Hence the music moving forward seldom relates to itself thematically, though its texture remains almost constantly undifferentiated. The dynamic level rises hardly above mezzo-forte, with little contrast and no climax until the final page when we hear forty-four inexorable knellings of an open fifth which denote the agony of the philosopher who, in the last two bars, expires with a sigh. The harmony, mostly triadic, is rarely dissonant, and never dissonant in an out-of-key sense except in a single "pictorial" section, again from the end movement, when the jailer presses Socrates's legs which have grown cold from the hemlock: here the words are colored with repetitions of a numbingly foreign C-sharp. So where lies the remarkability, the ever-renewed thrill of anticipation? It lies in the composer's absolutely original way with the tried and true. The music, written in 1919, is not "ahead" of its time, but rather (and of what other work can this be said?) outside of time, allowing the old, old dialogues of Plato to sound so always new.

What worked for Satie did not (to my ears) work for Virgil, for Virgil was a sophisticate faking naiveté while Satie was a true naif hoping for sophistication and achieving it despite himself. Virgil, like so many, misread the name Satie by inserting an "r" betwixt the "i" and the "e."

In case you've been wondering, Virgil and I never "had sex," nor did he ever make a pass. Except once. One winter afternoon, when I had to stay late to make corrections in something I'd botched, Virgil said, "I'm going to take a nap. Will you wake me at exactly four fifteen?"

At four fifteen I opened the door into his darkened room.

"It's four fifteen."

"That's no way to wake Papa. Come over and wake Papa with a kiss."

Am I supposed to say no? So I leaned down, as upon a great lady— a great *doughy* lady like, say, Nero—and kissed him on the lips.

"That's how to wake Papa," he said, quickly realizing he'd maybe done the wrong thing. I still hear the wistful voice now as he turned toward the south window through which the light was fading fast over our grimy city.

"It looks like Barcelona out."

Where is Barcelona? In Spain, the only country besides England that Virgil had visited outside of France during his long years abroad.

Six months passed before he was aware of Morris as more than a name I lived with, and who sometimes phoned to ask where the hell I was. The *Second String Quartet* had just been published by New Music Editions with, among its hundred-odd pages, one minor misprint where a flat was omitted. The thousand extant copies were delivered from the publisher. My job was to enter the missing flat into each copy, pack the whole into a foot-locker and deposit this hundred-pound object at the American Music Center at 250 West 57th, then bring the foot-locker back to the Chelsea. I said that my friend Morris Golde would help with the cab. When Morris showed up, all tough and eager, he hoisted the foot-locker like a feather onto his shoulders, and off we went. Virgil was thrilled.

That evening we dined *à trois* at Bleeck's. (Lucius Beebe was there and had a drink with us. He feigned remembrance of our Chicago orgy five years earlier, especially when I mentioned that Frank Van Antelek —now in the army and whom I'd recently seen in a gay bar called Ralph's on West 44th where he stole my new wristwatch—had stolen my wristwatch. *"Autres temps autres moeurs,"* remarked Beebe, blushing as much, or as little, as he ever would. *"Du côté de chez les voleurs,"* added Virgil.) If, as Virgil said of his first meeting with Gertrude Stein, "We got on like Harvard men," he and Morris hit it off like long-lost Jewish cousins, and remained close—closer than I ever was with Virgil, or at least in a different, non-competitive way—until the end.

Morris Golde lived and still lives at 123 West 11th, but now he owns the ground floor, while then he rented the one-and-a-half-room flat on the fourth story back. The half-room was mine, plus a rented upright, the decor was Mexican with a view onto a courtyard complex *en face* as in *Rear Window,* and the street remains one of the prettiest in the Village, with only eleven short blocks up Seventh Avenue to Virgil's to where I walked each morning. Each evening we ate out, usually at Drossie's, a good and cheap downstairs bistro on Greenwich Avenue run by a Miss Jeanne Drossie with her two Americanized Russian-born sisters who resembled the witches of Macbeth, only shorter and oh so warm. All the waiters were gay and so was half the clientele. The other half was high Bohemia. Joe Gould, for example, with his sweet darting eyes and bushy beard, toting the notorious manuscript of his ongoing *Oral History of the Universe;* he was the premiere intellectual homeless bum who one early dawn came to pass out on our floor. ("A myth is as good as a smile" wrote Cummings about little Joe Gould's winsomeness.) Or Maxwell Bodenheim, author of *Replenishing Jessica,* who would descend the five steps into the restaurant where, pausing among the candlelit tables, he lit his cigarette with a theatrical sweep of a wooden match up the back of his pants, then danced a little dance and vanished. Or the bitchy and likeable Dougie who, like Dante Pavone (another patron), proclaimed himself a "layer" of Djuna Barnes's Doctor O'Conner and who in fact had been immortalized by Kay Boyle in her *Valentine for Alan Ross MacDougall,* who had published a collection of Attic recipes called *And The Greeks,* and who—though twice his age—was now Alvin Ross's best friend (for Alvin too was now in New York). Or the sculptor Zadkine with his white granite hair. There was no liquor license, you could bring your own, but most people, even Bohemians, didn't drink on weeknights—*Americans* don't drink on weeknights and make up for it on weekends, which the French find infantile if not gross.

Morris and I were Americans, and he knew the city like the back of his hand—not just the concert halls and baseball arenas but the drinking holes. Of a gloomy snow-covered Saturday we might decide, before landing at Drossie's for the evening meal, to go pub crawling, starting at noon and working up Sixth Avenue bar by bar. But we'd seldom get beyond 14th Street since the pub grew more crucial than the crawling. Or we'd have a martini or two or fourteen, in a gorgeous orange-and-black Longchamps, perhaps the one on lower Fifth, where the walls are banked with pink glazed mirrors into which yellow lamps reflect their discreet heat, and you are in another world. Outside the sleet pelts the late afternoon and slush accumulates on the salt-strewn sidewalks, but here the gin in its funnelled tumbler protects you from reality—or rather, *becomes* your reality—and Morris tells me about Kafka. A sober Sunday, after such a Saturday, could be no less unreal. Do you remember—we were *there!*—when the airplane crashed into the Empire State Building, and hung like a maimed bat in a hole on the sixtieth floor? Elevators fell sixty floors in six seconds. We were too distant to make out what the radio reported: a woman's head—she had red hair—impaled on a girder.

Energetic, Morris rose early, rushed to the IRT local which whisked him near the 45th Street office where he ran a flourishing direct-mail and printing-press business with his older brother Michael, married with children. (A still older brother, Ben, a successful businessman, was gay). Among their many musical clients was the Town Hall's series called The New Friends of Music. For them, thanks to Morris, I made fifteen extra dollars copying the parts, astonishingly unavailable commercially, of Ravel's *Chansons Madécasses* directly from the full score, which Martial Singher accordingly sang with the Alberneri Trio. I emphasize "astonishingly unavailable," for in those days everything in music was available. You had only to walk into Chicago's Lyon & Healy store, Philadelphia's Theodore Presser store or similar "sheet music" outlets in any medium-sized city across the country and buy the always-in-stock complete works of Gabrieli or Griffes, Praetorius or Poulenc, not to mention standards like Stravinsky or Schoenberg, all for sensible sums. Today printed music must be sent away for; six months later your Gabrieli may arrive from Milan in a battered Xerox facsimile, with a bill for $200, or more likely a memo saying "permanently out of print." So much for the age of quick communications in the high arts.

Evenings Morris and I would dine out, usually at Drossie's, sometimes at the more expensive ($2.50) Waverly Inn where the chicken pie and the cinnamon apple tart *à la mode* were special lures, occasionally at the old Brevoort Hotel on lower Fifth Avenue which had an outdoor café in summer months. Two or three times we dined at Morris's parents' in the Bronx. Rumanian immigrants with marked accents, they lived comfortably on the Grand Concourse, doted on their three moneymaking male offspring and served gefilte fish which turned me off. Mrs. Goldenberg was domineering. Her husband, stricken with Parkinson's, was not ambulatory. He hummed little folklike melodies of his invention, which I notated properly on music manuscript paper. His pride in this physical evidence of his talent was touching; he made scrolls of the sheets and kept them in a crystal vase to show the neighbors.

During the eighteen months of our cohabitation Morris and I were never unfaithful, although there was habitual teasing and flirting, especially at all those after-hours all-boy dancing parties we ended up at, after a dogged ingestion of beer on Saturdays at the Welcome Inn or the MacDougall Inn, identical gay bars side by side on MacDougall Street. We quarrelled some, made love a lot—about eight times a week—and listened incessantly to music, usually all at the same time. The lovers' bed resembled a shipwreck, the room smelled of muscle, the phonograph heaved with *Der Rosenkavalier*'s horny evocations, as we fell panting to the floor, then rose to swill milkshakes with raw eggs and sherry. Often I'd copy my own work at home on the cedar table while Morris read aloud: Vincent Sheehan's *Personal History*, Denton Welsh's *Maiden Voyage*, Joseph Mitchell's *McSorley's Wonderful Saloon* about the landmark on East Seventh where we sometimes hung out.

Morris was friends with, and had been the lover of, harpsichordist Ralph Kirkpatrick, a patrician presence of massively organized intellect, already half blind and very tall. It would be hard to imagine two creatures more disparate, Morris with his darting wiry verbosity, Ralph all calm and cultured as he sat at his Chalice-made instrument. Kirkpatrick's series at the YMHA of Bach and Mozart sonatas with violinist Alexander Schneider was a landmark of performing excellence, as were his solo clavichord series at the Carnegie Recital Hall. Harkening to the clavichord is a craft in itself, knowing how to stay still so as to hear each silver teardrop tinkle in an ever-growing necklace miles away.

Ralph loved Billie Holiday, even knew her a little (a little is all anyone knew her). We visited the singer at the Onyx Club where I got drunk, and in adulation sank down to put my head 'neath her skirt which smelled like a Catholic church. Bringing her back in the early hours to Ralph's small flat on Lexington Avenue it became clear that Billie, in all her uneducated glory, could attend as astutely as any trained musicologue. She admired the harpsichord, its construction, its repertory, became a silent audience to Ralph the executant. Billie was a jazz star, never a blues singer except for a few forays, notably into Bessie Smith's repertory, and in her own *Fine and Mellow*. Like surrealism, which was a literary (sometimes by extension a painterly) movement which excluded the art of music as sissified and irrelevant, so the blues is a poetic form which can exist independently of the music that ornaments it—a series of A-B-A verses in iambic pentameter:

> My man don't love me treats me awful mean
> My man don't love me treats me awful mean
> He is the lowest man I've ever seen.

"Iambic pentameter," said Billie. "Yeah, that's it."

Had I gleaned anything during three-and-a-half years at Northwestern and Curtis, other than some practicalities about the craft of formalized sound? Certainly I had mild crushes on this or that male or female teacher, but I never forged such scholarly role models as Father and Paul Goodman represented in the outside world, or Debussy and Ravel from the evanescent past, or Virgil and Aaron in the very close future. But I did learn that, just as there's no one right way to play a piece (there are as many right ways as there are smart virtuosos, and even the composer's way is not final), so there is no one perception of any fact or concept or, indeed, "truth."

Having first-hand knowledge of homosexuality, and seeing that the world is mostly blind to, or wrong about, homosexuality, wised me up early. Jews must be similarly wised up.

I had a recurring nightmare which makes no plausible sense, and which began (again) in 1944. Today, putting myself in the Me then, the Me then puts himself in the Me of infancy when it all started. The dream does not concern human or animal rapports. Just a mass, immense, shifting with and against other masses, cloud-shaped and lugubrious. The counterpoint of mass-against-mass is like the motion in Messiean's music, as distinct from the line-against-line in Bach. No variety, no progress, no illumination. Only inexpressible fear.

And every year or so throughout my life I dream of being pregnant, literally. How I got in that condition, and by what route the child will emerge, I do not know. (Magritte's green apple fills a room.)

Seated for my daily stint between parlor and bedroom I observed Virgil Thomson running the world. When I arrived each day at ten, he would have performed his ablutions, and now, in clean orange pajamas from Lanvin, propped up and surrounded by an ocean of pillows with a sharpened pencil and a big yellow pad (he never learned to typewrite), he conducted the musical life of Manhattan from his bed. If it were Tuesday the phone would be off the hook as he scrawled (his handwriting was as infantile as his musical calligraphy) his Sunday sermon which he would then, with no revisions, dictate by phone to his secretary, Julia Haines, at the *Tribune*. The subject of the sermon, he explained to me, could materialize from anywhere: the previous month in concert halls (he reviewed three concerts a week), crank letters from strangers, reactions to the state of modern song in France, or from a question Maurice Grosser put to him *en passant*. On other weekdays he would spend the morning hours on the bedside phone, mostly on business for the paper: making assignments to his staff of critics (which included Paul Bowles), or telling them his reactions to their reviews from last night. He might otherwise extend or accept invitations involving Oscar Levant or Sir Thomas Beecham (whom he loved) or Ormandy, or simply gossip with his Franco-American cronies who included the art world as much as the music: the brothers Berman, Sylvia Marlowe, Philip Johnson, Tchelitcheff, Peggy Guggenheim. Since the bedroom door was wide open as I labored, naturally I overheard all this, often with a lifted eyebrow (I was the *bourgeois* he was pleased to *épater*), unless he specifically asked me to close the door, an academic gesture since his shrill voice carried.

On one such occasion his mother, Clara May Thomson, then aged seventy-nine and in New York for the first time, was present. She slept in a room down the hall but arrived at Virgil's each morning at 7:30 to help the cook—a large and humorless old-world Negro woman named Leana—shell peas or iron shirts on the other end of the table whereon I labored. Towards noon I was asked to close the door, and we all cocked our ears as Virgil dialed Paul Bowles.

"I have to bawl you out, Paul dear, so have you had your breakfast?"

"Breakfast at noon!" snorted both women with midwestern righteousness.

As for Paul Bowles being chided, it struck me as . . . as against nature that anyone could be in the driver's seat with Paul; Paul was just not accessible. I hadn't seen him yet since living in New York, but still thought of him with vague awe if not respect. Virgil's reprimand concerned what he called Paul's "pose," going around saying he didn't know anything about nineteenth-century German music, for this made mockery of criticism and by extension of the *Herald Tribune*. Of course, Virgil had no love for, or careful knowledge of, German music either, but when a review of, say, a Brahms symphony was needed it was assigned to Jerry Bohm or Arthur Berger or, *faute de mieux*, Paul Bowles, who was admonished to do his homework. Meanwhile Virgil took his mother to all sorts of recitals, including one of John Cage's for prepared pianos. Asked her opinion, Mrs. Thomson replied, "Nice, but I never would have thought of it myself."

Were I to dare interrupt a phone conversation with a query about some illegible smudge, Virgil would remonstrate either by amending the smudge to look worse than before, or by declaring, "That's baby stuff, baby. Don't bother Papa with baby stuff." "Baby" was one of his favorite words. So was "amusing" which in English rings more preciously than in French. Everything was amusing: Macbeth, a cherry pie, his mother's heavy overcoat. When he said to the stony Leana before she went out shopping, "If you see any vegetables that look amusing, buy them," she came back empty-handed.

In the afternoons Virgil, dressed, would receive in the parlor. Again I eavesdropped as he rehearsed his Violin Sonata with Joseph

Fuchs, or served coffee to the staff of *View* magazine who wanted an article from him, or chatted with his most frequent visitor, Maurice Grosser, friend and longtime lover from Harvard days, a topnotch realist painter of people (Jane Bowles), landscapes (the coast of Maine), and foodstuffs (mainly eggs and rounded fruits and vegetables like eggplants and pears, all vastly enlarged). Maurice, a Mississippi Jew, was in physical stature reminiscent of Morris Golde, sinewy, short, excitable; in mentality he was, arguably, the brains behind Virgil's brains. Have I already mentioned that it was Maurice who took the raw sketches of Stein's *Four Saints in Three Acts* and superimposed a scenario which blossomed into the ideal libretto, even as Alice Toklas wrote Stein's famous autobiography? But neither Stein nor Thomson gave credit its due, and their paramours were willingly silent partners. True, Maurice did have an independent career as a painter and a cult-public of sorts; he also wrote two intelligent and useful books about painting. True, too, that Virgil encouraged Maurice (his junior by a few years) by recommending him, talking him up, but only insofar as Maurice didn't grow too tall. Even long after, when Maurice Grosser died at eighty-three (of AIDS, astonishingly), Virgil was oddly mum.

Indeed, he was oddly mum about anything that might compromise him publicly, if not socially, especially sexual innuendo. Campy and gossipy and aggressively effeminate as he was at home, so he was circumspect in the world. This may have been due to the still-recent trauma of the arrest in that male whorehouse; more probably it was due to his cool rivalries and deluded notions of himself. Because my *Paris Diary*, published in 1966 a few months prior to VT's own autobiography, was unprecedentedly plain about my own homosexuality (it's not that I made a point of it—on the contrary, I didn't bother to pretend), he cut all references to me in his book for fear of being compromised. Who was he kidding! That book, an otherwise unique document on the economic history of the arts in contemporary America, has a faint but common stench, not just because he doesn't mention what Gide called *la chose*, but because, hypocritically, he does mention his passions for various women.

Virgil, who spoke as he wrote, economically and to the point, in whole sentences and paragraphs, had the wittiest English language repartee of anyone around. Even physically he had imitative gifts of cutting precision, as when he would rush across the room with tiny tight steps, imitating a Gibson girl in a hobble skirt playing badminton.

But he was no less competitive than most artists, as well as imperious about his lore. How often I saw him alienate unalerted folk he was meeting for the first time—a professional photographer or a brain surgeon, for instance, to whom he'd explain the craft of soft lens focus or the details of a scalp incision! For the young ("All young people look alike to me") he also had all the answers. What is this silly old fairy trying to say? they would ask. Of course, Virgil spoke always in French-style generalities which are anathema to literal-minded American children.

After six months or so of secretarial work *chez lui*, it was thought I needed more formal training. He never admitted it, but Virgil felt a vague sense of responsibility vis-à-vis my father; after all, he had talked me into foregoing my scholarship at Curtis in midstream, and moving to New York. And he was aware that the meager salary he doled out was my sole income. So he took it upon himself to give me lessons, no extra charge.

There is no such animal, according to Thomson, as the teaching of musical competition (do as your idols do, not as they say) which is an aesthetic study best left to analytical Germans. Composers become composers not because they take lessons, but because they beg, borrow and steal. Certainly I had learned counterpoint and harmony until they came out of my ears, while amassing a repertory was merely a question of answering to the heart (we wouldn't be musicians in the first place if we didn't like to hear music), and of attending a regular dose of concerts, thanks to the free tickets provided by Virgil. But academic instruction of the so-called creative arts is a non-existent process. Good teaching, the imparting of extant knowledge, is a healthy infection which leads students to rich mineral waters and makes them drink; but no teacher can cause a piece of music to be, he can only criticize it after it exists; if he is a composer he can teach only by himself being—by allowing himself passively to be imitated. But there is a craft, if not an art, the lineaments of which can be imparted, even from one untalented person to another, and that is the craft of orchestration. Instrumentation is physical fact, not theoretical idea. That is what Virgil intended to show me.

At first I was wary. What, after all, did the maker of all these simple-minded ditties I'd been transcribing know about teaching? But during the eighteen months I worked with Virgil I was to learn more than during the long years, before and after, spent in the world's major conservatories. In mastering the art of calligraphy a young musician becomes answerable for every note among millions, for the need for clarity on the page (because music, before it can be heard, must be visibly communicable), and the copyist eventually knows the score better than the author of the score. Meanwhile, if orchestration, unlike composition, is the study of specific balances—a study available to any layman—then Virgil, in placing before me the principles of this study, explained once, and only once, the sonic results of every physical combination of instruments. Just as overhearing the phone conversations—and thus his manner of behavior in a professional milieu—was an indelible instruction, so I can recall today as on a disc each word he spoke during our lessons fifty years ago.

His lucidity was due no less to an innate clarity of mind than to a voicing of that mind through an ideal language of thrift: he spoke French in English. Since he knew what he was talking about and didn't waste words, merely to be in his presence was to learn. And merely to think about him is to risk being influenced, as these pale phrases attest, for no one out-Virgils Virgil.

My ambivalence about both him and his work rose and fell with the years. I could live without his music, yet his two operas on Gertrude Stein's texts are arguably our *only* American operas. His music resembles, more demonstrably than with any composer I know, himself. It is impatiently terse, free of fat or padding, eschewing sensuality to a point of self-indulgence, and one absorbs it like an icy acid which bathes a core of hot prettiness. At its best his music is very, very witty—if that adjective makes sense when applied to non-vocal works.

I was Virgil Thomson's sole pupil, which makes me proud, and made him proud too, so far as it went, especially when he eventually heard my opulent scoring—so much more opulent than his—but which retained a transparency that only his training could have produced. (Transparency means that no matter how many instruments you use at any moment, each one—each group—is heard, nothing vanishes in the fray. This is French, as distinct from German where, since every instrument or group is doubled, nothing retains an individual stamp.) Still, Virgil, who was old enough to be my father, was always slightly jealous of whatever successes I may have had after I went to France where hitherto he had been, or so he imagined, America's only musical representative.

One spring night at Drossie's, Morris and I ran into Paul Bowles. He was sitting in a corner with his cousin, stage designer Oliver Smith, eating the homemade apple cake of which the restaurant was renowned. Learning that I was now Virgil's copyist, Paul asked if I'd be interested in doing a copying job for him. So next night we visited him.

Paul rented a small penthouse nearby, at 56 Seventh Avenue off 14th Street, with a spectacular view of downtown Manhattan. (Did you know that Seventh Avenue curves at a 35-degree angle while descending toward the Battery?) The larger of his two rooms was all in white: white sofas, a white piano, with long white curtains moving slightly in April's first warm breezes, and a white fur rug wall to wall. A white telephone with the number removed. Drums here and there. The room reeked of perfume, as indeed did Paul himself, wherever he went. He had spent the better part of his Guggenheim fellowship on raw ambergris which he combined with patchouli and other basic essences to confect heavy oils that imbued the furniture, never to disappear. A luscious cage of scent for him to hide behind. He brewed the gooey incense in various flavors and titled them for special exotic friends: a vial of *Evil Eye* for Hazel Scott, *Green Devil* for Elsie Huston. Garish books, with a careful casualness, were strewn over the floor: a tome of Goya's horrifying *Caprichos*, a collection of Weegee portraits of murderers. Paul reinforced his effect when speaking of Man Ray, who once showed him photographs of slaves somewhere in North Africa, chained to pillars and living in their own excrement. (Eight years later, when I knew Man Ray in Paris, I asked him about these photographs. He had never taken pictures of slaves, he claimed, never been in Africa, never heard of Paul Bowles.)

All this would be chitchat were it not relevant to another aspect of the man which grew clear in the next half hour, and which changed my life as *Socrate* and *Sacre* had changed my life. Paul asked if he might play for us a recent piece of his. This turned out to be an aircheck of a five-minute arietta from the zarzuela, *The Wind Remains*, which had been recently broadcast with Maria Kurenko intoning the Lorca text. I was bewitched and remain bewitched after fifty years. Would Paul enjoy comparing my state to that of Dorian Gray to whom Lord Henry lends a copy of *A Rebours*, precipitating poor Dorian's descent into "esthetic corruption"? Alas, Paul's music is the picture of health. A more proper analogy might be the *petite phrase* of Proust's musician, Vinteuil, which so colored the hero's life.

The *petite phrase* in this case was that most melancholy of intervals, a descending minor third, the "dying fall" that—I later discovered—threads all of Paul's music. This arietta was a mere bagatelle, after all, yet it had more impact on my thinking than any symphony of Mahler, who also favored the "dying fall" yet whose nature was the antithesis of Paul's. The little phrase was a mannerism which Paul is doubtless unaware of; we live with our signatures, so never think much about them. For me, though, it was a conscious expressive device which I appropriated and have retained. I have composed ten times more music than has Paul (with the 1949 advent of *The Sheltering Sky* he shifted, in the ken of the general public, from the role of composer-who-also-writes to that of author-who-used-to-compose), yet somewhere in my every piece lurks the rhythmic or melodic lilt, albeit disguised, of the invisible mentor. Influence, of course, is all art's fertilizer: thievery is embellished, then branded with the new owner's tic. Paul Bowles and I are separated enough in years for me still to wish, at this late date, for his approval. He would surely feign astonishment at this juvenile admission, especially since he might not see—or hear—himself in me.

If I stress Paul's musicality, it's because that musicality seems to have fallen away in our world. The bulk of his fans today are unaware that he ever composed, much less have they ever hummed his tunes: Americans are meant to be specialists. So for the record let it be said that Paul Bowles is, like Europeans of yore (Leonardo, Cocteau, Noel Coward), a general practitioner of high order. Unlike them, his two professions don't overlap—neither esthetically nor technically. Composers when they prosify (Schumann, Debussy, Thomson) inevitably deal with music or with autobiography. Bowles is the sole fiction writer among them, and his fiction is as remote from their prose as from his own music. His stories are icy, cruel, objective, moralistic in their amorality, and occur mostly in exotic climes; they are also often cast in large forms. His music is warm, wistful, witty, redolent of nostalgia for his Yankee youth, wearing its heart on its sleeve; and it is all cast in small forms. No American in our century has composed songs lovelier than his. None of these songs is currently in print. That fact echoes the indifferent world that he elsewhere so successfully portrays.

The only secretarial work I did for Paul was to copy an extract from a ballet, *Pastorela* (fifteen pages for fifteen dollars), but with the years I had occasion to examine piles of other work, including the beloved moment from *The Wind Remains*. If the sound of his music remains like the wind over an otherwise barren earth, the sight of it was like a beginner's. The manuscript was puerile in appearance, the spellings and placements on the staff were frequently incorrect, the orchestration seemed so unbalanced (according to my textbooks on instrumentation) as to sound like a smear. Hey, what was it with these trendsetting New Yorkers that they knew less than I about the basics of their profession!

The wheel turned, the spokes fanned out now toward such diverse stimuli that it's a matter of selection. Several events in the spring of 1945 immediately precipitated a new direction, which, all told, was a nice direction:

Morris kicked me out. After eighteen months of cohabitation he longed for a change of scene, a room alone, a lack of me. (Once when Morris was away I brought a sailor home "after hours" and played the phonograph full blast with the window open while making love. Billie Holiday's voice moaned in the courtyard, "You follow me around, build me up, tear me down," and the neighbors were not amused.) Morris was kind but firm, wanting me gone by tomorrow. Since I couldn't yet move into the little flat on 12th Street that had been promised as soon as a friend vacated, I stayed at George Garratt's big apartment on East 53rd. Morris and I remained close, saw each other nearly as often as before, and he was concerned about the adventure, attractive and frightful, of my living completely alone for the first time.

Then Father persuaded me to return to school. He would pay tuition, an allowance and rent (twenty dollars a month) if I would aim for a degree at Juilliard. A degree, as distinct from a diploma, meant attending various non-musical classes. At the entrance exams in April, I passed the musical tests with such flying colors that I was not required to take most of the theory courses. Still, to qualify for the "secular" curriculum at Juilliard I had to enroll for eight weeks of summer school, in General History and English Lit, at NYU. Which meant commuting from Garratt's down to Washington Square five mornings a week.

The upcoming school plans precluded further work with Virgil, with Harold Brown, and with Betty Crawford (at Juilliard I would be a double-major in piano and composition and would continue orchestration with the comp teacher). As with Morris, my new and strictly social role with Virgil would continue on the best of terms. My last day as Virgil's lackey, he took me in a cab to the Mary Chess boutique on Park Avenue and asked me to pick out the biggest bottle of any cologne I fancied. I didn't fancy any (Paul Bowles had gifted me with a lifetime supply of patchouli oil), but chose the Russian Leather because it brought back the past.

Virgil also suggested I contact soprano Janet Fairbank. Having looked over my songs he concluded that Fairbank, who specialized in arcane Americana, would love them. So I became Miss Fairbank's rehearsal pianist.

As for Betty Crawford, she was soon to leave New York anyway, as a bride. Her parting gift was to pass on her job playing for Martha Graham. This seemed too interesting for me to forego.

How I juggled these friendships, academic deadlines, and pianistic responsibilities while still finding time for the semi-weekly binges of a newly divorced narcissist, I cannot imagine. My body of today has shifted its resilience, and so has the century. But with my back to the mirror I can't always tell the difference.

VIRGIL THOMSON

Of Portraits and Operas

The making of musical portraits dates from at least the eighteenth century, when François Couperin drew hundreds of them for harpischord, chiefly of ladies denominated *L'Audacieuse, L'Aimable Thérèse,* and the like. Robert Schumann in his *Carnaval* for piano (1837) lightly sketched the composer Frédéric Chopin, and maybe others. Later in the century Anton Rubinstein made twenty-three piano portraits of the guests at an island house-party, toward the end of these adding a picture of the locale itself, Kamennoi-Ostrow. The best known twentieth-century group is Edward Elgar's "Enigma" Variations for orchestra, each of which, though not identified, is the likeness of some friend.

When I began to make musical portraits, back in 1927, I worked, as the others had mostly done, from memory. But shortly I found, as had many visual artists centuries before, that one gets a more living likeness in the presence of a sitter. Consequently, since that time, I have not done them otherwise.

As to what is a likeness in music, resemblance there, like characterization in opera writing, can come from divers directions. Music can imitate a gesture or typical way of moving, render a complexity or simplicity of feeling, evoke a style or period, recall the sound of a voice, or of birds or trumpets or hunting horns or marching armies.

It was Pablo Picasso, inquiring about my method, who found an explanation of it in the mere fact of proximity. To my answer that I sketched very much as he did, which is to say, by first looking a bit and then letting my pencil put down what came to my mind, he replied, "Ah, yes, of course! If I am working and you are in the room, anything I draw is automatically your portrait."

There are by now a hundred and more of such portraits, all but the first six drawn from life, and each one bearing, in the judgment of persons acquainted with the sitter, some resemblance to its model. All have been sketched in silence too, usually at one sitting, save for those that comprise several sections, in which case each movement has been composed without interruption. And I do not stop to try out on a piano, to hear, correct, or criticize what I have done. Such adjustments are left for later, as is orchestral elaboration should this occur. Descriptive subtitles, such as Lullaby or Hunting Song, are also subsequent additions. My effort while at work is to write down whatever comes to me in the sitter's presence, hoping as I transcribe my experience that it will, as the painters say, "make a composition."

The result of this disciplined spontaneity, for I do think one may call it that, has been in all cases an instrumental piece. Instrumental also is likely to be any musical characterization for choreography, since singing is rare in the dance theater. In the opera, however, where singing is the basic operation, that without which there is no opera, characterization has from opera's beginnings, and emphatically so since Mozart, been a chief duty of the vocal line. Even in Richard Wagner, where themes and motives are passed from voice to voice and back and forth from orchestra to voice, Siegfried does not sing quite like Fafner, nor Ortud like Elisabeth. Each works in character and vocally paints his own portrait, this portrait remaining strongly marked even in the ensemble pieces. It is noticeably so, for example, in the quartets from Mozart's *Don Giovanni* and from Verdi's *Rigoletto.* Also in the *Lucia di Lammermoor* sextet, where the heroine proclaims frustration by singing in syncopation against the others.

Instrumental illustration also can exist in stage works, from some villain's heavy-footed entrance to the threatening trumpet-calls of Cherubino's impending military service. But these are likely to have more to do with the drama—as description of a locale or the kinetics of a situation—than with the immediacy of a character's nature and presence.

Nevertheless, orchestral style and color are not excluded from characterization. I tend in my own practice to use them as extensions of the vocal self-portrait, as when, in *The Mother of Us All,* the shining militancy of Susan B. Anthony is constantly pointed out by a blend of trumpets and strings; and whenever Lord Byron, in the opera that bears his name, takes on a bardic pose, the harp and its idiomatic ways are clearly indicated.

In the vocal line itself, a florid, or coloratura, style, so often judged to be meaningless, can actually express many things—cruelty, for instance, or lightness of heart, or cold anger, or (for contraltos) villainy, or (for basses) pomposity, for tenors either insincerity, as in *Rigoletto,* or, as in *Don Giovanni,* the suavities of true love and joy in faithfulness.

My first portrait was of a Spanish girl who was staying with her mother in a small hotel near St.-Jean-de-Luz, where I was also staying, having just completed there my first opera, *Four Saints in Three Acts*. She had a grand and very Spanish way of walking, like a dancer coming out on stage, as she would enter our dining-garden, her mother, as is the Spanish way (the American too, for that matter), following just one step behind. She also played the violin. So, wishing to offer a gift that she could play, I made a musical portrait of her walk and gestures for unaccompanied violin, which I entitled *A Portrait of Señorita Juanita de Medina Accompanied by Her Mother*, for that was exactly what I had essayed to depict. But the mother, who was also a musician, asked thereupon my permission to compose an accompaniment for it. So that the piece became, in their version, a portrait of the señorita accompanied by her mother on the pianoforte.

The last of my early portraits for violin alone, of which there are seven, was of the composer Henri Sauguet, which I entitled *Sauguet, from life*. And the next hundred or more were all so drawn.

A portrait usually takes me an hour or an hour and a quarter. That seems to be about the limit in time of my ability to keep my mind on the subject, to work rapidly, and to bring the piece to a close. Later I may correct, if need be, fill in the sketched patterns of some complex harmonic texture, or, if I have been garrulous, cut out measures. I have no principles against reworking an inspiration to improve detail. But unless the piece turns out to be a whole piece and embodies what I esteem on later examination to be a good musical idea, I treat it as a painter would an unsuccessful effort. I discard it.

J. D. McCLATCHY

Laughter in the Soul

"Anyone Can Whistle." . . . Some songs seem to be parables of their creator's imagination. *Anyone can whistle* might as well be the poet's arch opinion of his collaborator, the composer—or, in Stephen Sondheim's case, one talent idly accusing another. *So someone tell me / Why can't I.* It's not that Sondheim can't, of course: the song's own lilting melody itself dismisses the question. But his point turns on a further dilemma: *What's hard is simple / What's natural comes hard.* It's not that music, what anyone can whistle (and "natural" is a musical term), is hard for him to write— though tin-eared critics have complained his shows lack tunes an audience of Anyones might begin whistling while they walk toward the lobby. (Those critics miss the point: for one who grew up on Richard Rogers' music, hearing Sondheim's is like listening to Stravinsky after years of Rimsky-Korsakov.) But music's impulses toward clarity of structure and force of sentiment conflict with the quintessentially ironic energies of Sondheim's lyrics. Those lyrics, on the other hand—where words can dance tangos or slay dragons—are of a complexity Sondheim had simply mastered from the start. The "difficulty" lies not in concocting their cleverness, but in manipulating an intractable medium. Simplicity of utterance alone is suitable for song; and in addition, show tunes have narrative responsibilities, a psychological duty to reveal the character of the singer, and the dramatic business of opening up that part of the musical. To have seen to all that, with a breath-catching thoroughness, and still to have those words take on an independent life in a listener's imagination, not merely to have amused but to have puzzled and challenged that listener, puts this lyricist in quite another class. Sondheim is more than the true poet of our theater. He is one of those rare writers by whom our language lives.

The best lyricists in the long tradition of American musical theater—Ira Gershwin, Lorenz Hart, Cole Porter—shared a fondness for wordplay, for elaborated conceits, for brilliant turns of phrase that Sondheim is clearly heir to. I wouldn't say that Sondheim is cleverer than those men. I'd say he is cleverer than *any* lyricist—and that includes one with whom he has, to my mind, an overlooked affinity: William Schwenck Gilbert. I've heard grumbles that Sondheim's lyrics are *too* clever, too intellectual." That seems an odd charge, considering that a song represents precisely that moment when our feelings are brought to the pitch of thought.

But of course the wit of Sondheim's lyrics is of a very high, a very self-conscious order. It's not just the bravura patter of, say, "A Little Priest." It's not just the metrical ingenuity and beadchain of rhymes, where variety and substitution help both to sustain and toy with our expectations. I'm thinking too of Sondheim's extraordinary ability to create a dramatic scene within a song. From *West Side Story*'s "America" to *A Little Night Music*'s "Now—Later—Soon" or "A Weekend in the Country," these extended numbers are Sondheim's *coups de théâtre*, their exhilarating tensions drawn from a melody's shadow-side but turning finally on the exigencies of language, one phrase plucked from the implications of another. Smaller songs can likewise turn themselves inside out: the way "sell out" is modulated from an over-the-top noun into a menacing verb in "It's a Hit!" from *Merrily We Roll Along;* the way a threatening "leave you" slides into a predatory "leave me" in "Could I Leave You?" from *Follies*. Valéry once said that poetry is not speech raised to the level of music, but music drawn down to the level of speech. That is what these songs do: music becomes speech, speech that flickers and gleams within the glass lamp of form.

One advantage Sondheim has over his peers is that his first mentor was Oscar Hammerstein. If Gershwin and Hart and Porter together comprise the smart set, all snappy sophistication and innuendo, then Hammerstein's great strength was his command of metaphor and the vivid or tender details at the heart of his lyrics. So often the effect of a Sondheim verse depends not on its quick-wittedness but on a homely detail lifted from context into wrenching significance. Here is one instance—one that sounds like Millay imitating Dickinson:

> Every day a little death
> In the parlor, in the bed,
> In the curtains, in the silver,
> In the buttons, in the bread,
> Every day a little sting
> In the heart and in the head.

Every move and every breath,
And you hardly feel a thing,
Brings the perfect little death.
      —"Every Day A Little Death," *A Little Night Music*

The plot and tone of *Pacific Overtures* are built out of a series of metaphors, indirectly finding direction—east and west—out. The delicacies
of the haiku, the enigmas of court language, the flimflam of diplomats
and courtesans . . . the entire show is a view back from inside the metaphor toward its subject:

It's the fragment, not the day.
It's the pebble, not the stream.
It's the ripple, not the sea
That is happening.
Not the building but the beam,
Not the garden but the stone,
Only cups of tea
And history
And someone in a tree!
      —"Someone In A Tree," *Pacific Overtures*

The dark satanic mill that roars under *Sweeney Todd* is a brilliant metaphor for the engine of Commodity that the show anatomizes. The forest
of *Into the Woods* is both psyche and text.

It was Gerard Manley Hopkins who claimed that a poem's style
should read as "the current language heightened." That's exactly the
sound of Sondheim, the idiom of the cocktail party, the bedroom, the
shrink's office, the nail parlor, the idiom of foreplay and daydream, of
fashionable attitudes and childhood fears, of love's resentments and
anger's scruples, the idiom of the lust inside our liberal principles, the
rabid fears behind our pieties, your idiom and mine: the way we live
now, the way we speak with each other and with ourselves. But heightened, yes.

How does a Sondheim line work? It is hard to separate technique
and tone in his lines, but together they account for the high wit of his
work. Sondheim commands a prosody of astonishing virtuosity. (In an
age when the fashion for shaggy, sprawling poems forced formal verse
underground, you sometimes wonder if song lyrics haven't been a ref-
uge of the kind of sensibility that prefers the epigram to the ego trip.)

His metrical skill is such that his measures create the character of the lyric's voice and are an extension of its moral tone. Without their musical settings, most song lyrics are as lusterless as pebbles carried home from the beach. Not Sondheim's. Usually the lines are short, crisply accented, adding appositional layers of ironic commentary to the song's thematic refrain:

> Someone to hold you too close,
> Someone to hurt you too deep,
> Someone to love you too hard,
> Happily ever after.
>
> Someone to need you too much,
> Someone to read you too well,
> Someone to bleed you of all
> The things you don't want to tell.
> That's happily ever after,
> Ever, ever, ever after in hell.
> —"Happily Ever After," *Company/Marry Me A Little*

> And while it's going along,
> You take it for granted some love
> Will wear away.
> We took for granted a lot,
> But still I say:
> It could have kept on growing,
> Instead of just kept on.
> We had a good thing going,
> Going,
> Gone.
> —"Good Thing Going," *Merrily We Roll Along*

When the phrases are stretched to sentences, and ideas more leisurely entertained, the wit can be more exquisite than biting:

> Too many people muddle sex with mere desire,
> And when emotion intervenes
> The nets descend.
> It should on no account perplex, or worse, inspire,
> It's but a pleasurable means
> To a measurable end.
> —"Liaisons," *A Little Night Music*

This sort of skill, a verse that is pleased with itself and is endlessly entertaining, would put Sondheim in the company of poets from Praed to Ade, masters of light verse. One of the best is Samuel Hoffenstein. Let me quote one of Hoffenstein's poems to demonstrate the family resemblance:

> Your little hands,
> Your little feet,
> Your little mouth—
> Oh, God, how sweet!
>
> Your little nose,
> Your little ears,
> Your eyes, that shed
> Such little tears!
>
> Your little voice,
> So soft and kind;
> Your little soul,
> Your little mind!

You can imagine, though, how Sondheim would have arrived at the same twist with altogether more intricate and pungent, more sharply observed means, with fresher rhymes and a more studied enjambment.

What Sondheim shares with a Hoffenstein or a Dorothy Parker is their instinct to invoke conventions—both poetic and social—and then subvert them. This is a part of the *realism* I would cite as the hallmark of his work. It is to this point that Sondheim's intelligence and seriousness converge, and his model here might as well be Brecht or the Auden who wrote "Calypso" or "Refugee Blues" ("Stood on a plain in the falling snow;/Ten thousand soldiers marched to and fro:/Looking for you and me, my dear, looking for you and me."). The realism of Sondheim's lyrics may be either cynical or rueful. They work variations on the abiding problem of loss: the lost paradises of childhood and first love, the loosening grip of age, the losing battle between the self and the world. His ironies are aimed at the most intimate ways we betray ourselves and then live with the fact. When sex is his subject, he will look at it from those angles which drive us to it, love and loneliness; then trace each motive back to its heartfelt illusion or heartless need. Big ballads like "Losing My Mind" or "Send in the Clowns" do so in a grand manner, with grown-up ambivalence. Their romantic music posits what the lyrics disavow. Which is why, of course, we need the music. Sondheim's poems are made of the musical precisions in his words and the moral discourse of his melodies.

Even by themselves, his lyrics work wonderfully—not because they so readily evoke their settings but because they so readily reveal us to ourselves. When we recall his songs, we think of their quicksilver lined with clouds. But we think too of their ebullient charm. His scrupulous technique is a wonder because it has a temperament. Only rarely has he used wit to substitute for feelings, or merely to control them. In his best work, wit *is* feeling, the feeling that tempers others; that can both astutely caress the contours of experience and then, with a sharp turn of phrase, sound its depths; that assures us suffering is not final, while warning us that joy is transient. "The size of a man's understanding," said Dr. Johnson, "might always be justly measured by his mirth." And it is Sondheim's *understanding* I want to stress, because it most aptly characterizes his mirth and his verse. There is a penetrating intelligence and clear-eyed humanity here that can accommodate and balance the absurd and solemn, the painful and frivolous. It is, finally, a laughter in the soul.

HOWARD MOSS

ILLUSTRATIONS BY EDWARD GOREY

Johann Sebastian Bach

"Thunderation!" Magda exclaimed. She'd just climbed the one hundred and seventeen steps to the belfry. "Do you have to sit here and compose all day just to prove you're a Christian believer?" She dodged one of the bells that began to sway ominously. Another metallic, clangorous, deafening concert! Why couldn't they all just shut up and pray quietly, the way she did? All this singing and howling! This ostentatious clamoring about the Lord! Wasn't there more true religious feeling in baking a pie than in constantly proclaiming the glory of God? Yes, there was, she said to herself, as she set Bach's simple lunch down on the table next to the organ.

"Sardine and salt-smelt sandwiches again?" Bach queried, his kindly face creased by genius and consternation. Sometimes he felt the iron hand of alliteration directed Magda's culinary impulses. Such as they were. Sometimes he felt nothing.

"I thought you liked them," she said, about to burst into tears. Her emotions were close to the surface, on the few occasions when they weren't on it.

"Ach," Bach said, "I was only joshing. Sardine and smelt are my favorite fish."

Actually, Bach was being polite. He was getting tired of Magda's unimaginative recipes. She was a sweet and devoted creature, but the lip-smacking sensualities and heady subtleties of the true gourmet were beyond her.

"How are the cantatas coming?" Magda asked. "I see you're up to No. 198—(*Trauer-Ode*)."

Bach smiled. "I have twenty-two mouths to feed, *meine Kleine*. Not counting my own."

"Ruppert Feinshting is waiting for his organ lesson," Magda replied. "And I have to get back to the kitchen. I hope you haven't forgotten that the Kappelmeister is coming for dinner tonight. You know how fussy *he* is."

"Tonight?" Bach asked, incredulously.

"We're having rabbit and rice and radishes and roast ram," Magda confided. And rats and ropes and riffraff and reefs, she went on compulsively, to herself. "Ruppert has written a prelude and fugue." *She* knew where to get the knife in.

"Tell him I will be down—in a day or two," the great composer riposted.

For a few moments, Bach's mind had been diverted by small talk. But once Magda was gone—he could hear her falling down all one hundred and seventeen steps—he leaped from the table to the writing desk. The great chords and giant sonorities of the opening of the B-Minor Mass had just thundered through his head. What did it matter now whether the sandwiches had been smelt or not?

HOWARD MOSS

ILLUSTRATIONS BY EDWARD GOREY

Frédéric Chopin

The Majorcan afternoon, streaked like a tomato tulip, enveloped the island in a beneficent blaze. Each stunted tree seemed to thrust itself up with a pert starchness, and the sea, glinting irremediably in the distance, added a touch of the mysterious to what was already a mystery. Would the "Prelude" ever come right? Chopin thought, his fingers idly straying across the keyboard. The piano was out of tune, as usual. The dampness of the island had turned the strings into veritable nerves—nerves sensitive to the slightest change in pressure, the merest alteration in the alchemy of water density. Suddenly, she was on the stairs, standing there looking down at him, the whole force of her figure concentrated in one galvanizing full-length portrait.

"Why don't you cough more, Frédéric," she said. "Then I could stay up the *whole* night." Slowly she descended the stairs. He stared at her.

"*Again?* You're going to be like this *again?*"

"I don't know what you're talking about," she replied. "Dolcilita has prepared breakfast?" Her Spanish, he noted with envy, was improving. It was still light-years away from the Castilian glitter.

"Am I supposed to run the house, *too?*" Frédéric asked, and instantly regretted it. It could just possibly be true.

In truth, they were getting on each other's nerves. Little had George Sand reckoned what it would mean to be sequestered in a house on an island with someone who played the piano more than half the day. Its tinkle, as she referred to it, had become abhorrent to her. She was afraid that, finally, she would come to detest music, even really *serious* composers like Massé and Tagliafico. Besides, *François le Champi* was going badly. That was something she could never admit to him—she felt her powers were failing. Alas, what lack of communication exists even among the great! For her fear was, *au fond,* his fear as well. He could compose now only in the key of A minor—he who had once been the sovereign of B flat major, who had had every nuance of the scale so firmly under his finely pointed fingertips that it had been said of him, "Chopin breathes B flat major." He was no ordinary Pole.

"Dolcilita!" George Sand shouted, but her voice was drowned out by a louder sound. Someone was insistently pounding on the door. They were united now in a common fear. Could it be her publisher? Or *his?*

III

BABS GONZALEZ

Paying Dues

I arrived back home in August of 1944 and since my wardrobe and my bread was cool, I really expounded on about my success. Most of the names that I hadn't known through Mom's restaurant, I met in L.A. so I decided I was ready for New York. There was only one hang-up—the Army. I reported to the local board and they told me to go home and they would call me in due time. I was by no means to leave Newark, I'd been home six weeks and still I never heard from them. My being a big shot every night had put a big dent in my bread, so I went and told them they would have to give me a date for my physical or I was leaving town, jail or not. They gave me a date for a week later.

I'd already made up my mind, so the day before my physical, I borrowed a pair of ladies' panties from Ike's wife. That night I stayed at the home of another friend, Gus Young. His wife straightened and curled my hair, painted my toes and fingernails red and gave me a brassiere stuffed with cotton to put on. At seven in the morning, I decided to test my outfit on my mother so I visited her for breakfast.

When I walked in, she nearly fainted. All she said was if you want to stay out that bad go ahead. I asked her to ride the bus with me but not to sit with me, and test the reaction of the people. She did and when we parted in front of the induction center, she said "if you're not home for lunch, I'll buy you a new suit."

I poured a bottle of Wood-hue perfume down my neck to get my aroma and walked in. A big sergeant put his hands to his nose as I asked him for directions. I thanked him in my practiced feminine accent. As I proceeded to my destination, pandemonium broke out as everybody was trying to get a look at the freak. A security guard took me upstairs and put me in a room with about twenty more fellows. He said alright sister take off them clothes for an X-ray. I told him I couldn't disrobe in front of all those men. He informed me that until I left the building, I was in the Army.

I slowly sat down and took off my shoes and socks. My red toe nails and curled hair caused quite a commotion, but when I took off my shirt and pants and they dug my breasts and panties, I was rushed out in two minutes. Without any examination I was taken to a psychiatrist. He told me to sit down and relax and that he'd seen my sort of case before. He also explained that anything I told him would be between him and I. His first question was "you look dazed. Are you drunk?" I said no. I had been smoking marijuana. He made a notation then asked me where I got it. I told him on any corner in Harlem if you had the money. His next question was "did I like girls and did I have a girl friend?" I jumped out of the chair screaming never to mention girls to me. He asked why did I wear female garments. I told him I was a female impersonater on the stage and wore my attire in the street, too.

He was just sitting there talking when I touched his hand saying, "You sure are an understanding man, I wish I could visit and talk with you some place after you're finished working." He snatched his hand away and promptly began stamping papers telling me to get out and wait in the next room. In fifteen minutes a guard came up and gave me a card marked "4FH" and told me to go home.

I got my revenge on quite a few of the guys that laughed at me as I watched them being taken direct to Fort Dix without a chance to go home. I told them through the bus windows not to worry, I would take care of all the lonely wives and girlfriends. It had taken just under two hours and I was home free. That night everybody in town was talking about my "act" but during the next six months about seven big name musicians came and borrowed them (dig?).

I was now ready to tackle New York City. One day I saw Billie Holiday in our restaurant and I told her about my wanting to come over. She was real great. She told me to go to her mother's house in the Bronx. When I arrived at her mother's pad, I offered to pay a month's rent in advance. She just smiled and said "Billie called me about you, make yourself at home, you don't have to pay anything until you start working."

My first few months was an introductory period. I'd eat breakfast, take the subway down to Harlem and hang out all day. I would start at the Theresa, then backstage at the workshop (Apollo), then up Seventh Avenue to the Savoy. I didn't tell Mr. Buchanon I'd moved so he kept giving me publicity and I kept throwing them away, as I didn't want to have to start paying to get in. Whenever I didn't go to the track (Savoy) I'd go down to Minton's. This was where the "new" music was being spawned. On any evening you could catch guys like Monk, Sonny Stitt, Charlie Parker, Dizzy, Kenny Clark, Lockjaw Davies or Oscar Pettiford, jamming. There was another guy we called Stokowski. He came in every night like he was working. Every time the band would be playing he'd sit on the bandstand with his violin. To look at him one would think he was playing his ass off. His fingers would be moving, he'd make all sorts of grimaces, etc., and when intermission came, he'd be dripping with perspiration. In five years I never heard him play one note because the bow never touched the strings. No matter how much people laughed, he did this every night. He was allowed to do this because he always brought five dollars ($5) a night to buy the other cats drinks and pot. During my turning I had met Charlie Parker occasionally but we'd never said more than a "what know man." I was down at the Onyx club to see "Lady Day" one night and "Bird" asked me was I going uptown. I told him yes. He said "C'mon I'm taking a cab, you can ride with me." All the way up through the park, I thought, "Bird sure is nice people." When we reached 116th Street and Seventh Avenue, he told the driver to pull over and keep the meter running while he delivered a message. Bird was gone a half hour before both the cab driver and I realized rigor mortis had set in. The cabbie was fuming but I didn't have but twenty cents so he couldn't take out nothing. I caught my subway and headed for the Bronx a little wiser.

January of 1945 I was out of bread and I hadn't scored musically so I had to find me another day gig. I talked to two clothiers (F&F) and they gave me a salesman's job. This was really sweet. I started at ten and worked until five with an hour for lunch.

As part of my job, I had to stay sharp, so I got seven vines (suits) right away. In three months I had twenty bands buying their uniforms there. Whenever I wanted to hang out on Fifty-second Street, I would tell the bosses I was courting a new account and they'd give me expense money. I'd been working four months before I noticed there were no Negro tailors, cutters, etc. I asked the bosses and they said it was because none had ever asked for jobs. I spoke to a friend and he came down one day and applied. When the ten Jewish employees found out this Negro tailor was even LOOKING for a job, they threatened to walk out. Finally the bosses broke down and told me. "Look, Babsie. It's not us, we're not prejudice but if we hired one we wouldn't be able to get any linings, buttons, or anything, plus the help would all leave." They also said they had a lot of pressure on them for having ME as a salesman.

By this time, the happenings had all moved to Fifty-second Street. Coleman Hawkins and Lady Day were the king and queen. Dizzy and Oscar Pettiford had a band in the Deuces, and Clark Monroe the only colored owner had his joint and was featuring Bud Powell and Max Roach. Miles Davis had just come to study at Juilliard and was the envy of everyone because his father sent him seventy-five ($75) dollars a week which was as much as the guys working were getting. The new sound got to me so I found myself there every night. I began to get gigs on weekends going up to Bridgeport and New Haven.

The street was really something in those days. The war was on and there were always loads of sailors and soldiers who wanted to and did fight every time they saw a Negro musician with a white girl. I'd seen a whore uptown beating her man with her shoe heel and him just holding his eyes screaming. When it was all over I asked her why the guy didn't fight back? She answered, "Just get a box of red pepper for a dime and throw it in his eyes and you'll win."

I took her advice and until today, I've never been without it.

The guys all laughed at me at first but after I saved Oscar and Bird's life with it, quite a few more colleagues copped some. There was one Irish bar on the corner of Sixth Avenue and Fifty-second Street that wouldn't serve colored even though the law said so. One night four of us went in with our white girls. After refusing us, the girls ordered. The owner called them all kinds of tramps, bitches, for being with niggers, etc. There were about thirty ofays there so we left. At 4:30 that morning, we took trash cans and broke out all his windows. We did this five times in a year before he finally got the message.

Another incident involved Ben Webster. At that time Ben weighed two hundred and forty pounds (240 lbs.) and was always ready to fight. Baby Lawrence, the greatest jazz tap dancer that ever lived ran into the Downbeat and yelled "the sailors are beating up Bud Powell." We all rushed around the corner to the White Rose bar and there was Bud in the street unconscious and bleeding. Ben grabbed two sailors, one in each hand by the backs of their necks. He ran them both from the curb straight through the plate glass windows and the rest took off like track stars.

I stayed on the job at the clothing store until November. Nat Cole had made it and was playing the Apollo. I went by to see him and when he dug my clothes, I had to take the whole trio down to get wardrobes. To show his appreciation, he found an open date in his schedule and told me to hire a hall and do the publicity and we'd split after expenses.

I went to Mr. Buchanon and rented his other ballroom The Golden Gate. He laughed and said I'd lose my shirt using a Wednesday night. The place could hold seven thousand people. When I arrived at eight o'clock to open the box office, the complete block was filled. Traffic had to be rerouted. By eleven o'clock I had sold five thousand tickets, when a police captain told me to shut down. I explained the fire marshall had okayed seven thousand, but they made me close anyway. The other two thousand people had come out to go to a dance so they just walked down one block and by midnight, the Savoy was full (dig it?).

Nat and Nadine were staying with Andy Kirk and that morning over breakfast we split twenty-eight hundred dollars. With all this bread I'm now really Mr. New York. I moved to Sugar Hill took a kitchenette on Hamilton Terrace. All the professional and good doing people were in that block. I invited Dizzy and Web by and reached under my bed and shocked them with a suitcase full of money.

My name was going around. All the high powered broads were "shooting" on me. I'd let them think they were going to con me out of my bread until I had made it with them. I'd ran through about ten before the word got out that "Babs ain't gonna spend nothing, but the evening." Lucky Thompson left Lionel Hampton and moved in with me and two weeks later Trummy Young who was ducking the cops for non-support moved in. The old West Indian landlady tried to give me trouble for having two extra people, but with my money I just gave her an extra ten. Trummy got out to Hawaii in a couple of weeks and Lucky got a gig in New Haven and took me on it.

We had a ball in New Haven. There were a lot of Portuguese chicks and beautiful little untouched colored orchids. I had been watching Billy Eckstine, and I began to realize that to make long bread one needed to be a singer and look pretty for the girls. I started my singing career up there with Lucky and when we came back after three months, I was cool with about twenty tunes.

In May of '46 I started rehearsing my first group. It was "Babs Three Bips and A Bop." I had Tad Dameron, who'd already made a name as a great arranger for Basie on piano and vocal. Pee Wee Tinney guitarist and vocal and Art Phipps bass and vocal. I had me a set of drums made so I could stand up and play them out front. We rehearsed at Helen Humes' pad in the basement of the Douglas Hotel every day for a month. I copped a gig at Minton's and one night Alfred Lions came in to dig us. He said we gassed him, but we were too far out for the people. We closed at Minton's and went back to rehearsing. Tad had to cut out and travel with Basie so I replaced him with Bobby Tucker, who was idle because Lady Day had gotten busted.

Nat came in town and this time he gave me two open dates. I told my guys not to worry that I would send them fifteen dollars a week while I made this money with Nat. I booked two places. The Convention Hall in Atlantic City and the Newark Armory. Nat gave me three thousand for expense bread so for six weeks I was shuttling between Newark and Atlantic City. I was a big man. Chicks in both towns were mine for the asking if I promised to introduce them to Nat.

Convention Hall could hold fifteen thousand people and at six o'clock the night of the dance, I got a call from Nat that they were "stormed in" in Milwaukee and no planes were leaving. I kept my hopes up until eight o'clock then decided to go to the hall and watch all the money we could have had. It was a beautiful August night and since it was going to be his first appearance, I watched eight thousand people come and then turn around.

The hall and expenses were a two thousand dollar ($2,000) loss and the next night in Newark we only made three thousand ($3000) profit so it was six weeks of running practically for nothing. Nat took two thousand to get even and gave me all the other grand so I could get me some uniforms for the guys and chalked it up to *c'est la vie* . . .

Nothing exciting happened for the next seven months—just rehearsing and hoping. I had one thing in my favor. All the guys in the group, except me, were living at home with their folks and didn't need nothing more than cigarette money and carfare. Early in 1947, I persuaded Al Lions to give me a record date. I added Rudy Williams on alto for soloing and we cut our first date.

The tunes were "Oop-pop-a-da." "Pay Dem Dues," "Lop Pow," and "Weird Lullaby." "Oop-pop" was an instant hit around New York and the metropolitan area. Freddie Robbins, a disk jockey, of note at the time, played it every night for a couple of months.

At that time Bluenote was a very small record company and had been doing a mail order business in Dixieland jazz. The result was our record wasn't heard outside the radius of Freddie's station unless they ordered it. Our jobs picked up around New York and we were booked into the Onyx club with Billie Eckstine. *Metronome* picked us the number one vocal group in the country.

We worked all the clubs along the street during the next few months and it was during a rehearsal at the Onyx one afternoon when Dizzy came in and said his big band was auditioning for Victor. He said he'd played a lot of tunes but hadn't moved the big brass. I told him to do "Oop-pop." Dizzy went back and did it for the big brass and they signed him immediately.

We left town to play an engagement at a lounge on the north side of Chicago. When we arrived at the club, the manager counted us and said we had one too many.

I showed my contract which read "Babs and His Three Bips and Bop" which came to five people. He told us to go straight to the dressing room in the rear. The dressing room turned out to be a storage room for empty bottles and we had no mirrors, chairs, or anything to hang our clothes on. While we were changing, we could hear the solo colored pianist playing "the nigger" and the white man played five up, the "nigger" won the money and was scared to pick it up. We all looked at each other knowing this was going to be a drag. As we were going to the bandstand, the customers were yelling "All right niggers get hot."

During our first set behind their long bar, we could see gangsters and police officers trading money and were called twenty-five "black bastards." All the big name jazz groups were playing this room and I wondered had they received this sort of treatment or had they been just waiting for us. Back in the storage room I asked all the guys did they want to quit and since nobody had any dependents, everybody agreed to split. I went up to the boss's office and asked for my transportation.

My contract read I was to receive it upon arrival. He told me "Nigger, can't you see I'm playing cards? I'll give it to you tomorrow." I went back and told the fellows what was happening, and that we were in trouble. I had a .32 pistol and my bass man had a .38. We knew we couldn't carry the instruments and protect ourselves too, so we decided to leave them. We'd only gotten about ten feet when the boss and two of his cronies confronted us. I told him we were leaving. He said "Look you black bastards, all the big names play here and they don't mind being called a few Niggers." I told him they were getting two and three grand a week, but for seven-fifty we wasn't going to take it. We both reached for our heat at the same time and I told him even if he got me, I'd get him. You'd be surprised to know that even a big gangster is humble looking down a .32. I led my men out while the bass player covered us from the rear and made it back to the south side.

We were stranded in Chicago, so the next morning I went to see the president of the Colored local. He was the first of several "Uncle Tom" officials I was to encounter later in life. The white boss had already called him and gave him his orders. He berated me about being late and flirting with white women, etc. I knew I wasn't going to get any cooperation from him so I called the New York office of my local.

When I recorded "Pay Dem Dues" the union officials thought I meant "union dues" so I was held in regard at that time. I spoke to the president and told him of our plight. They wired us three hundred to pay hotel bills and get back. We were almost finished packing when the "spade" delegate showed up at our hotel. He said, "Why would you call the national office, I told you I would look into the matter." I told him, "Look my man, my men are out here stranded and we can't wait while letters take two or three months to be argued before the boards. We'll do our talking from New York." (Bye!)

As we were waiting for a cab, Dinah Washington rolled up with her entourage. After conversing with her, she explained she wouldn't be needing her station wagon for a while and if I drove it back to New York, we could save our train fare. I accepted her offer and we cut out in style with wheels.

I turned on the radio and was almost shocked to death. The first thing we heard was "Oop-pop" and the D.J. was praising this great new hit. All the way back we heard it at least ten times, even on square ofay stations in Indiana and Ohio. We were all happy for Dizzy because with a hit he could keep his big band. Soon as we got back and I'd garaged Dinah's wheels, I went to the record store to buy the record. Soon as I walked in, the cat from Victor was bringing another five-hundred order in. He explained that in two weeks, the record had did fifty thousand and expected it to go to four hundred thousand.

I copped my record and looked under the title for my name and where I was supposed to be credited as the composer, there was Dizzy's name too. The next week was one of the most hectic ones I've ever had. I spoke with Dizzy, his manager and the front office of Victor. They all had the same bullshit, that they didn't know how the mistake was made. I wasn't worried about my royalties, I wanted my name where it belonged. If the world saw my name on the record, it might have helped my group.

I sued Victor and thereby started my education concerning a nobody trying to sue a big concern. They got angry because I made them call back ten thousand records and reprint the labels with my name. This took time and also they lost sales, so my name was mud.

I was signed to the same agent at the time so I soon found there wasn't any gigs for a smart nigger. The only satisfaction I got was watching Al Lions of Bluenote as he watched Dizzy's record soar while rigor mortis set in on my record simply because he wouldn't promote it.

Around this time Bop was commercial so a new joint was opened called The Royal Bopera House on Broadway. I hadn't gigged since I instituted my lawsuit so naturally I was bitter. Here we were a number one group and couldn't get arrested. One night I ran into Max Roach and he told me, "Man they're using your shit down at the Bopera House you better go check it out." I went down and out front they had a huge sign which read, "THE NEW BOP MUSIC.—Hear 'Oop-pop-a-da.'" There was no name of the artist, just that sign. I went in and spoke to the idea man for the joint. He was very indifferent and even a drag as he told me, "Man you suing Victor, if you don't like it sue *me*." I told him "I got a suit for you and I hope it fits." I threw my pepper in his eyes and broke his nose with a beer bottle and told him if he pressed any charges, I would put him under the ground.

This idea man was a good friend to a big disk jockey who was the only one spinning progressive records over a big station.

This D.J. approached me and told me unless I gave him ten percent of my earnings, he wouldn't play my records any more. I'd known this bum when he'd spent a year in Newark hanging out with us spades and trying to pimp off colored broads. I told him in "Negronese" what I thought of him and that he wasn't big enough to stop me from eating. Charlie Ventura was the first to emulate our style and in two months of constant plugging by this snake, he became the "originator" of the "Bop" vocals.

The gigs were non-existent for us for the next few months but I got a reprieve when Nat came in to play the Paramount. He was in the process of courting his second wife, Marie. He invited me down and told me of his intentions to divorce Nadine and marry Marie. I told him "If that's what you want, go ahead," but to remember the financial dues he'd have to pay. He told me Nadine was coming in from Los Angeles that night and gave me instructions to be with her daily to keep her from getting lonely.

He'd give me fifty dollars a day to take her out with. During our first night out she explained "Babs, you go get a hundred every day" as fifty wasn't enough. During the two weeks he was at the Paramount,

Nat gave me twelve hundred dollars of which I never spent a penny. Nadine told me to just keep it as she didn't want nothing he had. She used her own bread. I would never do it again because everyday he'd ask me her plans and at night she would do likewise. The fellows in my group had gone to work in other groups because they had to make a living, but with about a thousand dollars I ushered in 1948 not feeling too bad.

I moved out of my kitchenette to a nice room on One Hundred and Fifty-Third Street. I'd gotten the message the big booking offices weren't going to give me any jobs so I began to figure a way out. I bought a bus ticket to Boston. I stopped off at Bridgeport, New Haven, and Hartford. I'd canvass the town and talk to club owners. These were small clubs in Negro neighborhoods and couldn't pay but twenty dollars ($20) a night. The money wasn't the issue, I'd been inactive six months and I wanted to work. My record had reached most of these cities so the owners were glad to use a so-called name for twenty dollars. It took me two months to reach Boston after two and three weeks in each town on the way.

A friend I'd met in Atlantic City, named Sabby Lewis, had a cookin' little band at the Hi-Hat club. I was still cool with bread so I checked into a white hotel downtown. That night I went by the club and did a couple of numbers with Sabby and the boss gave me a job. I felt good, I was in a big city again. During my third week I met a fine Back Bay socialite ofay chick. I wasn't hip to the Mass. laws so one morning I took her home with me. About four o'clock the house detective knocked on my door. When he entered and saw the girl, he told me it was against the law to have a girl of any color in my room unless it was my legally married wife.

It's a good thing we hadn't gone to bed as I found out later they would beat a spade to death when caught in bed with an ofay broad.

I "Tommed" for him and explained we were only listening to records. He told the girl to go home then and asked me how much bread I had. My California experience had taught me a lesson, so I told him one hundred dollars. He got fifty and told me to leave town, which I promptly did. As I was leaving I noticed him and the desk clerk splitting the fifty and laughing. From that night on I have never checked into a hotel or motel again in America.

KEITH JARRETT

INTERVIEWED BY KIMIHIKO YAMASHITA

In Search of Folk Roots

*M*iles said that many people misunderstood what John Coltrane was doing.

> I don't understand this talk about Coltrane being difficult to understand. What he does, for example, is to play five notes of a chord and then change it around, trying to see how many different ways it can sound. It's like explaining something five different ways. And that sound of his is connected with what he's doing with the chords at any time.
>
> —*Miles Davis*

Miles is never wrong. But, there's always more to say about it.

> I think a movement in Jazz is beginning away from the conventional string of chords, and a return to emphasis on melodic rather than harmonic variation. There will be fewer chords but infinite possibilities as to what to do with them. Classical composers—some of them—have been writing this way for years, but jazz musicians seldom have.
>
> —*Miles Davis*

Miles talked about Ahmad Jamal's use of space. Is this the same thing you've talked about—space and melody?

No, this is space with tempo. I'm talking about space with space. Ahmad plays with a rhythm section so the space he uses is taken up by the rhythm section. That's not space the way I was talking about it.

> Listen to the way Jamal uses space. He lets it go so that you can feel the rhythm section and the rhythm section can feel you. It's not crowded . . . Ahmad is one of my favorites.
>
> —*Miles Davis*

I was talking about the kind of space when there is no sound and no pulse. This space can have a pulse anyway. It depends on what came before it and what comes next. The spaces can start having their own melodic position.

Miles was intrigued by Monk's masterful and idiosyncratic manipulation of mysterious-sounding chord progressions, but he was especially fascinated by Monk's use of space in his solos.

—Eric Nisenson

Monk's concept of space alone was one of the most important things he taught Coltrane; when to lay out and let somebody else fill up that space, or just leave the space open. I think John was already going in that direction, but working with Monk helped him reach his goal that much faster.

—McCoy Tyner

Did you have something special in mind you wanted to accomplish with Miles's band?

I had heard his band just before I started to play with it. I heard it with Tony [Williams] and Wayne [Shorter], and Herbie [Hancock] or Chick [Corea].

And everybody sounded like they were playing alone, they didn't sound like they were playing in a band. They were only hearing themselves and it sounded so much like an ego trip.

Then when Miles played it sounded so refreshing. He would play these short solos and go off the stage and the rest of the band sounded like, "Let's try to be me," "I'm going to be me now." I didn't think Miles deserved this kind of thing, so that night I thought, "Well, there's gonna come a time when I'll work with him for a while." That was a little before the time I actually started to play with him.

So, after you joined his band, what did you feel?

That's a big, big, question. I mean, what did I feel about what? Everything in the world [he laughs]?

What you were trying to do in the band.

He asked for me, so he had already had heard me—many times. I didn't think I was there to be pretending I was someone else. He knew who he was getting. He knew who he had heard play, so I didn't have to do anything special except stay myself there.

Bill [Evans] and Keith Jarrett were different. Chick Corea is different. Chick knocks me out at that tempo [Miles taps out a medium up tempo]. Then you get Herbie; Herbie can do anything. He and Keith, I think they must have drunk the same dye [he laughs].

—Miles Davis

He was not so happy . . . he wanted more funk in the band; so I knew I could be a part of that. I think that's one thing he didn't believe Chick could do.

> Miles is trying to get further out (more abstract) and yet more basic (funkier) at the same time.
>
> —*Tony Williams*

Jack [DeJohnette] was in the band and Jack and I had played together . . . we knew each other very well and we knew we could play together and have a good time . . . But I was temporary, I knew I was temporary.

> *Keith played so nice I had to give him two pianos. He'd go like this. Miles imitates Jarrett in a pianistic frenzy. I'd say, "Keith, how does it feel to be a genius?"*
>
> —*Miles Davis*

> *The music that Miles had wouldn't have worked with acoustic piano. You couldn't play chords (functional harmony)—it wasn't chordal at all. It was just . . . sounds . . . I thought the band was the most egocentric organization I had heard musically . . . except for Miles. Miles was still playing nice, beautiful things, and the rest of the band was in boxes. So in a way . . . I just wanted to do something a little bit to change the feeling. And I knew Jack DeJohnette was there, so we play well together.*
>
> —*Keith Jarrett*

I didn't want to play electric keyboard but that's the way it was. I could have played electric typewriter, that would have been o.k., too. Same thing.

I have this funny vision of people pulling electric keyboards away from keyboard players while they're playing and putting different ones in front of them; they all feel the same and the last one is a typewriter but they're so into it they don't know it's a typewriter.

I collect watches because I'm very interested in time. Now with everyone wearing a digital watch, it says time goes in a straight line . . . one, two, three, four, five, six. Time does not move like that. It's never perfect either . . .

Digital time is like record production. In record production we have the bass, then you say now we add the vocalist, now we have the conga drums, we go this way—one, two, three, four. Real music, when people play together, is like this: you come together, you go away, you come together. There are no edges, no sharp edges.

Even when people talk they are not spontaneous, they prepare. You prepare, like putting a frame—I'm going to say this first, and I'm going to say this second, and then I'm going to say this . . .

But if you're spontaneous you talk about everything—on a good day you talk about everything all the time. So for me a watch is a symbol.

There are many kinds of time altogether.

Time is subjective . . . See, music can tell you many things, if you listen well. Different drummers can prove that time is subjective because none of them plays the same tempo, at the same tempo. They find their own time. If time was the same for everyone, every drummer would play the same . . . But there are many kinds of time . . .

When I hear Miles play with his new band, the new band is like a digital watch. Miles comes and Miles is round, he is alive. He just plays one note.

Someone could say, "Oh, anyone can play like Miles." He has a trumpet sound that is almost like a student has when a student is learning trumpet. You get that same sound—almost—for a while and then you get more brassy and then you play more and more and you lose this "innocent" sound that Miles has. So the whole world can say, "anybody can get that sound," but nobody can get it.

And the reason Miles gets that sound and no one else gets it is because Miles wants the sound more than they do, he wants that sound. He wants it with this ferociousness, so he gets it.

I don't know what other word to use . . . ferocious is just . . . I can't think of a better word . . . it's not enough to say Miles wants the sound, because everybody can say they want things, but Miles wants it with all his energy.

The ferociousness can't be egotistical, that's why I used that word. An animal doesn't have an ego like we do and animals can be ferocious . . . They need to eat, they are ferocious. They don't let anything get in their way. But they are not doing it for an ego, they're doing it to survive or for something to survive . . . maybe their kids . . . their little baby lions.

I'm using that word because a poet was talking about one of my favorite writers, who's Persian, and he, this poet, said something about how no one understands how ferocious this writer is. If they understood that, they would see more about what he's saying. And that was the first time I heard someone say the right word for this, so I'm using it because it's true.

I'm trying to get out of this thing where "want" means something like "desire." I don't mean desire. Ferocious is too fast for desire. Desire is I'd love to do this. The kind of want that would make me play the note I hear isn't ego. That's not ego, that's a sort of harmonizing with reality in a powerful way.

Miles can play soft and it's powerful, other trumpet players play soft and it's weak. There is ferociousness even in the soft note.

But it's not anger or ego, it's the whole note—"I *want* this note. Not for me but for the air." The thing that makes it ferocious is what happens before he plays the note. He has to be ready for the note, for his own note, not someone else's note. Not the note on paper, not the note somewhere in the air above him, but *his* note. He has to be ready for this. And that's very difficult . . .

> Underneath his lyricism, Miles swings. He'll take care of the lyricism, but the rest of the band must complement him with an intense drive. And it's not that they supply a drive he himself lacks. Actually, they have to come up to him . . . As subtle as he is in his time and phrasing and his courage to wait, to use space, he's very forceful. There is a feeling of unhurriedness in his work and yet there's intensity underneath and through it all.
>
> —Gil Evans

> Miles's conception of time has led to greater rhythmic freedom for other players. His feeling, for another thing, is so intense that he catapults the drummer, bassist and pianist together, forcing them to play at the top of their technical ability and forcing them with his own emotional strength to be as emotional as possible.
>
> —Cecil Taylor

Miles said something in one of his interviews about your playing . . .

About Irish melody?

Yes, how did you feel about that?

I kind of knew what he meant.

Can you explain it?

No [he laughs].

> Years later Miles would say that Jarrett was "the best pianist I ever had." Jarrett's technique was awesome, but his imagination was often annoyingly eclectic. Left to his own devices, he would show off all the styles that he had mastered.

He could play bebop one moment, then switch to a Bill Evans romanticism, and then suddenly leap into a frantic, "outside" Cecil Taylor pandemonium. He could also be extraordinarily lyrical, playing what Miles called "those beautiful Irish melodies."

—Eric Nisenson

That's just what he heard in some of the things I played. I remember though that when I wrote compositions like "Metamorphosis" and other things on *In the Light*, I remember always thinking that there was a section of each piece that sounded Irish.

I also think of it ["Metamorphosis"] as Universal Folk Music.

—Keith Jarrett

Jazz is getting too far from its folk roots.

—Miles Davis

Jazz today is closer to classical music than it is to folklore music, and I'd rather stay closer to folklore music.

—Miles Davis

Miles saw vital connections between rock and jazz, and expressed the opinion that rock wouldn't fade away, because, like jazz, it's folk music.

—Ian Carr

Miles lamented back in the seventies that jazz was getting further and further away from its folk roots. How do you feel about that?

Well, now he went pretty far from it too. Now he has pop roots [he laughs]. Maybe he lost the way back to the folk roots, you know. But it's true, jazz did that.

So you think jazz relates to folk roots?

Jazz is folk music. Now it doesn't seem like it is, but the thing that I would call jazz is still a tribal language. A local thing.

Many people think that the world should speak the same language eventually, every country would speak the same language, and many people think that would be a really good thing to happen. But I don't agree. If that was the way the earth was two hundred years ago, we would have no jazz. We would have no folk music to listen to from anywhere else. We would only have one thing, it would be like New Age music forever. So to me something local is very important. Something that's only in a certain geography.

Nobody would play anything that anyone else would learn from. Everyone would hear the same thing and play the same thing.

Because language, the way we talk, is connected strongly to how we hear—so if everyone spoke the same way, the same words, they would be all hearing the same sounds.

Geography makes the language. I don't think people just come up with some imaginary language from nothing. I think the sound of the language comes from the colors in the sky and the landscape.

If you go to beaches in Belgium, it's very gray all the time. There's not much color in the sky and there's not much color in the ocean. The shells don't have much color. If you go to the South Pacific where the ocean is very blue then the shells are very colorful. People aren't immune to that. People are affected by the geography. So if we are all forced to speak the same language we won't even see our own geography anymore.

So when the indigenous people of each country—the Indians of North America, African natives—when they become civilized they lose what they can give to us. I can see that very clearly here in the United States.

If I see a black man and I hear him talk like a Wall Street executive who is white, there is something he cannot give me anymore. He's traded. He gives himself, and he gets this Wall Street image, but he can never get back his local sound again.

So maybe the trio with Jack DeJohnette and Gary Peacock needs to exist for one important reason that is not musical. We are keeping this language alive. We are not saying, "Well now, it's modern day, we move to fusion or we have to change our language." We are keeping this language no matter what the pressures are around us.

There is a funny story from when I was with Miles and Gary Bartz was with the band. Gary is black and I'm white. Gary and I went into a coffee shop to have some food before we played and the man comes up with the sandwiches and says, "So you're musicians." We said, "Yes." He said, "What kind of music do you play?" And Gary said, "We play black music." I said "Wait a minute, no, no, no, wait a minute. Gary plays black music and I play Hungarian music." [laughs] I said, "Let's be fair. We have to be fair."

AMIRI BARAKA

Diz

I was into the Orioles. Ruth Brown. Larry Darnell. Louie Jordan, The Ravens, Ya know, the late '40s, just going into high school. When my first cousin George let me have his older brother Sonny's BeBop collection!

I got those old Guilds, Manors, Savoys and a whole world unfolded before me, beginning with the names: Dizzy Gillespie, Thelonious Monk, Charlie "Yardbird" Parker. The names, Bud Powell, Max Roach, Klook, Kenny Clarke. The names, the language, another world had opened.

Oop Bop sha Bam (a koo koo mop!) the language, another world. The Land of Oo Blah Dee. Me and Joe Carroll went there and hung until they sicked Dooie Blah and Dooie Blee on us. Swing Low Sweet Cadillac. (Didn't one of them dudes in the horn section answer after "wadie wadie wadie wadie yo wambo. . . . YO MAM—OO!")

And from the beginning of my entrance into that world, it was Diz who was the central figure, the beckoner, sitting there looking out at me from *Esquire*, the beret and hornrimmed BeBop glasses. "To Be Or Not To Bop" the caption said, and called Diz the "High Priest of BeBop." And that was it for me, then. All the wild stuff they sd about Diz, trying to make you think this or that, escaped me. What I saw was my leader. The twinkle behind the rims, I thought I understood what he was signifying. That's what Diz taught fundamentally, how to nut out on the square world. That word Hip! That was with it, too, from the beginning. They, and I got in it, too, were Hip. Hip cats. Cats. I rather be a cat than a dog, right now!

The Square versus The Hip, and I never forgot that. Even now in this square and ugly world, to be hip in a square world, would make some square call you dizzy.

The Ethiopians called the Pyramid "the angle of success." They called the Square "the angle of failure." The culture continuum even across the middle passage. Like

Oop shoobee doobee
　　Oop Oop
Oop shoobee doobee
　　Oop Oop!　　You Dig?

A lovers' conversation. In "Kush" or "Nights in Tunisia" or approaching "Tin Tin Deo." We could also dig the funk of burning *Manteca!*

Dug the cirle as
　　the whirl
　　O world
the pyramid as
the rising focus
of endless energy. I
and I.
　　So the square, goes
no where. Like the box
we in. It might rock but
it sure can't roll (censored censored
censored censored censored censored censored)
no matter how high it go
it always resemble its lowest self-

And I went to work then, trying to find out what was really hap-
pening. That language too. What's Happening? I had gotten Max
Roach & His BeBop Boys. Charlie Parker and his Reboppers. Stan
Getz. Opus De Bop. *Thriving On A Riff.* I copped Bird's *Repetition* w/
Strings. Wow.

The titles of the songs drew me in further. They were so . . . yeh,
weird. Then I dug the real high priest, in shades and another tam, looking past all of us into the hipnopocity of everything. Monk. Diz was the
leader. The speaker. The political cadre, pushing the music by his playing, by his Diziness. He was His Royal Dizziness. Monk, on the other
hand, was inside the deepness, the heaviness of what it was. He made
no statements, no daunting alarums (yeh) he was the High Priest, but
Diz was royalty.

And Diz titles always carried you somewhere up the street and
around the corner where the hip shit was. "Tin Tin Deo," "The
Champ" were two of my 1st self-reliant purchases. Now I was in high
school and cd get an after school gig.

"A Night in Tunisia," "Kush," "Con Alma," and with the Ooo Bop Sha Bams and then Woody Herman's "Lemon Drop," and Babs' 3 Bips and A Bop, the language of BeBop became easily my own, and still to this day remains.

Diz BeBop. The beret, Bop glasses, and a goatee, dont forget that. For a couple of decades journalists around the world would sum up the music, or make cracks about it, using that stereotype of early Diz. Bopper jokes became the norm, for alluding to the crazy, the wild, the frantic, and thats what they called us, because thats what we said.

The language registered our psychological expressions of our social life (and the U.S.'s). We were "wild," "crazy," "frantic," as opposed to trained, nor/mal, static, like regular bourgeois culture.

It was an emotional expression of the common psychological development of urban AfroAmerica.

But that language was a shower of new images. Diz and Bird and Monk and Max and Klook and Bud. "Un Poco Loco" was what Bud said and everybody thought that's what Bop was—craziness.

But like the Zen masters knew, inside Diz's laughter was an absolute rationality, as to How corny this bullshit white face slavery exploiting society was, is. We needed Diz's assurance that it all could be laughed at. And if you wadnt doing anything else, you least needed to do that. Dig?

Dig? the language. Like Thelonious, you dig? It scrambled me shot some disparate colors into my mind trying to make me understand some stuff I needed to grow. Things, feelings, revelations, my own acts. That I was entering a higher intellectual culture, in which art was validated as personal experience.

To Be Or Not To Bop. But Diz was already Bopping. He & Bird, Bud, Monk, Klook, then Max, Miles, Sonny had created it, as a new speech, a new song. Like a dialectical expression of the new feeling the times demanded, in contrast to the careful dead arrangements the corporations had coopted swing into.

The big classic swinging jazz orchestras had created a fresh expanded contemporary form for Afro American music. But soon the big band became a commercial and artistic jail, as it was subsumed by the commercial largely white swing (as a noun) bands. Like '60s jazz was coopted by fusion.

Diz and the others had worked the big classic bands. Teddy Hill, Lionel Hampton, Earl Hines, Cab Calloway, &c. After working those gigs, Diz, Bird and the others would wind up uptown in Harlem after hours, in Minton's and Monroe's uptown houses, the black night laboratories of sound, the smoke and whiskey academies of soul, where they gave a new generation their self consciousness.

The bullet-sharp experimentation in wailing, the sound's language. To get the blues back into the music, to get the polyrhythms of Africa back, to get improvisation back as primary, these were the essence of their experiments. To get away from the deadly charts of commercial swing. The tin pan alley plantations.

This was one of the catalysts for Bird and Diz and the young boppers beginning to improvise off the harmonic structure, the chords, or cliched standards, rather than play those tired melodies.

And those terrible groups that came out of that. Diz, Bird, Klook, Blakey, Max, Miles, Bud, Monk. It was blazing and yes, weird. That was an acknowledged constant. Frantic. Yeh, we called it that. We was trying to get frantic trying to get away from Kay Kayser and Sammy Kay. The music turned us on. And it was already Gone, if you dug it!

Our language told where we was coming from and where we was trying to go. *Frantic, Crazy, Wild, Out, Gone,* We was hip not square. We walked that way, the bop walk, used to dance the bop, these squares talking about you couldn't dance to it, shit we danced to all of Diz's shit. We were Boppers. My father even asked me Why I wanted To Be A Bopper. You mean why did I want to be conscious??

But Diz always held the paramount stature in the music. Bird was the great innovator and genius. But Diz was the leader of the whole shit. Of everybody. The speech and the song. The music and the life-style.

Plus, from the beginning Diz, himself, was a musical innovator of great impact. He was a theoretician, a teacher, a performer, a composer, an incredible instrumentalist. Dig, of the two U.S. world ambassadors, they choose Louis and Diz, both the same kind of bloods. Both great musicians and great communicators. No matter how jive and bloody the U.S. would be, here come Louie and Diz, and like Louis said, I'm the real ambassador!! Nobody could put them down. They were loved around the world.

Dizzy's groups have always been signal. His big bands among the most innovative in the music.

Like Diz said when he signed my copy of *To Be Or Not To Bop,* "For My Idol" . . . Hahaha. That's the kind of ambassador Diz was. He was one of my largest culture heroes. And so he rewards me with assuming my regard for him. Incredible.

But the lames always purposely misread Diz, being Lames. They confused his domination over squareness as lack of seriousness. To be serious about squares one needs a gun. But in his autobiography Diz says his hero was Paul Robeson. And in the '40s there was a whole group of black youth, who called themselves the Paul Robeson Movement. And Diz was undoubtedly part of that.

The '40s when ww2 made it seem, again, like there might be equality in the offing. There was a social consciousness movement that swept through the black arts as it had done in the '20s and again in the '60s.

It was the worldwide resistance to fascism that had undergirded it. So that the music Bop was also a conscious attempt to tear away from the grim corporate establishment that locked the music up just as it did the people.

I have always thought Bop language, Ooo shoobie doobie oop ooo OO shoobie doobie oo oop, for instance, was an attempt to respeak African language. Like the unknown tongue, the African language still glued in our consciousness with our history and the syntax of African American language and culture. The scatting (which Louis raised earlier!) and the Bop talk that Diz brought, both were attempts to put the instrumental language back into vocal language, and that unknown language of the black unconsciousness was and is "African" or AfroAmerican.

Diz was always into Africa. As the titles of his compositions attest to. (". . . Tunisia," "Kush", &c.) Diz also hooked up the PanAmerican funk to its African origins. Diz was the one who set out the larger expression of what was to be called AfroCuban music.

Its internationalist focus is unmistakable. Diz hooked up with Mario Bauza, Chano Pozo, Candido, Machito, Mongo Santamaria, and other great Latin American musicians to reconstruct a new AfroLatin sound. Called AfroCuban music. What Jelly Roll alluded to as "the Latin tinge" Diz brought all the way into full sight. Bringing both the Latino and English Caribbean into focus in AfroAmerican music. "Manteca" is a classic, as is the still-not-well-known "Cubana Be Cubana Bop."

Years later Diz came back from Brazil with what the commercial people tagged Bossa Nova, again linking the Brazilian Samba with AfroAmerican jazz.

Now, it's too weird to think that even Diz is gone. All the others of that generation, almost, have booked. Only the great Max Roach of the original funkateers remains. And a few of the close communers, Sonny

Rollins, Roy Haynes, who were younger and among the first disciples. But where there was a deep deep sadness for all the departed, Bird, Bud, Klook, Monk, Miles, like part of myself had left, certainly my youth, and the bright unshakeable hopes of my generation. But with Diz's departure, there is not only a sadness, still not completely raised. (I mean, I dont know whether I even believe it yet. Diz might be jivin, and he might just pop up somewhere. I heard Jon Farris play the other day at St. John the Divine and I thought maybe Diz was somewhere cracking up.) But with Diz gone, it's like you dont even feel safe around here no more. Really, like you dont even feel safe!

AL YOUNG

We Jazz June / We Die Soon:
Jazz Film Thoughts

Now that our jazz musicians—like novelists, poets, filmmakers, and business execs—are increasingly the products of jazz institutes or college and university jazz studies curricula, the meaning to audiences of recent films about the music and the lives of some of its colorful practitioners must certainly be up for grabs.

Think about all those self-taught players and originators, stylists, whose lives were often in shambles, their personal habits shocking, yet who—under dreadful working conditions and without benefit of fellowship or grant—developed techniques so uniquely expressive that their recorded legacies and personal histories are scrupulously studied all over the world.

After expatriate tenor saxophone great Dexter Gordon surprised everybody by starring in *'Round Midnight,* the 1986 film directed by Bernard Tavernier, dramatic movies and documentaries about jazz musicians have been appearing with unusual frequency. While Clint Eastwood's *Bird* and Spike Lee's *Mo' Bettah Blues* have generated controversy in more than just film and music circles, documentaries about jazz personalities haven't fared badly at all. *Straight No Chaser,* a remarkable documentary on the legendary Thelonious Monk (Clint Eastwood was executive producer), and Bruce Weber's *Let's Get Lost,* which takes a close, unblinking look at trumpeter Chet Baker's career, hold up well and continue to fascinate under repeated viewings.

The character Dexter Gordon plays (supposedly inspired by the saddening lives of bebop pianist Bud Powell and saxophonist Lester Young) is an alcoholic jazz has-been who has abandoned New York for Paris in the 1950s to live out his final professional days. Living at first at the Hotel Louisane, which seems to be jammed with expatriate American musicians, under the all-too-watchful care of an ex-lover turned manager, Gordon allows his drinking to get so far out of control that he can no longer function. It is only after a devoted French admirer and single parent (François Cluzet) takes Gordon home to live with him and his young daughter, and nurses him adoringly, that Gordon recuperates. The handsome, wobbly, hoarse-throated Gordon is as personable as an actor as he was in so-called real life. But despite the spirited, somewhat anachronistic music provided by Herbie Hancock, Bobby Hutcherson, Wayne Shorter and Gordon himself, among others, the message seems to be: Jazz musicians are helpless, hapless, and childlike; incapable of taking care of business or caring for themselves.

Why is it that the documentaries tend to be more convincing than fictional films about jazz? In the half century that I've been exposed to the music itself and to on-screen portrayals of the jazz life, I've had occasion to do a lot of thinking about this. For one thing, all music speaks for itself and tells its own story, which varies from performance to performance and from listener to listener. This means that the music of Charlie Parker or Amadeus Mozart have taken on lives of their own that ultimately have little to do with their creators' personalities.

Parker (who used to say he "attended Lester Young University," just as Bud Powell was a graduate of Charlie Parker University) along with Dizzy Gillespie, Thelonious Monk, and drummer Kenny Clarke, played a major role in redefining modern music. And these were all African-American musicians who understood the artistic significance of their innovations. And yet in jazz mythology much is made of Parker as a twentieth-century trickster figure, the consummate put-on artist; his gargantuan appetites for drugs, drink, food, and sex, his off-hours penchant for reading and movies, his riotous lifestyle.

So overwhelming are the handed-down, carefully sifted details of Parker's eccentric, disorderly existence, his self-destructiveness, that he tends to come across in the movie *Bird* as thoroughly humorless, although larger-than-life. His music, however, quivers and squeals with humor, warmth, and jubilance. "He was one funny dude," Max Roach once told me. "That's why people liked to be around him; that's how he got to take advantage of them again and again." Joel Oliansky's script never gives us a clue about why its subject behaves as he does. For a flickering spell, after he and his pretty wife Chan (Diane Venora) fall genuinely in love, set up house, and start their family, things look as though they might begin looking up.

But, like the pitiful stumblebum of a character Dexter Gordon depicts in *'Round Midnight*, Bird is hopelessly, perhaps fiendishly, childish and helpless. Except when he has that almighty alto magic sax working its magic for him, he must be looked after and indulged, especially, it seems, by long-suffering, genius-conscious, sympathetic lovers and well-wishers. Except for his embarrassment at being hooted off the stage during an early jam session, events and family relationships that traumatized Parker's Kansas City childhood aren't even touched. In fact, you would never gather from watching this movie that heroin addicts actually enjoy getting high; that the whole idea was to shoot up, kick back, and have a little fun.

Forest Whitaker performs Charlie "Bird" Parker winningly, and yet it is never made clear in the movie what might have motivated Bird to give his short life over so completely to drugs and excess. That he was able to play with such brilliance and produce so much beautiful music—quite in spite of his pain—is what astonishes. Mozart, by the way, wasn't exactly an ascetic, either. He seems to have been, in personal affairs, as pleasure-driven, perhaps even wilder than Bird, but time has tempered the composer's reputation; it is no longer Amadeus that matters so much to us as it is the music he left. Parker's music, with its blues-suffused exuberance, shows every sign of outlasting its composer's outcast status and juicy notoriety.

As notorious as Hollywood has become for the broad array of stereotypes its movies have drawn and projected, their magnetism and raw appeal continue to flourish. The South African-born trumpeter-singer-composer Hugh Masekela once described in a radio interview how he became interested in jazz, while he was a grade school kid in Johannesburg.

"At school they showed us that movie, *Young Man with a Horn,* with Kirk Douglas. I saw him playing that trumpet and I said, 'That's what I want to do—play trumpet, play jazz, and be a jazz musician.'"

I've been mulling over that one for a long time, too.

As it happened, the first dramatic motion picture I ever saw about jazz and jazz musicians was the 1950 Warner Bros. feature, *Young Man with a Horn,* an adaptation of Dorothy's 1930s novel inspired by the life of cornetist-pianist Bix Beiderbecke, the first white player to qualify for genius status in a musical culture virtually created and developed by black Americans. Smooth, handsome Kirk Douglas starred as the colorful, sound-obsessed but doomed young trumpeter. Doris Day and Lauren Bacall played the women in what little love life our hero's smoke-and-drink-drenched existence permitted. And you can guess which actress got the "good girl" part. Betty Grable's husband Harry James dubbed in all the trumpet licks for Douglas to mime. And under the amazing Michael Curtiz's direction, Douglas didn't come off looking all that bad. Yes, Hoagy Carmichael—who had actually done some serious hanging out with Bix himself back in the 1920s—was up there on the screen, as heroically world-weary as ever, yet personable. He tickled the ivories and stoically hoisted neat shots of whiskey or gin between numbers.

Jazz was over a half-century old by then; I was eleven. As early as 1937, the European-born musicologist Alfred Einstein, in the first edition of *A Short History of Music*—to this day an influential and enduring work—had described jazz as "an orgiastic dance-music in quick-march time—the most abominable treason against all the music of Western civilization." Einstein cites as contemptible the deliberate adoption by European composers of ragtime, tango, foxtrot, shimmy, and jazz ("erotic and barbaric dance-music") as elements of artistic music. Like World War I, in his view, such vulgarity was "symbolical of the spiritual disintegration of the world." "Yet even in jazz," he goes on to say, "there lurks a European and decadent desire—that desire for the natural, primitive and barbaric, a desire that often lifts its head in 'contemporary' music." I can hear some waggish Negrophile of the era wisecracking to Einstein: "You ain't heard nothin' yet!"

As for my contemporary pals and younger siblings, we were always lifting or shifting our heads to see over or around someone else's. Or ducking down in our seats to avoid flying popcorn boxes and other matinee missiles. Saturdays we always ended up at the Astor Theater, 12th Street, Detroit. At nine cents a pop we could afford to sit through anything; the same as when it came to records, we'd listen to anything. Spike Jones, Perry Como, Kay Starr, Bull Moose Jackson, Lily Pons, Billy Ward and the Dominoes, Vaughn Monroe, Kate Smith, Louis Jordan, Stan Kenton, Sugar "Chile" Robinson, Gene Autry, Duke Ellington, Georgia Gibbs, Frankie Laine, Thelonious Monk, Frankie Yankovic and his Yanks, Jerry Lester, Ella Fitzgerald, Mario Lanza, Howlin' Wolf, Woody Herman, Sister Rosetta Tharpe, Billy Daniels, George Shearing, Earl Bostic, Harry James, Doris Day, and even Mickey Katz, whose band did strange Yiddish send-ups of the day's pop hits. For example, when Jo Stafford hit it big around that time with "Shrimp Boats Are A-Comin'," Katz came back with "Herring Boats." We'd all learn the Yiddish lyrics without even knowing what they meant.

I'm reminded of Fat Boy, the slow kid from midblock, who once stayed on at the Astor past the matinee. It was customary for the management to run Yiddish-language films Saturday nights. Fat Boy was curious. Most of us would be busy clearing out of the theater when the titles and opening scenes would come on-screen.

"How was it?" I asked Fat Boy at school the following Monday.

"I liked it," said Fat Boy. "It was pretty good."

"What was it about?"

"I don't know, but I liked it a lot."

Neither I nor my listening and movie-going buddies knew what jazz was about, but, like Fat Boy at the Yiddish screening, we liked it. I had grown up with a father who played jazz bass and tuba, and who collected records the way other people collected pennies. In those days no one really talked much about jazz as an art form or jazz as America's classical music. The music itself was all around us, and at a time when bop jokes, leopardskin jackets, berets, goatees, and coal-black sunglasses were creeping into vogue.

But the movie theater was the last place we expected to see anything about jazz. Every now and again, Mr. Victor, who ran the Astor, would treat us to some of those old-fashioned, all-Negro short subjects—most of them made back in the 1940s—with Duke Ellington, Louis Jordan, Herb Jeffries, and other musicians. But we, as delighted as we were to see people our color up there on the screen, we knew those movies weren't as serious as *Young Man with a Horn*. When Kirk Douglas pressed that horn to his lips and blew his way into Doris Day's and Lauren Bacall's hearts, we kids adroitly perceived it as another way— besides being fast on the draw or good with your dukes—to get over; that is, to score where it counted. In the parlance of that Detroit neighborhood, fast becoming black, Kirk Douglas was bad.

Badder yet, we thought, was Marlon Brando playing the leader of a rebel motorcycle gang that takes over a small California town for a weekend. The movie, of course, was *The Wild One,* which also starred Mary Murphy as the good girl, and Lee Marvin as the new kind of beer-guzzling bad guy: the slob psychotic. What drew me into the theater to sit through this movie a dozen times was the film's jazz score by Shorty Rogers and His Giants. It wasn't that we even liked Shorty Rogers all that much, but the idea of there being a jazz score at all seemed to mean something. Maybe things were changing. Several of us went out and bought the RCA Victor album and, for good measure, brand new Harley-Davidson motorcycle jackets. Looking back, it's easy to see now how, by substituting motorcycles for horses, and leather jackets for cowboy gear, producer Stanley Kramer and writer John Paxton had come up with a twist on the old cowboy-or-gangster format that would catch fire. By then it was 1954, and adolescence had definitely drawn me and my pals into jazz with a vengeance. Jazz was, after all, in our view, a powerful way of telling the world what it could do with its insufferably square, corny, uncool self.

"We real cool. We/Left school," is how Gwendolyn Brooks begins one of her most popular poems, which ends: *"We/Jazz June, We/Die soon."* So Al Wardlow, his brother Don, and I thought it was pretty cool to cut school one icy afternoon to take the bus downtown to the Fox Theater, where Frank Sinatra was playing a junkie jazz drummer in Otto Preminger's *The Man with the Golden Arm.* Based on a novel by Nelson Algren, the film had a musical score by Elmer Bernstein. The three of us were in band together and—when we weren't faking our way into clubs that featured live local talent—we spent hours listening to the likes of Clifford Brown, James Moody, Thelonious Monk, Dinah Washington, Charlie Parker, Miles Davis, J.J. Johnson, Chris Connor, Sonny Rollins, Tito Puente, Charles Mingus, Gigi Gryce, Dexter Gordon, Sonny Stitt, Gerry Mulligan, Chet Baker, Lee Konitz, Stan Getz, and Bob Brookmeyer.

After the scene where Frank Sinatra quits heroin cold turkey, Hollywood-fashion, with lots of shivering, screaming, sweating, and throwing up, the most dramatic scene in *The Man with the Golden Arm* has Sinatra (as drummer Frankie Machine) auditioning for a record session. The studio band just happens to be Shorty Rogers and His Giants and, as you might expect, Frankie—badly in need of a fix—blows it altogether. Kim Novak hangs in there with our boy, though, and so does Eleanor Parker, his crippled spouse.

We came out of the theater depressed and more than a tad baffled.

"Sinatra was bad," said Don, "but they didn't even have one colored cat in the band."

"Hell, no," said Al, "they'd steal the show."

"Can you imagine," I said, "what a picture about people like Bird and Diz and Monk or Bud Powell would be like?"

"No, I can't," said Don. "White people wouldn't be capable of understanding nothing like that."

Even then, sophomores in high school, we knew and cherished all the wild stories about our sonic heroes. And there were plenty of them in circulation, just as there was plenty of local music, dope, and trouble to be had for the taking. The one thing I'd noticed thus far about the depiction of jazz musicians in Hollywood films was this: they tended to prefer passion and self-destruction to going along with the social zombification.

Later that same year, 1955, Steve Allen starred with Donna Reed in *The Benny Goodman Story*, which was about as Hollywoodized a jazz movie as they come. The music swung; it had to. Contributing to the soundtrack were Lionel Hampton, Teddy Wilson, Gene Krupa, Buck Clayton, Ziggy Elman, Harry James, Stan Getz, George Duvivier, Urbie Green, and singer Martha Tilton. It also had some "colored cats" in it. Sammy Davis, Sr., played Fletcher Henderson, the great arranger responsible for many of Goodman's biggest hits. Lionel Hampton played himself. Goodman dubbed Allen's clarinet and Allen, himself a highly listenable pianist, played a low-keyed, watchable "King of Swing." Moreover, Steve, a popular TV-show host and all-around entertainer, somehow was our idea of a white boy who was hip, smooth, cool, and with it. We didn't blame Steve for the hokiness of the movie; we blamed Hollywood, which, as everyone was beginning to discover, seemed to have a vested interest in *not* being with it; *not* getting anything right, most of all minorities and subcultures. After all, it was Hollywood's MGM that bought Jack Kerouac's San Francisco-set novel, *The Subterraneans,* about an affair between a genius Beat writer and a stunning Negro goddess named Mardou Fox, and in 1960 came out with a slick, sickening movie of the same title, in which George Peppard plays the novelist and Leslie Caron his beatnik paramour. Yet they did have sense enough to get André Previn to score the thing, and we are treated to some artfully shot glimpses of Art Farmer, Art Pepper, Carmen McRae, Shelly Mann, and Gerry Mulligan in action.

I've watched *Straight No Chaser* and *Let's Get Lost* several times now; mostly alone, but sometimes with others. For all the sad facts they reveal about their subjects' lives, these films somehow are a joy to both the eye and the ear. Monk's dark lapses into silence, his mental illness, his compulsive spinning around and dancing, both on-stage and off, his devoted wife Nellie, their son and daughter, his close and abiding friendship with the Baroness Nica de Koenigswarter with whom he lived after he quit playing altogether several years before his death in 1982. Thanks to footage shot by Michael and Christian Blackwood for a German TV special in the late 1960s, we get shots of Monk at work, at play, at home, on planes and buses—always in motion—and even in bed. One of my favorite sequences happens to be the one that has

Monk, still in his pajamas under the covers, working out a meal order with a room service attendant at a German hotel.

Chet Baker's storybook rise to fame in his early twenties is hauntingly captured in *Let's Get Lost*. "My first job was with Charlie Parker," he tells us. "In 1955 I even tied with Nat King Cole [in the *Down Beat* poll] as best male vocalist." We see clips of him performing on the "Steve Allen Show" in the late 1950s, hear varying versions of how he came to have his teeth knocked out by "five black dudes" in San Francisco while he was working the Trident in Sausalito during the sixties, after he'd been kicked out of Italy and 86'd from the continent of Europe. We learn of his first wife from Compton, his Pakistani wife, Halima, and we meet his English wife, Carol, their three children, his torch-carrying girlfriends, as well as his tearful Oklahoma mother. We see how, in many respects, Baker's drug habit led much of his life for him and how—like his screen counterparts in *Bird*, *'Round Midnight* and *Young Man with a Horn*—Chet Baker was also a charmer and confidence man *par excellence*. But, as his last legal wife Carol, a dancer, beamingly assures us: "He could play!"

They all could play, that generation of imaginative musicians, and they didn't seem to do badly at playing themselves and the roles that our society had unconsciously scripted for them. They lived as hard as they played, and they all died young. Of course, the ones who led healthy, reasonably respectable lives don't make the glory rolls as readily as the maladjusted, the scoundrels and the tragically flawed. If present trends continue, we'll soon be surrounded by a mature generation of clean-living, clinically trained, conscientious jazz artists. Wynton, Branford, their father Ellis, and the other Marsalises have certainly been blazing an exemplary trail.

Branford Marsalis, Terrence Blanchard, and composer Bill Lee are musical contributors to the lovely, seductive soundtrack of Spike Lee's controversial film, *Mo' Bettah Blues*, the first dramatic motion picture about the jazz life to be written and directed by an African-American. While Lee glosses and glamorizes the life of fictional trumpeter Bleek Gilliam as mythically as any of his filmmaker predecessors, he also taps into the jazz sensibility of the antiseptic eighties, when the importance of proper training, physical fitness, juicy club and recording contracts—plus, an all-around luxurious lifestyle—triumphed over traditional jazz self-righteousness. But I'll run through those changes another set.

IV

CHARLES SIMIC

No Cure for the Blues

*It seems that we learn something about art
when we experience what the word solitude
is meant to designate.*
— MAURICE BLANCHOT

A cold and windy day in New York City thirty years ago. Outside an
A&P market plastered with signs of that day's specials, a beautiful old
black man with a beat-up guitar, dark glasses, tin cup, and an equally
ancient seeing-eye dog lying at his feet. He sings in high tenor voice:

> "Santi Claus, Santi Claus,
> Won't you please hear my lonesome plea.
> I don't want nothing for Christmas,
> But my baby back to me."

Later that day, crossing Central Park, I see a young woman lying
on a bench, her face hidden in her hands, her white party dress just covering the backs of her knees, one of her red shoes fallen off to the side.
She is sleeping, or more likely pretending to. In any case, I feel obliged
to walk past her almost on tiptoes.

No one else is around, and it's still cold and windy. I walk briskly,
looking back now and then, the last time when there's no chance I can
see her from so far away.

"Doing something wrong," sings Walter Davis.

> You show your linen to any man . . .
> You come home walking like a goose
> As if somebody turned you loose.

The chief preoccupation of much country and urban blues is the
relationship between men and women. Love, unfaithfulness, jealousy,

hard times, good times, happy sex, bad sex, and everything else that keeps people awake tossing and turning at night, is the subject.

You'll need me some morning when I won't need you.

Or,

> You've been a good ole wagon, Daddy,
> But you done broke down.

Or, there's the blues song Jelly Roll Morton claims is the first one he ever heard back in New Orleans in the early years of this century:

> Stood on the corner
> With her feet soaking wet,
> Begging each and every man
> That she met.
>
> If you can't give a dollar,
> Give me a lousy dime.
> I want to feed
> That hungry man of mine.

That's the blues at its most tragic. But the same Morton can also sing on another occasion:

> If you must go, sweet baby,
> Leave a dime for beer.

A kind of comic realism is at work in many of the songs, especially when the subject is love or sex. No wonder churchgoers called it devil's music. Everybody knows the devil likes to fool around. The comic seriousness of these songs understands the coexistence of misfortune and laughter. It is in that joyful irreverence and freedom that one must seek their truth.

> Your nuts hang down like a damn bell clapper,
> And your dick stands up like a steeple,
> And your asshole stands open like a church door,
> And crab walks in like people.

This is from the blues singer Lucille Bogan, who sang about sex with such abandon and humor that it seemed her purpose was to intentionally terrify the prudes.

There was a commercial angle to it, of course. How else do you entertain a bunch of drunks in a dive? The critics who say sexual themes were forced on black performers are talking nonsense. I guess they were forced on poor Boccaccio and Rabelais, too. Money is not the whole explanation. There is poetry in some of that smut.

"I have something between my legs to make a dead man come," I overheard a woman once say to the young preacher at a wake which had turned boisterous with drink and good food. It was improper, but very funny, like this music which knows only the truth of laughter and no inhibition.

They played blues records in Berlin in the 1920s. They heard "Jazzin' Babies Blues" on the banks of the Nile, "Mean Old Bedbug Blues" by the Yangtze River. I first heard the blues in Belgrade in 1947–48 when one could go to jail for listening to American music. We heard Louis Armstrong sing "St. James Infirmary." We lay on the floor next to the record player with the sound turned down low and the mother of my friend fretting in the next room.

> Some people call me a hobo, some call me a bum,
> Nobody knows my name, nobody knows what I've done.

Bessie Smith, Eva Taylor, Bertha Chippie Hill, Alberta Hunter, Sippie Wallace, Ada Brown, Ida Cox, Victoria Spivey—addicts of the blues know them all. I played Ethel Waters's "One Man Nan" till it hissed and skipped terribly. I could not play that record or most of my other records for anyone else. They would not understand my forbearance. At their best my records would sound like rain, a summer downpour in the city when everyone runs for cover, at their worst like a sausage patty being fried in a pan. It didn't matter. Sadness and happiness would well up in me with the first few notes. Why is it, I said to myself one night, that listening to the music I feel a homesickness for a vanished world that I was never a part of?

The blues prove the complete silliness of any theory of cultural separatism which denies the possibility of aesthetic experience outside one's race, ethnicity, religion, or even gender. Like all genuine art, the blues belong to a specific time, place, and people which it then, paradoxically, transcends. The secret of its transcendence lies in its minor key and its poetry of solitude. Lyric poetry has no closer relation anywhere than the blues. The reason people make lyric poems and blues songs is because our life is short, sweet, and fleeting. The blues bear witness to the strangeness of each individual's fate. It begins wordlessly in a moan, a stamp of the foot, a sigh, a hum, and then seeks words for that something or other that has no name in any language and for which all poetry and music seek an approximation.

The friendship of solitude, late night, and the blues. In 1959, I lived in a fleabag hotel in Greenwich Village in a room no bigger than a closet and just as dark. There was a window, but it faced a brick wall. My nights were interrupted by creaking beds, smokers' coughs, and moans of lovemaking. I didn't sleep much. I lay in bed reading, chain-smoking, and drinking wine. I had a radio and a cheap portable record player.

> Nobody loves me but my mother,
> And she could be jiving too.

Some old sage claims that the soul is made between one or two in the morning. I agree, especially if you're listening to the blues. I owned a few records, but it was the radio that brought me surprises and delights from time to time. Playing with the dial, I'd come across an unknown voice, a cornet, and a piano that would make me turn up the volume in my excitement. I lay with eyes closed, astonished that such a fine song existed and regretting already that it would end. Very often the D.J. would not even name the performer, and what I'd heard would haunt me for years, until in my manic record-buying I would come upon that very cut.

One night I was listening to a program devoted to Leroy Carr and Scrapper Blackwell, that great piano-and-guitar duo that made so many records back in the 1930s, when there was a soft knock on the door. It was quarter to three. I thought somebody had complained to the night clerk about me, but why was he knocking so softly? I didn't budge. Carr could have been singing something like:

> Ain't it lonesome
> Sleeping by yourself
> When the woman that you love
> Is loving someone else?

Finally, I opened the door a crack. Outside, an old man stood as if shivering in his T-shirt, pants, and with nothing on his feet. "What's that beautiful music?" he asked me with a heavy Italian accent. I told him. Carr went on singing, so I let him in. He sat in my only chair and I sat on the bed.

> In the wee midnight hour
> Long before the break of day,
> When the blues creep upon you
> And carry your mind away.

My visitor listened with a serious, even pious expression. He didn't say much, except to call the music nice, very nice, much too nice. We parted when the program was over, and I never saw him again.

> Some people tell me,
> God takes care of old folks and fools,
> But since I've been born,
> He must've changed the rules.

The guitar player who sang this recorded, under the name Funny Papa Smith, some twenty sides between 1930 and 1931. They say he wore a stovepipe hat and work-overalls, but not in the picture I have of him, where he wears a suit, bow tie, and the kind of hat a traveling salesman might wear. A good-looking young fellow with a sensitive, even melancholy, expression. I can well believe he was a gambler, but I'm surprised to learn that he murdered a man. I read someplace that he ended up in an electric chair, but I've no idea if this is true. All I know is that he sang an astonishing two-part hoodoo blues called "Seven Sisters."

> They tell me Seven Sisters in New Orleans, that can really fix a man
>   up right,
> And I'm headed for New Orleans, Louisiana, I'm travelling both
>   day and night.
> I hear them say the oldest sister look like she's just twenty-one
> And said she can look right in your eyes and tell you exactly what
>   you want done.
> They tell me they been hung, been bled and been crucified
> But I just want enough help to stand on the water and rule the tide.

It's bound to be Seven Sisters 'cause I've heard it by everybody else.
'Course I'd love to take their word, but I'd rather go and see for
    myself.
When I leave the Seven Sisters I'm piling stones all around
And go to my baby and tell her there's another Seven-Sister man in
    town.
Good mornin' Seven Sisters, just thought I'd come down and see
Will you build me up where I'm torn down and make me strong
    where I'm weak?

I went to New Orleans, Louisiana, just on account of something I
    heard.
The Seven Sisters told me everything I wanted to know and they
    wouldn't let me speak a word.
Now it's Sara, Minnie, Bertha, Holly, Dolly, Betty and Jane—
You can't know them sisters apart because they all looks just the
    same
The Seven Sisters sent me away happy, 'round the corner I met
    another little girl;
She looked at me and smiled and said: Go devil and destroy the
    world.
[Spoken: I'm gonna destroy it, too . . . I'm all right now]
Seven times you hear the Seven Sisters, will visit me in my sleep,
And they said I won't have no more trouble, and said I'll live twelve
    days in a week.
Boy go down in Louisiana, and get the lead right outta your being.
If Seven Sisters can't do anything in Louisiana, bet you'll have to go
    to New Orleans.

Small masterpieces by nearly unknown performers are the rule
when it comes to the history of recorded blues. Again, it must have been
the usual makeshift recording studio in some hotel room on a street of
pool halls, whorehouses, and dance halls. The year was 1931. Around
the corner, probably, there was a soup kitchen with a line of unem-
ployed black men and, inside, a straight-backed chair and a bottle of
whiskey for the musician.

There was nothing customary about what Smith sang. Here was a
blues song about the secret world of voodoo, eroticism, crime, and god-
knows-what-else, in a lingo both poetic and obscure. In this blues, as in
many others, one glimpses an unknown America with an imagination

and imagery all its own. The blues poet has been where we are all afraid to go, as if there was a physical place, a forbidden place that corresponds to a place in ourselves where we experience the tragic sense of life and its amazing wonders. In that dive, in that all-night blues and soul club, we feel the full weight of our fate, we taste the nothingness at the heart of our being, we are simultaneously wretched and happy, we spit on it all, we want to weep and raise hell, because the blues, in the end, is about a sadness older than the world, and there's no cure for that.

HAYDEN CARRUTH

Good Old Wagon

Perhaps the best-known of Bessie Smith's recordings today—justly so, because it's one of her most sensitive performances—is "You've Been a Good Ole Wagon" with Louis Armstrong on cornet and Fred Longshaw on piano (New York, January 14, 1925, Columbia 14079-D). But it presents problems worth thinking about for both their musical and historical implications.

The original title was "You've Been a Good Old Wagon But You Done Broke Down." According to *American Popular Songs,* edited by David Ewen, it was composed in 1896 by Ben Harney, who introduced it as a "stick dance specialty" with a minstrel company. He performed it at that time and for some years thereafter. I'm not certain, but I think a stick dance was the kind done with a cane or walking stick, which became a stand-in for a human partner, in this case the good old wagon, thus female in the original interpretation. Anyone who has seen a minstrel show or a tent show or second-rate vaudeville from the 1920s or burlesque from the 1930s or 1940s or for that matter a club act in Las Vegas today can imagine the lascivious way in which Harney worked his stick dance to a laughing audience. No doubt he was in blackface and possibly he was cross-dressed as well, in which case the stick/wagon would have been male and sexual ambiguity would have been part of the act, a source of "humor" as much then as it is now. Later May Irwin, without the stick, turned the song into an extremely popular number for vaudeville and made the wagon patently male. Evidently Bessie Smith learned the song from Irwin or someone like her. Ewen notes: "Because of the success of this number after publication, coon and ragtime songs began to flourish in Tin Pan Alley," i.e., around 1910—and one knows too well the dismal history of such songs in popular culture after that.

"Good Old Wagon" is a sixteen-bar composition divided into sections of four bars each, common enough in white popular music of the last century, a short form of the thirty-two-bar ballad that later became standard pop fare at the hands of Gershwin, Berlin, Kahn, and many others. Early in this century the sixteen-bar form became assimilated to the blues and was widespread in African-American music before the twelve-bar structure became dominant in the blues of the 1920s—compare Jelly Roll Morton's "Buddy Bolden's Blues" and "Winin' Boy Blues." Certainly "Good Old Wagon" is a blues in Bessie Smith's interpretation of it. She gave it a decidedly bluesy diminished modulation between the eighth and ninth bars of each stanza, and I don't know if this was part of the original music composed and published by Harney. I doubt it. As Smith sang it, these are the lyrics:

Looka here, daddy, I want to tell you,
   please get out of my sight.
I'm playing quits now
   [right] from this very night.
You've had your day,
   don't set around and frown,
you've been a good old wagon,
   daddy, but you done broke down.

Now you better go to the blacksmith shop
   and get yourself overhauled,
there's nothing about you
   to make a good woman fall.
Nobody wants a baby
   when a real man can be found,
you've been a good old wagon,
   daddy, but you done broke down.

When the sun is shining
   it's time to make hay.
Automobiles are the rage,
   you can't make that wagon pay.
When you were in your prime
   you loved to run around,
you've been a good old wagon,
   honey, but you done broke down.

There's no need to cry
   and make a big joke.
This man has taught me more about loving
   than you will ever know.
He is the king of loving

> [and he wears] a double crown,
> he's a good old wagon,
>   daddy, and he ain't broke down.

Not great poetry, and of course the printed version gives no indication of the musical phrasing, essential to the metric and prosody of the song. I place brackets around the words which try as I may, either on the original issue or on the cleaned-up CD released by CBS in 1989, I cannot make out clearly. For that matter I'm not sure what or how much was meant by the "double crown."

But the real problem of the recording is the discrepancy between Smith's vocal and the accompaniment by Louis Armstrong. (Longshaw's piano is primarily rhythmic and unexceptional.) "Good Old Wagon" was a piece of common bawdry. As far as I can make out, this is not only what it was but what it was deliberately intended to be. Yet Smith saw in it something more serious. From the Pindaric ode down to our own time, the poem of succession has been a notable part of literature, the poem that laments the fallen hero or victim-king and celebrates the new conqueror or victor-king, to use the terms of *The Golden Bough*. Smith saw in this song, with its reference to the supplanting of the horsedrawn by the motor-driven vehicle, not only a narrative of sexual transition but of social and historical transition. I don't say she "saw" this clearly or consciously, though she may have—she was a damned smart woman. In fact, since the original song was written in 1896, the reference to the automobile could not have been part of it; someone added this later, and I'd lay odds that Smith was the one who did it. One way or another she felt the human implications of the narrative and gave them force in her rendition of it. The good old wagon, after all, has indeed been a good old wagon. The song is addressed to him throughout, "daddy" and "honey," even in the final stanza where his replacement is proclaimed and glorified. The song is not quite an elegy, not quite a eulogy, certainly not an exaltation. It is, precisely, a poem of succession. And no one in her audience, black or white, doubted that she was singing as a whore and that her song—a dirty comic song—was addressed to her pimp. In this milieu Smith found, as have others, the materials of pathos. Her greatness permitted her to find in them, mysteriously and ineluctably, a source of dignity. In the end it is a function of incalculable personality.

I wrote such a poem myself once about the night at Minton's when

Dizzy Gillespie finally cut Roy Eldridge—and now Gillespie himself is gone.

Armstrong plays his accompaniment on a cornet with a plunger mute. (In 1925 he hadn't yet switched to trumpet.) He begins with a wah-wah effect, to which he returns from time to time throughout. In the final stanza after the line, "There's no need to cry," he makes a horse laugh, à la "Livery Stable Blues," and after the next line, "or make a big joke," he does a very rough, toneless growl, and he follows these effects with the staccato triple-tonguing that was obligatory background for any reference to lovemaking in those days. In other words Armstrong's innuendoes totally miss the import of what Smith was attempting, and in general throughout the piece he not only misses but collides with both Smith's emotional attitude toward her material and the whole melodic and chordal structure of the number, which he skates over as if it hardly existed.

Now one must say plainly that Armstrong was not doing anything that other musicians, especially brass players, did not also customarily do when accompanying blues singers in that era. One can hear plenty of silliness, vulgarity, and coarse mercantilism on the old records. Armstrong's performance is less offensive than many, and in parts, the middle parts, his responses to Smith's phrasings are at least somewhat original and interesting. Moreover his work on this date in no way detracts from his absolutely fundamental place in the evolution of jazz a year or two later. But the facts remain that Armstrong seems to have been unaware of what Smith was up to on "Good Old Wagon" and that his ineptness turned what might have been a staggeringly great recording into something still worth listening to but seriously flawed in the minds of all devotees. Such is the power of reputation, however—in this case the reputations of both Smith and Armstrong, the former having been greater than the latter in 1925—that the blunder has gone unnoticed, as far as I know, except for one paragraph in Gunther Schuller's *Early Jazz* (pp. 236–237). Now that jazz criticism is finally becoming more rigorous in at least a few quarters, we may hope that such misunderstandings and delusions will become less cumbersome in the minds of those who love America's only internationally persuasive, native music.

This is not, I emphasize, a question of musicology in the narrow sense, scholarship, biography, dating, merely technical derivations, etc. Rather it is a question of establishing and continually re-establishing good judgment and some significant modicum of consensual taste. We must know the superb musicians and the superb performances; we must know as well the less than superb and if possible why they are less. Often this isn't possible, at least in detail, but if criticism in the arts has any function, it is this—the attempt to discriminate and analyze, for our greater keenness of sensibility, the near successes. Smith and Armstrong experienced a failure of communication in recording "Good Old Wagon." Since Smith was the better-known musician at the time and the leading performer on the record, which was issued in her name, presumably the failure was hers. She and her accompanist did not talk about what they were going to do before they did it. Why? One can think of many likely reasons. Because Smith didn't have good enough direction and assistance from the producer. Because she didn't know what she was going to do before she began to sing, though this seems improbable to me: she had sung the song fairly often outside the studio. Or let's say she relied too much on the convention of recordings by female blues singers, a convention which had become well established in the few years since 1921 when Mamie Smith (no relation to Bessie Smith) recorded "Crazy Blues" and began the whole history of recorded vocal blues, a convention moreover which pretty well dictated what the vocalist and her two or three accompanists would do. Or did she simply not care? We don't like to think of this, she was so fine an artist. But what would motivate her, an African-American woman in the years after World War I at the very bottom of the social scale, to think of herself as an artist, a self-conscious creator of music? Nothing. How could she take herself seriously? It is one of the wrenching paradoxes of our history: the source of her intense, complicated awareness of suffering, which made her music what it was, was the same phenomenon that prevented her from realizing her music in the full artistic sense. But she was not unique. Most real jazz musicians of her time, white as well as black, were afflicted in the same way.

Nevertheless I prefer to think that in some way she knew what she was doing and had some inkling of its importance. If this were not true, I believe she could not have done what she did with "Good Old Wagon." She had her limits, of course. Not much musicianship, for one thing, not much technique. And though she had the fullest, richest voice of any blues singer ever, Gunther Schuller has pointed out that she often sang a whole blues within the first fifth of the scale. Yet she met and overcame these limits superbly, she was almost never trite or imitative, and this in itself must indicate some degree of self-consciousness. At any rate the tough pathos of "Good Old Wagon" led in the direction of her finest recording, "Young Woman's Blues," which she wrote herself and recorded with Joe Smith, Buster Bailey, and Fletcher Henderson—three accomplished musicians who were more amenable than Armstrong—about two years later. Here she was not at all impeded by her accompaniment, and she sang with a passion that she never quite matched elsewhere, though she came close. It is a wonderfully expressive performance. Had she learned in the meantime to communicate better with her fellow workers? No one knows. Was she the great sensibility that can rise to its culmination only in conjunction with inferior collaborators? Sidney Bechet, her contemporary, was something like that. All these possibilities and others are part of the mix, I believe. They are worth thinking about, as I said at the beginning, and I hope worth writing about, if we are to understand African-American music, the most vigorous and often the most expressive component of American culture in our time.

V

DOC POMUS:
A SPECIAL FEATURE

WILLIAM BRATTON

A Note on Doc Pomus

Though often over-used, the term "founding father" is totally appropriate in describing Doc Pomus's relationship to popular music. "As one of music's most gifted and prolific songwriters, Doc Pomus helped invent rock 'n' roll," pronounced *Rolling Stone Magazine* in the 1991 year-end issue.

Born Jerome Solon Felder in 1925 in the Williamsburg section of Brooklyn, he became Doc Pomus in part to shield his middle-class family from his nocturnal activities as a rhythm and blues shouter. For it was as a singer, braced on crutches (Pomus contracted polio at age six), that he entered the world of music which was to become his life.

George's Tavern, a small, smoky Greenwich Village music spot, was the setting for the eighteen-year-old Pomus's singing debut. His rendition of his life-long idol, Big Joe Turner's, "Piney Brown Blues," backed by trumpeter Frankie Newton's band, was successful enough to launch a ten-year career. From 1944 to 1955 Pomus performed in clubs throughout the metropolitan area. Leading a band which included legendary guitarist Mickey Baker and saxophonist King Curtis, Pomus recorded for the Savoy, Atlantic, Coral, and Chess labels. At first penning songs for his own recordings, he soon became a major song source on the New York scene and a regular at the new Atlantic Records' office, creating classics for Laverne Baker, Ruth Brown, Lil Green, Ray Charles and Big Joe Turner. He enjoyed his first rhythm and blues top ten hit with "Lonely Avenue" by Ray Charles. Hooking up with a team of two other young songwriters, Jerry Leiber and Mike Stoller, he hit big with the Coasters' "Young Blood."

Pomus, by coincidence, met a talented teenaged fledgling songwriter Mort Shuman, who was dating Pomus's cousin. He took Shuman under his wing and eventually the two became full partners despite the fifteen-year age difference between them.

Ultimately, the pair enjoyed a wonderful nine-year association resulting in a major body of work which, collectively, became a dominant force on the record charts and led to sales of well over one hundred

Doc Pomus, ca. 1948

Doc Pomus, ca. 1989

million. The songs included, "This Magic Moment," "Save The Last Dance For Me," "Teenager in Love," "Can't Get Used To Losing You," "Turn Me Loose," "Hushabye," "I Count The Tears," "Sweets for My Sweet" and "Seven Day Weekend," among many others. For Elvis Presley, they produced a series of major hit songs, including "Little Sister," "Viva Las Vegas," "His Latest Flame," "Surrender," "Suspicion," "A Mess of Blues" and "Long, Lonely Highway," to mention a very few.

During the mid-sixties, Pomus teamed on different projects with Otis Blackwell, Ellie Greenwich, Phil Spector, and Leiber and Stoller. His union with Spector produced the memorable "Ecstasy" and "Youngboy Blues" for Ben E. King, and with Leiber and Stoller "She's Not You" for Elvis. Toward the close of the sixties, the Pomus/Shuman team dissolved, with Shuman leaving for Paris and Pomus entering semi-retirement for almost ten years.

In the years between the Pomus/Shuman break-up and his re-emergence in the mid-seventies, Pomus, as Bette Midler's musical advisor, brought her national attention by booking her first "Tonight

Show" appearance, and was instrumental in her signing to Atlantic Records. He also figured significantly in the creation of Belushi and Akroyd's Blues Brothers.

Pomus created some of his most beautiful and adult work during the final decade of his life. His collaborations with Dr. John, Ken Hirsch, and Willy DeVille produced tracks for Ray Charles, Joe Cocker, Marianne Faithful, Johnny Adams, Irma Thomas, José Feliciano, and B.B. King (whose Pomus/Dr. John-penned "There Must Be A Better World Somewhere" album won a Grammy Award). Pomus also wrote original material for such motion pictures as "Dick Tracy" and John Waters's "Cry Baby."

As a crusader for the many forgotten and overlooked, Doc was dedicated in particular to helping R&B artists who had fallen on hard times. Mike Stoller called Doc the "arch angel of rhythm and blues." He was a founder and trustee of the Rhythm and Blues Foundation, and was the recipient of their prestigious Pioneer Award (the only white honoree to date).

Doc Pomus was truly a writer for all times. He holds the distinction of being one of the select few songwriters to have been inducted into The Rock and Roll Hall of Fame and The Songwriters' Hall of Fame.

PHIL SPECTOR

The Induction of Doc Pomus
Into The Rock and Roll Hall of Fame

It gives me great pleasure to thank you for the privilege and honor of inducting my dear and beloved friend, mentor, and teacher, Doc Pomus, into this illustrious Rock and Roll Hall of Fame—without question the greatest hall of fame in the world. And Pete Rose, if you're listening and they don't want you in *that* hall of fame—yeah, we like guys who've done some time, gambled . . . And it's obvious the Baseball Hall of Fame doesn't give a damn how well you played the game, so why the hell should we? Come on!

First of all, to put things in perspective, I should mention the fact that I imitate Doc's voice and I think I was the only one he'd allow do it; he said I made him sound like a cross between Daffy Duck and Elmer Fudd, but folks, he sounded like that. So you can better understand the Doc Pomus I knew, I'll tell you a short story about me and Doc that occurred soon after I met him in 1960. While I know it is not a serious way to start this, I know he would not mind if I shared it with you, and you will excuse my imitation of him. I lived in New York and Doc used to call me up on the telephone. He befriended me and took me in; he would invite me to dinner and he'd take me to Joe Marsh's Spindletop. Now, Joe Marsh was an alleged, you know, an alleged, an alleged, an alleged—but I don't know. Doc would say to me, "I'll buy you a steak. C'mon." So I would go down to this restaurant for the finest meal in the world and conversation and memories that were lovely. His wife at that time was working in Fiorella's; she was a big star on Broadway. One day we're sitting in there eating and I don't know, but out of the corner of my eye I saw something happen—I thought it took five hours, but it took like a second—a guy in a raincoat walks in with a hat, walks in and goes up to a guy and BOOM BOOM BOOM, three booms in the head and the guy slumps over dead, just like that. I mean I couldn't believe it. I'd never seen a murder, an execution in a restaurant. When Doc called me up the next time, I told him, "I can't go back in that place

/ 153

ever." And Doc says, "What's the matter babe?" "There was a murder! In the Spindletop Restaurant." I came from Los Angeles, and I was born in New York, but I'm telling you, . . . And the scene was ten years before the *Godfather*! So Doc says, "You gotta understand something babe. You see life is up and down, up and down." I said, "What does up and down have to do with it? A man got murdered." He said, "The place is incredible, right, the salads, I mean how about the service in that restaurant? You have to look at the up side." I said, "I don't get it, I don't get it at all, a man got murdered, man, his brains were splattered all over." He said, "You're looking through those funny glasses babe, you gotta see things on the up side, up up up." I said, "I don't see anything up about a man being murdered. I don't see anything up and I don't know what it has to do with the murder. How do you explain anything that has to do with the murder." "Well the murder—that's the down side of the restaurant, you understand, that's the down side."

As I said before, I met Doc in 1960, he befriended me at that time. While he was alive, he was the light of my life. Now that he's gone that light has gone out. His passing has made me realize much I don't understand. See, I know that love comes from the heart, but I have no idea where love goes when the heart dies. Nor do I know what it is within the heart that breaks so badly that it's impossible to repair. Doc's love was of a higher standard than that which I had ever previously known. He was uncompromising and totally committed, and I'm going to be a better person because of Doc Pomus, if you can believe that. What was so remarkable about Doc's love was that it came from the body of a person who never experienced a childhood or even a life on a physical level as we know it. Nor did he have much about which to be physically joyful, grateful, or even loving, if you will, since most of his life was spent in physical discomfort. It was not nearly fulfilled and I will be remiss if I do not mention how personally upsetting and distressing this was to him, and how completely inexcusable it is to me that Doc Pomus during his lifetime was never inducted into The Songwriters' Hall of Fame. The Hall of Fame generally seems to be sponsored by BMI and ASCAP and has been in existence for years. This giant of a songwriter, one of the world's finest, the songwriter I wanted to meet when I came to New York, the songwriter John Lennon wanted to meet, was not in The Songwriters' Hall of Fame. They ignored Doc Pomus. This is a man who before the end of 1960 had already written such classics as "Lonely

Avenue," "Youngblood," "Teenager in Love," and "Save The Last Dance For Me." And this man was more than a songwriter. He was a poet, for I need not remind you that while he wrote "Save The Last Dance For Me," he never experienced the thrill or the emotion of that wonderful feeling. For him not to have been admitted during his lifetime into The Songwriters' Hall of Fame is inexcusable, and shame on those people who allowed it to happen. It hurt his zeal and kept his life unfulfilled. But you know, even with his life unfulfilled and all the physical discomfort, he still approached life and lived every day with the happiness, the spirit, and the giving of love and friendship, which he gave to each and every life he entered, and everyone who knew him knows that's true. It was then and still is beyond my comprehension, something I've never seen before. Therefore I now know that that kind of love and strength and desire exists and I will settle for giving or receiving no less.

At this time, I would like to briefly mention and discuss something which I think is relevant to Doc Pomus the lyricist and Doc Pomus my friend; it is inside of me and I have to say it. Doc knew my two youngest twins; named Philip, Jr. and a little girl Nicole, aged nine. Doc was their friend as well and often sent them gifts and spoke to them on the phone. He was particularly fond of little Philip, Jr. as they had a camaraderie—little Philip, Jr. suffered a great deal of physical discomfort from an illness and he knew that Doc too had an illness he got as a little boy and was unable to walk. I mention this because on Christmas Day, 1991, my little son, Philip Jr., aged nine, passed away after a nine-year battle with leukemia. It was Philip, Jr., who, with his sister Nicole, told me not to be sad when my best friend Doc Pomus died. Because when he was alive he could not walk and now that he had died he was in heaven, walking with God. Well, I hope Doc and his little friend, my son Philip, Jr., are walking together.

You know it was years before I realized that Doc Pomus was what we referred to as "handicapped," or "physically challenged." He just never made me aware of it. He spoke, lived, and moved with such grace and such command of his life that I never saw him as handicapped in any way. I'm telling you he made it a privilege to be in his presence and to receive his love and friendship—what I would not give for one more time to share the pleasure of that company. And if the little we know about the universe and life can be simplified, perhaps there is something to be learned or gained by Doc's passing. We know, for example, that when the sun moves down it leaves its beautiful warmth on the land, and we most assuredly know, as Irving Berlin said, if I may paraphrase him, that when the song is ended, the beauty of the melody lingers on. So by that knowledge we know that for every joy that passes, something beautiful remains, and when I think of Doc Pomus, I will find, as should you, comfort in the beauty of his memory and his songs. Yes, he was taken away, but more important than the fact that he died, which took but an instant, is the fact that he lived, and because he lived, we are much better.

As a final thought, when you go home tonight, each and every one of you say to yourselves, for the noble deed you have done this evening, "Score one for the good guys," for that's what Doc Pomus was. That's what all of you are.

DOC POMUS

The Journals of Doc Pomus (1978–91)

My father used to sit in bed surrounded by piles of notebooks. He worked in bed and often "held court" there, as well. The T.V. was always on, the phone ring-ing, five or six people in and out, a dog, and music going all at the same time. If I walked in and he was in the middle of writing a song lyric, he'd squint his eyes for a moment, maybe turn down the T.V. volume, and say, "Just a second baby, let me finish this up." He was fast—the T.V. went back on and time resumed. He wrote everything in his notebooks. He loved to buy them in different colors, sizes, shapes. His notebooks had to be accessible to him at all times. Even in the last month in his hospital room, there was a notebook, for his thoughts and song ideas. In his large, loose handwriting his notebooks are filled with stories about his favorite singers, legendary characters, love, sex, family, card players, poli-tics, and autobiographical notes. When the royalties dried up in the mid-seventies, my father supported me and my brother by running poker games in his apartment, playing cards nightly in and out of the apartment. He kept score of many things: card games, baseball games, boxing matches, and who owed him money—always on the same pages as his beautiful lyrics.

—Sharyn Felder

I always believed in magic and flying and that one morning I would wake up and all the bad things were bad dreams and Daddy would be alive and heroic and Mama would understand and be proud of me only because she understood me and my kid brother was a kid again and I would sing to him and he would have that 10-year-old-I-worship-you look in his eyes. And I would get out of the wheelchair and walk and not with braces and crutches. And I would walk down all streets and no one would stare at me and young girls in see-through dresses would smile at me, dazzled by my appearance and glow, and men would listen to my words carefully and I could wander around all night without fear in my soul and I could sit by a lonely stoop at 1:00 am with friends and have a convertible top open at 2:00 am and walk or park in Prospect Park or Central Park. I would always sing and everybody would love to hear

me sing and my children were little children in my arms and the woman
or women in my life would stay young forever and love me in a young
way forever.

* * *

Every night I dream
when I wake up I'll fly
but when the morning comes
I still can't reach the sky

I just can't grow no wings
and do those kinds of things
cause since you left you see
the magic's died in me

Once I burned the sky
the mountains and the sea
the whole damn crazy world
the mountains and the sea
that all belong to me.

* * *

I used to get up and sing the blues—not thinking I was black or white—
just closing my eyes and leaning back on the crutches. I got to the point
where I sensed audiences learned show business tricks—pacing—
openers, closers. Little mannerisms that became identifiable—swinging the mike from hand to hand, swaggering the body in rhythm. Eventually developed a style. And learned how to introduce numbers and in
an emergency could emcee in a passable but professional way.

And all the time I was writing blues—mostly for myself—but occasionally I'd go around to the record companies and they would take a
song for Joe Turner or Laverne Baker, or Gatemouth Moore or Lil
Green and then I started recording myself. I always had a record going
on the jukebox—no hits—but there was always one out.—

I was beginning to get a reputation but underneath—I was always
trembling and screaming. My hotel room was always the scene of endless trips in and out of the bed.—In and out of the bathroom—
Constantly changing clothes always on the phone—anything to keep

me from quietly living with myself and thinking about what was going to happen.—Always trying to maneuver a girl in the room—talk to her—make love to her—or write a song—or write an article—or write a story or listen to the blues—on the radio on records—and listen and lose myself.

* * *

I'm boring, I'm boring, boring
It's a natural fact
I'm an opening act.

* * *

He was one of those white kids who heard the blues and got fucked-up forever. He thought there was blues in the bottle and blues in the dope and so he drank too much and he stuck needles in his arm and burnt out his nostrils with cocaine and his soul never got a little black.

And he only got more fucked-up. And his singing and playing got a great big "I" for superior imitation. And the white kids never knew the difference and they paid big money to hear him, and bought his records and idolized him and he hated them because he knew they knew nothing. They mistook his hatred for eccentricity and a famous blues singer said he was great because this was a way to get a gig for more money than a blues singer ever makes. And everybody was happy—the famous blues singer, the white junkie musician, and the audience.

* * *

Some people are lonely all the time—

* * *

Losers with no hope in their eyes get on every night and torture my thighs.

* * *

Everything I touch
turns to nothing

Everything I hold
breaks away

Everyone I love
loves another
all my tomorrows
are yesterday

No matter where I go
there's no one that I know
and when I open some new door
somehow I've seen it all before
I've been there once or twice before

*　　*　　*

There's a street that the especially isolated people live on. The people who feel like they're always fighting the battle of life with limited physical equipment. And it's always them against the rest of the world and they're always on the outside looking in.

And they keep trying and fighting but most of the time they feel like puppets being manipulated by a demonic puppet master or battling dragons with swords made of tin.

It's a huge army with the blind and the crippled marching hand in hand with the blacks and the other disenfranchised.

My room has got two windows but the sunshine never comes?

Cause I live on a (lonely avenue)
Suspicion—1,086,983–1,144,691
Save the last dance—2,871,970–2,995,492
This magic moment—1,453,708–1,545,524
Teenager in love—743,807–792,141
And young blood—474,899–504,376
Little sister—893,094

[Numbers refer to airplay.]

*　　*　　*

Lonely Avenue

Now, my room has got two windows
But the sunshine never comes through.

You know it's always dark and dreary
Since I broke off, baby, with you.

I live on a lonely avenue
My little girl wouldn't say I do
Well I feel so sad and blue
And it's all because of you.

I could cry, I could cry, I could cry
I could die, I could die, I could die
Because I live on a lonely avenue, lonely avenue.

Now my covers they feel like lead
And my pillow it feels like stone.
Well I've tossed and turned so ev'ry night
I'm not used to being alone.

I live on a lonely avenue
My little girl wouldn't say I do
Well I feel so sad and blue
And it's all because of you.

I could cry, I could cry, I could cry
I could die, I could die, I could die
Because I live on a lonely avenue, lonely avenue.

Now I've been so sad and lonesome
Since you left this town
If I could beg or borrow the money
Child I would be a highway bound.

I live on a lonely avenue
My little girl wouldn't say I do
Well I feel so sad and blue
And it's all because of you.

I could cry, I could cry, I could cry
I could die, I could die, I could die
Because I live on a lonely avenue, lonely avenue.

*　*　*

There's a thin little man
with gray streaks in his hair
who sits every evening
in his favorite chair.

His wife brings him tea
and loosens up
his tie—and she smiles as
he talks about his
day that just went by

The adding machine broke down
so he took off for an hour
and walked through the park and picked
his queen a flower

He's the king of 10 Geronimo Place
and his throne is that worn-out favorite chair
and his palace is the six rooms that he shares
with his queen and a prince, and a princess and his dog
you can tell by the pride
that's written on his face
that he's the king of 10 Geronimo Place.

* * *

I knowing I'm getting older every day
but I'm not getting wiser in any way
I keep on making all the same mistakes
and I keep blaming it on just bad breaks

But one day I'm going to open my eyes
and then the world is going to realize

* * *

Loneliness has chased me into strange corners
where there are no friends only mourners
but once in a while the sun shines on me
yes once in a while the warm winds call me
then I feel a little stronger
and I hang on a little longer

Memories are spiders spinning long midnights
but once in a while a rainbow finds me
yes once in a while its colors blind me
    then I feel a little stronger and I hang on a little longer where's the
    promised kiss of yesterday
that somehow lost its thrill along the way

*   *   *

The important thing is to be the poet—not the famous poet—there are
so many uncontrollable intangibles that make up recognition and success.

It's the life we choose that sets us up in the hierarchy of humans—
that proves our courage and understanding and sensitivity. I'd rather
be the worst poet than the best agent.

And a creative life is so much more important than a structured
shadowed existence.

Later—Saroyan represents all that is noble and sad in life—the nobility in maintaining the poetry and the sadness in always feeling the
inevitability of failure and death.

Much later—I'm not running a glue factory to patch up frag-
mented lives.

*   *   *

She's a *midnight lady* in a five o'clock town
trying to make it through the night

and a short order cook who loves to fight
and her eyes keep getting dimmer
and her mouth is a tight, tough line
and she's trying hard to forget
that she once knew special men
and vintage wine

She's a midnight lady in a five o'clock town
living a lie she calls her life
and in another world she was (mother and wife)

"I'm Temporarily Insane"
and Permanently Blue

(1)   I'm goin' round in circles
           till the squares don't think I'm cool
           if heartbreak was a schoolroom
           I'd be an educated fool
           since I broke off with you
           I'm temporarily insane
           and permanently blue

(2)   My coffee's filled with whiskey
           so my breakfast keeps me stoned
           if it wasn't for the DT's I'd be bored, numb and alone
           since I broke off with you
           I'm temporarily insane
           and permanently blue

(Middle)   I see your face on my ceiling
           and your body on my bed
           there's a ghost in my room
           and a creep show in my head

(3)   I'm going to hit the highway and ride it night and day
           if I could find a new brain I'd give the one I have away
           if I could hit the highway I would ride it night and day
           till I could air my brain out
           and give my blues away

           Cause/since I broke off with you
           I'm temporarily insane
           and permanently blue

* * *

It was only last night but it feels like a thousand broken dreams ago—
nonchalant and want—

* * *

Every time I see N . . . I'm reminded of the ugliness of the music *business* and you notice I underlined the word business, where the grossness of the deed is always justified by its enormity. (N . . . did to B . . . Records what Richard Burton did to Elizabeth Taylor, what some rock guitarist is doing to some wide-eyed waitress early every morning every a.m.)

Steve Goodman pixie singer songwriter was dining with me at a Soho gourmet watering establishment that was filled with better dressed professional followers practicing the unmanly art of wishy washy and fagdom. We were engaged in flights of fancy about songs, songwriters, singers and other motley carousings when I mentioned N . . .—He maintained seriously that N . . . was a hero and dear friend. Conversation ended on an ugly note—there's no accounting for bad taste and stupidity.

* * *

Joe Turner and Frankie Newton—my two early musical idols and inspirations—my life had direction, hope and meaning. Frankie died so young and before I could repay him. But Joe is still and I make myself always available and I'm always scheming how to make his life a little better—financially or emotionally—let him have the security of knowing I'm always there. And without making him feel I'm doing him a favor—

The world should be like this—

Offer everything not just stingy pieces.

* * *

Early in the morning—I realize I only feel safe and secure with Shirlee.

Later—Athletes and people in general have progressed from scientific advancements and I think today's athletes are the best ever. Training and diet have been tremendously advanced, accounting for so much of this. But recording advancements and electronic advancements have helped the sound of records and voices and instruments—but they have not made the singer sing better or the player play better—if anything—it's had the opposite effect. Things can be patched and doctored so beautifully that laziness can prevail and mediocrity does not necessarily have to sound like mediocrity.

* * *

Angel of the evening
angel of the evening
keep me in heaven tonight
spread your wings and hold me
and shut out the neon lights.

Angel of the evening
make all my prayers come true
I've prayed for a true love
please let me find it with you.

Midnights are getting longer all the time
loneliness is trying hard to twist my mind
and the devil's reaching out to touch my soul.
Angel help me keep my self-control.

Angel of the evening
stay here till the morning rolls round
if the sun is shining
stay here till the sun goes down.

*   *   *

You're Going With Me

Don't let me kiss you
unless you're going all the way
I mean commit your heart
for more than just today
cause I got to know
if I let myself go
you're going with me

If fame and fortune
looks like it's hiding anywhere
I'll go and find that place
no matter where out there
and you better know
if I'm going to go
you're going with me

Why can't we get lucky
and hit the numbers when we play
and have a pocket full of money
"live the good life" every day

Like every day in a penthouse
instead of this tenement way
like night clothing and night everywhere
the high roller plays
keep our pockets full of money
chasing those low down blues away.

And if you leave me
you know you've said your last goodbye
and I don't care at all
but any kind of why
you better know—if I am booked to go
you're going with me.

* * *

I'm gonna get a room with three steps leading to the door and high ceilings and a large step leading to a huge balcony. And there will be low chairs on the balcony and a fence with sagging boards.

One morning I will wake up and realize so much has been a dream and I will casually walk into the room and stroll on to the balcony and gently lean against the fence and laugh at all the people in the street below and then sadly shake my head as I watch them race madly about in their losing battle with time and space.

And then again I may never wake up a different person. And I'll have to keep fighting invisible tides and dragons and dress in my people disguises and battle and battle.

* * *

The Real Me

No one ever saw
or wanted to see
the real me.
I was hiding
and sometimes sliding
from the real me.

No one ever found
a reason
to take a moment
or a season
to find the real me
the real me.

No one ever knew
or wanted to know
the real me

When you stood beside me
and somehow got inside me
and you found the real me

You got through all the surprises
all those defences and disguises
and found the real me
the real me.

Your gentle touch
made me strong
showed me the strength
that I had all along

And you made all those tangled pieces unwind
when you found the real me
the real me.

When I look in the mirror
I no longer see
the man I used to be

now looking back at me
all I ever see

is the real me
the real me

all I ever see
is the real me.

[From the Pomus/Rebennack song "The Real Me" (© 1987, 1991
Stazybo Music/Skull Music). Recorded by New Orleans singer Johnny
Adams a/k/a "the tan canary." All rights reserved. Used by permission.]

Prince Valium and King Toot

(Chorus)   I'm a citizen of the kingdom of neon
presided over by Prince Valium and King Toot
I'm flying wildly through the night skies
and I ain't packin' no parachute.

(1)   It's midnight and it's time to get movin'
I'm fighting a ton of blankets trying to quit the bed
It will take five cups of coffee and a toke
to rejoin the walking dead

(2)   There's a waitress over at Charlie's tavern
who's got big legs and very little self-control
she'll give me ten dollars walking money
if I keep telling her she really ain't too old

(4)   A bad dude in the neighborhood pool room
swears he got my name on his blade
he got me down for ten losers
I'm leavin' that bill unpaid

(5)   A dealer in a tenement hallway
with a toothless grin on his face
sells me a fistful of shortcuts
for quittin' the human race

(6)   My son's in the loop of Chicago
in a run-down orphanage home
no crowds of people around him
can stop him feeling alone

(Middle)   I'm a citizen of the kingdom of neon
             ruled by Prince Valium and King Toot
             I'm flying wildly through the night
             and I ain't wearin' no parachute

             It's midnight and it's time to get movin'
             I'm fighting a ton of blankets trying to quit the bed
             It'll take five cups of coffee to rejoin the living dead
             in the kingdom of Prince Valium and King Toot

             That waitress at the castaway's tavern
             the one with the great big legs
             and next to no self-control
             she's good for some walkin' money
             if I tell her she ain't old

             Got an ex-wife in the east of St. Louis
             ain't seen in a thousand or more years
             cursing the day she filled out
             that contract for endless tears
             I used to dream about a perfect girl
             like I used to dream about the perfect world
             it had nothing to do with reality
             so I was unprepared for you and me

             Or my soul is goin' gone
             and to Hollywood Babylon
             sneakin' in and freakin' out
             in the gay underground
             is what Hollywood is all about

             I'm goin' the route
             of Prince Valium and King Toot

[Draft Lyric by Doc Pomus. © 1984]

*　*　*

There is a surge towards redneckism—that means an involvement with
narrowness—macho silliness—drunken stupors—and regionalism to
such a degree that universality and its tendencies to spread knowledge

and ideas become secondary to the worst kind of insulation and self-absorption.

The blues person thinks of the blues song the way the pop person writes or [pop] singer thinks of the pop song. For example, "Moonlight in Vermont" is no more a pop song to a pop person than "Goin Down Slow" is a blues song to a blues person.

* * *

Red wine and blues
It goes together like push and shove
like you and me and love
a combination you can't refuse
red wine and blues

it gets you through the
black heart of night
my favorite kind of music and booze
red wine and blues

High on a plane
on a sea cruise
bruise

* * *

Children

Cause we're children, children lost in a world we never made, no matter how hard we try, we're goin' to cry till we die, and never, never, make the grade, cause we're children.

* * *

Never forget that people get into business because they like to make money. People play ball—because they like to play ball. People write songs cause they like to write songs—and it's always us against them. And somewhere along the line the businessperson loses perspective and thinks that he does everything and the ballplayer or the musician are like puppets on his string and he actually causes them to do their thing.

Later—Sometimes you're infuriated by some people's tactics. But maybe they're just aware of their limited equipment and are trying to make the most of it and then their way of doing it comes out so strange and rotten, but it's all they got. And they're trying to make the most of it and sometimes no matter how rotten it gets—you can't blame them for trying.

* * *

Gerry Goffin called me yesterday and apologized for "copping so many of my songs." I told him he was silly and I invited him over. He said he would bore me and every time I spoke he answered, "What did you say?"

* * *

Protégé

(1)   I was kind of hip and sly
          I had that faraway look in my eye
          you came along and grounded me
          your choice of words astounded me
          you put me under your wing
          and that sort of thing
          and from that day
          I became your protégé

(2)   You told me I'd go far
          I had it in me to become a star
          and if I was real nice to you
          we'd make a million dollars or two
          so I sold my Oldsmobile
          cause stars don't need wheels
          and from that day
          I became your protégé

(Middle) I moved into your Hollywood luxury pad
          the kind that only superstar managers had
          with mice and cockroaches and neighbors that drink

I've been here for six months now
it's gonna to get better I think

Cause I got a job today
I got to feed this hungry protégé
my manager still has to eat
the grocer don't give us free meat
my genius still got high hopes
I support two dopes
(won't you please be
a protégé for me)
I curse the day
I became a protégé.

[Draft lyric by Doc Pomus. © 1980 Stazybo Music. Pomus/Rebennack. All rights reserved. Used by permission.]

* * *

Songs like movies should serve all purposes—from light and frothy to deep and lasting—the one thing they should have in common is professionalism in terms of structure and creating the desired effect. As to a hierarchy of songs, that may get tricky—there are all degrees and one person's frothiness is another person's deepness.

* * *

Stewart Levine was here and we discussed the B.B. King and Count Basie versions.

I told him the nine songs I suggested for the album and he agreed with me as follows: (1) I want a little girl (2) Every day (3) Goin' to Chicago. These are three Count Basie standards.

(1) Three o'clock in the morning
    Thrill is gone
    How blue can you get
    B.B. standards

Suggested new ones:
I started—(1) NY City blues minor blues about NY starting with Harlem and mentioning Dr. Clayton "Harlem must be heaven" line

(2) Blues Hall of Fame—possible title
(3) Funny shuffle blues

Two sides to every story, Ruth, your side of the story and the truth.

We talked about inability to consistently cope music business types—because we're never certain about what nights we are unable to function with the proper type of rapport necessary for maintaining equilibrium in the conversation—instead of rage or turning away.

Material for B.B. and Basie should be material Carson, Vegas can relate to and stuff that ghetto blacks won't feel is coming from a completely different world.

* * *

I quote Robert Palmer—from his book *Deep Blues* page 103 (discussing Muddy Waters slide techniques) "Musicians trained in say the classical music of India which puts the premium on the ability to hear and execute 5 microtonal shadings, would recognize in the astonishing precision and emotional richness of the variously flattened thirds and fifths sprinkled through the solo something close to his own tradition. Literacy, which trains one to focus on the linear continuity of words and phrases rather than on their intonational subtleties, tends to obliterate such minutely detailed and essentially non-linear modes of expression. Perhaps this explains why many of the young city-bred blacks who have taken up the blues in recent years have had almost as much trouble playing music as subtle as Muddy's as the legions of blues-smitten whites."
      Hmmmmmmm
I do declare—
      I think I'll read this to Joe [big Joe Turner] and get his academic reaction and find out if there's any validity or reality or maybe he'll write a treatise for Robert Palmer, Jerry Wexler, and Muddy Waters—or Gary Giddins or Robert Christgau or Dave Marsh or Lightnin' Hopkins or John Lee Hooker or Dr. Clayton—oops he's dead and anyway Palmer never heard of him. At least he never mentioned him in his book *Deep Blues*.

Still July 19, 1981. My working Shirlee is out on the streets—ripping. I hope she gets successful real quick and she'll have confidence—I realize now how much I need her and love her and it's too late—I always figure things out a little too late.

* * *

Elizabeth is one of those self-righteous, self-absorbed females who leads a life of serious silliness—hovering between petulance and haughtiness and her life double framed from the inside and outside with insecurity and an inability to act out.

* * *

Bob Dylan once said he's like an antenna that takes songs from the ozone.

When I'm in between songs, most of the time, I have no idea where they come from—how I invented them—and whether they'll come again.

I know what he means—I have similar feelings. Though I don't feel like an antenna—I think that at the times of productivity a chemical combination or chemical or metaphysical or physical combination or some strange reality or unreality becomes grounded enough to come from my body to my voice or pen or pencil.

* * *

You can't take yourself too seriously—those are the negative as well as the positive aspects of criticisms. I mean it has a lot to do with what people say about your work—whether they like it or dislike it.

* * *

I may be bruised
I may be used
I'm gonna to rise again.

Tinsel stars on a sequin sky
it's always Christmas or the 4th of July

Keep the swinger sweet
thrill your senses and kill that pain

Hollywood Babylon
where have all the superstars gone
love too hard and you die real quick.

*   *   *

Paul Case where are you? I need somebody to run with songs—give me
business advice and stroke me when I need it and get rough with me
when I need it. And evaluate my songs and discuss them with me—

*   *   *

Kafka said a book must be an axe for the frozen sea in us.

*   *   *

Performer gets juice every time he does a good performance and crowd
responds. But I don't get juice on old songs because that's old applause.
My juice could only be with new songs.

*   *   *

Some kids are miracles—no matter what's going on around them,
there's some part of them that internally resists everything and they are
not too adversely affected.
     And other kids are devastated and scarred by every little thing that
happens around them.

*   *   *

Hello Stranger

Hello stranger, hello stranger
who is that person in the mirror—it's not me.
Whatever happened to the man
that I used to be?
Is he just another faded memory?

Hello stranger, hello stranger
every night you're always in my bed.

Every day you stay inside my head.
Oh how I wish I was there instead
of some sad stranger, some sad stranger.

(Middle)   You're a stranger
who could never be a friend,
you're trying to convince me
that the good times have come to an end.

Hello stranger, hello stranger
how can I make you, how can I make you go?
I don't wanna know you any more,
I'm tired of living with or for
some old stranger, some old stranger.
Hello stranger, hello stranger.

[From the Pomus/Rebennack song "Hello Stranger" (© 1986, 1988 Stazybo Music/Skull Music). Recorded by Marianne Faithful and Walter "Wolfman" Washington. All rights reserved. Used by permission.]

*   *   *

I guess things never really change—Ralph Ellison's great book, *Invisible Man*, said it all.

At first I was invisible because I was crippled and then I became invisible because I was old plus crippled—

It's strange. I can handle how I feel cause I'm 64 but I can't deal with the way people act because I'm 64.

*   *   *

Don't be a trivial person. Don't be more concerned with your external than with your internal.

Don't let your spirit become mean and small.

The great singers like the great athletes sang within themselves and when they're not reaching to the farthest point within themselves their work suffers.

*   *   *

French hip expression practiced too often today and confusing people's feelings "je t'aime mais je ne suis pas amouroux."

* * *

To the world, a fat crippled jewish kid is a nigger—a thing—the invisible man—like Ralph Ellison says.

* * *

They Call Me the Barber, or, the Barber's Blues

(1) When you see the barber's pole
you know the barber's just behind
when it comes to high-class trimming
I'm the best you'll ever find

(2) I'll part your hair in the middle
or maybe on the side
and I'll even use my blower
until you're satisfied

They call me the barber
cause I got a barber's pole
it's like a rare antique
getting better as it gets old

(3) If you're in my neighborhood
you can't miss my barbershop
my pole stays out in front
(and there's a sign on it saying)
(we work around the clock)
they call me the barber
cause I got a barber's pole
it might be rusty and bending in the middle
but Lord there's no way it's goin' to fold

(4) You can come by once a month
the old-fashioned way
but if you need trimming real badly
you can come by every day

They call me the barber
cause I got a barber's pole
it's like a rare antique
getting better as it grows old

[Draft lyric by Doc Pomus. © 1980 "They Call Me the Barber" Pomus/ Rebennack.]

* * *

Fragments

I know that livin'
is part of dying
but it ain't all over till you're dead
I know that hating is part of loving
but there's so many things that are never said

Teach me to feel again
make the world real again
help me find my place
and still give me space

* * *

The roots of pop music should be classical, jazz, blues, and evergreen pop writers like Berlin, Gershwin and not ancient rock writers like Berry, even myself etc. That is why the current music is so silly and meaningless and *second rate*.

* * *

Lincoln said—you cannot strengthen the weak by weakening the strong. You cannot help the poor by destroying the rich. You cannot help men permanently by doing for them what they could and should do for themselves.

* * *

When businessmen found out there's limitless money in R&R—they got involved and then figured out what kind would bring them the most money and then they perpetuated it (non-musical, soullness, bad music easily replaceable) "when one group dies another three or four similarly bad groups are available to take its place." And that's what happened.

Years ago because it wasn't a gigantic endless money maker the music business had something more to do with music that is *really really* music and sometimes even good—great music.

*　*　*

Obscene silly doggerel. The Ballad of Doc and Lulu

You heard about girls who made love
Like it was their last day on this earth
And it was so wild and unique and so thrilling
That there was no way to value its worth
And that was the girl they named Lulu
The flower of old Budapest
And she conquered the hearts of all comers
Until she met the good Doctor
The pride of the 70s gone west
They paired and sparred and they twisted
In a night made specially for love
With risers and downers and vibrators
And the only witness the mirrors above
And the morning found them exhausted
The victims of technique and pride
And the lust that they'd sown
And all they had left for each other
A song called, "The next heart you break is your own."

*　*　*

The Victim

I was born in the country
raised in the ghetto street
I was born in the country

raised in the ghetto street
and since I was old enough to be one
I've been a victim of every girl I meet.

Every time I meet a pretty girl
I lose my self-control
It's bad enough with self-control
but it's always followed by my bankroll

The country girls are slick
the city girls are slicker
and the way they keep on slicking me
it keeps getting me sicker and sicker.

I got a room in a third floor walk-up
The landlady fell in love with me
I couldn't pay the rent for three months
she said romance don't make the rent free.

It was so cold outside
and the ground was covered with snow
but she threw me and my stereo out the window
and hollered "Victim coming! Look out below . . ."

[Draft lyrics by Doc Pomus. © 1980 Stazybo Music. Pomus/Reben-
nack. Recorded by B.B. King. All rights reserved. Used by permission.]

* * *

This is the age of the underdog and the minority fighting and achieving
recognition and rights and respect. But my minority group, the physically handicapped, are still stumbling around, falling down subway
stairs and high pavements and staying home because half of the good
places aren't accessible and half of the good people never see us and
know us. If I wasn't a hit songwriter I might have ended up on relief in
some third-rate hotel room with a visiting nurse coming in to help me
once in a while.

* * *

A World I Never Made

The late show is over
and the city's fast asleep
and I'm lost in a world
that's just too cold
too cold and deep.

I've turned so many ways
I'm spinning like a top
I wish that I could get off
or that the world, that the world would stop.

I'm a stranger and afraid
I'm a stranger and afraid
in a world I never made.

I'm always chasing dragons
with a sword that's made of tin
so I know in my soul
there's no way I can win.

I try, oh, how I try
but there's no place
no place to go
there's no one here who knows me
and no one here I know.

I'm a stranger and afraid
I'm a stranger and afraid
I'm a stranger and afraid
in a world I never made.

[From the Pomus/Rebennack song, "A World I Never Made" (© 1981, 1988 Stazybo Music). Recorded by Johnny Adams, B.B. King, Ruth Brown. All rights reserved. Used by permission.]

* * *

I want to be somebody's hero sometime
not just a loser till I die
I want to know there's a girl waitin' somewhere
and if she don't see me she's gonna cry.

I tried to change my ways
I even started working days
I learned how to sleep at night
feeling right
I did it in the name of love
then you started seeing other men
I'm hangin' out in the bars again

* * *

I can't shake the shadows and memories keep on crowding me. Am I
somewhere in between a never-was and a used-to-be?

* * *

Let the sweet sadness fill my soul because the world is sweet, sad, and
bittersweet and I can't cope no matter how hard I try and I'm always
on the outside lookin' in. The sweet sadness covers and fills me and the
world is always my master and I never control anything. Especially me.

* * *

And each book I read tells me there is so much more for me to know and
it goes on and on—I'm never quite holding on to anything except bits of
a puzzle that never gets completed.

* * *

Take your losses and move on
what's dead is rarely gone
and don't look back
your shoulders were my rock
and your arms held me round the clock

[Doc's last journal entry. He died March 14, 1991, at N.Y.U. Medical
Center, surrounded by his family]

* * *

Save the Last Dance for Me

You can dance every dance with the guy who gave you the eye:
let him hold you tight.
You can smile every smile for the man who held your hand
'neath the pale moonlight.

But don't forget who's taking you home
and in whose arms you're gonna be
so darlin', save the last dance for me.

Oh, I know that the music's fine, like sparkling wine,
go and have your fun
laugh and sing
but while we're apart, don't give your heart to anyone.

But don't forget who's taking you home
and in whose arms you're gonna be
so darlin', save the last dance for me.

Baby don't you know I love you so?
Can't you feel it when we touch?
I will never, never let you go
I love you oh so much.

You can dance, go and carry on till the night is gone
and it's time to go.
If he asks if you're all alone, can he take you home
you must tell him no
'cause don't forget who's taking you home
and in whose arms you're gonna be
so darlin', save the last dance for me.

[Copyright protected. Words and music by Doc Pomus and Mort
Shuman.]

JIMMY SCOTT

INTERVIEWED BY JEANNE WILMOT CARTER

An Interview: On Himself and Doc Pomus

While compiling the Doc Pomus journal entries with his daughter Sharyn Felder, I began reminiscing with her about the night Jimmy Scott sang "Some-one to Watch Over Me" at Doc's last birthday party. It was only ten months later that Jimmy was singing the same song at Doc's funeral. I saw Jimmy after the funeral at his apartment in Newark and told him about my conversation with Sharyn, and he started talking to me about Doc and the old days and what it is to be what he and Doc are.

— JEANNE WILMOT CARTER

JWC: Aren't we both from Cleveland? What was your Cleveland?

JS: Very mixed. It never touched us, the racial thing. One area, two or three streets from where we lived, was Italian; a few streets on the opposite side were Jewish; then there were the Hungarians. There were also a lot of Slavic and Polish in the area; we were like centralized in the east side area where all the Afro-Americans were living. There were a lot of poor families, it was a mixed atmosphere, because the richest guy could live next door to you. In fact, six doors down the street from me lived Jesse Owens.

The attitude in my family was that the racial situation wasn't a problem. The problem was not being able to feed your kids, or keep a decent place for them to live—something like that. That was foremost in my family—keeping the family together, seeing to it that everybody ate and had clothes on their backs. But the racial thing never really touched us then. It touched me and reached out to me more or less after my mother passed.

My father wasn't a home-type guy, you know. Some of the kids looked at it as though it was a horrible thing because he wasn't home. The devastating thing was that when my mother died the bottom fell out of the money. My father didn't want to be responsible for the situation . . . there were ten of us . . . so that left the kids to be divided up for a period of time. The younger ones spent more time in foster homes than the oldest. . . . I stayed in a foster home until I was sixteen.

Yeah, the little kids knew Mom 'cause they were able to look at her; but to study and understand what she represented, or what she was, they didn't fully get the message. I had started working. I had like newspaper routes; then I had coal and lumber—we would go around and get all the old boxes, break them up, tie the wood in bundles, because people used this for firewood. Then we'd get a wagon and go along the train tracks. They had the old coal trains. When these coal trains would come sometimes they hit a bump and slow down. I'd sneak up there and knock some coal off and sell it to somebody for 50 cents. Those little pennies helped out at home. And then, we had to have coal, too. It was a means of survival. We had this old big upright piano and at night, to comfort herself, you would hear my mother play. After we all went to bed she would be playing the piano.

JWC: What kind of music did she play?

JS: Well, a lot of classical and gospel.

JWC: Did she sing at church?

JS: Yeah, we sang at church as kids, you know.

JWC: Was that where you first sang?

JS: Yes, I can say, in a way, yes.

JWC: In a way no, too?

JS: Well, actually, in the church it was like an occasional thing, in church your turn comes. But where I actually got into it was in school. Yeah.

JWC: In what context? School plays?

JS: In school plays, that's it exactly.

At the time I was coming up I had this teacher, a dramatic teacher, a white teacher who liked the arts and the theater. She created themes for her plays and we would take that theme; once it was the Red Cross, for example, and I played the role of the nurse—I was in an all boys' school, so the boys had to play the nurses. We'd go from that to the comics. The big comic back then, I don't know if you ever heard of it, it was one of those comic strips like Disney's things—"Ferdinand the

Wolf." I played the role of this delicate wolf, and had to sing the song, "Ferdinand, the Delicate Wolf." So this began my thing.

JWC: Did they let you sing it any way you wanted?

JS: Any way. Uh huh.

JWC: And what kind of music were you doing then?

JS: Jazz. This was the infancy of our life interest. Being a product of the roots of jazz was what we were all about. I remember us kids would get together and put on shows. Finally, some of us met up at a theater that was run by an old timer who was in business, in show business, one of the great old-time dancers who was in show business here in New York—he had come to Cleveland. His name was Teddy Black. He convinced this theater chain to start a circuit. That's when Cleveland became part of the chitlins circuit. Because when Teddy Black came to Cleveland and went into this metropolitan theater in Cleveland, he started bringing in Buddy Johnson, the Erskine Hawkins Band, Cab Calloway, Duke Ellington, Count Basie—all of these old bands were coming into Cleveland, which gave us an opportunity.

JWC: Did they let you guys open to the bands?

JS: Well no, here's what it was. We worked in the theater. Everybody who was interested in entertainment naturally wanted to work there. Now the girls were working the candy counters. Myself and some of the fellas were working as ushers, and cleaning up the place, and what not. So I volleyed myself into a position to have a concession backstage; I would dust up each of their rooms at night and put fresh towels in for the next day, which was one of my little hustles. You know. So he [Teddy Black] says, well now, you know you're making too much money and I can't pay you. So I said, just let me have the back room. So I made my salary back there with their little tips and things. But at the same time I was always checking out the scene. Then the owners of the theater finally decided to bail out, and when they decided to bail out, all of us got to Teddy Black and said, why don't we put on a show.

JWC: And a lot of people came to hear you?

JS: Yes, it was so great. A great beginning. I myself, I went on to professional entertainment; then Barbara Taylor, she went on to professional entertainment, she was one of the dancers with the Norma Miller troupe. She was one of the most important dancers with that troupe.

Lester Johnson, he did a record, one record on RCA, but he never did no more, that was his first and last, and they didn't really promote the record that big. But I ventured on and out into the field. I had been telling these guys backstage that I wanted to sing, so finally two dancers, Lem Neal and Dickie Sims, said how would you like to come and go with us . . . they were a tap dance team . . . they wanted me to go with them and be their valet. I didn't know anything about what they were talking about. Valet, what is that? I was running around, saying what does a valet do? Show business? I'm going, I'm gone. So I have to live with them. They went up to Buffalo, okay they did Buffalo, and came back. Back to Pittsburgh, because they lived in Pittsburgh at that time. Came back to Pittsburgh, then they got an engagement to go to Meadesville, Pennsylvania. Now the unique thing about Meadesville is that the band playing for that show was Lester Gallin, Coleman Hawkins, Howard McGee, Joe Jones on drums, Sir Charles on piano, and Slam Stuart on bass, this is bad. You've got those cats and I got the itchy feet I want to sing so bad. So Lem and Dickie eased over to Lester and the others . . . "Okay, they're going to call you tomorrow."

JWC: What year was this?

JS: Oh, it has to be around '44. I was like 20. Not quite. I was 17 or 18. So I got on, I sang "Talk of the Town" and "Don't Take Your Love From Me"—two numbers. Boy, the place just roared. So I went on, they sent me off, and now I'm standing backstage. I'm anxious for these guys to come off stage and say, you know, you did a good job. Because I want to know from them did I do all right? That was my anxiety. I was just bubbling over, and I'm standing like this in the doorway where they come off stage. So Lester comes off, he comes off with his saxophone up to his shoulder and under his arm, and he said, get on back in the dressing room, you're a valet, you ain't got no business up here. No compliment. No nothing. I was looking for this, this was the greatest thing that happened to me in my whole life. And I'm telling you baby, there's something funny about the way old timers pass the teaching down. If they liked you, hurting your feelings was more important to them, conveying that message. Now if you're hip, down the line you digged why they did it. No big deal. It isn't no big deal because you went up there and sang a couple of numbers. I was waiting out there backstage thinking, yeah, I did a damn good job. But no way. They took my feathers down so quick, yes. You know I was quite hurt. I was quite hurt and disillusioned that, hey, I didn't hear anything about what they thought of my singing until about a year. After that, I wound up in New York at the Baby Grand.

JWC: Babs, *I Paid My Dues*, Gonzalez?

JS: That's right, that's where I met Babs. How'd you know Babs?

JWC: I used to know him in the seventies.

JS: Baby Grand was where I met Doc [Pomus], too. What happened was, Redd Foxx had spoke to Joe Louis and Ralph Cooper in Baltimore, where Redd and myself were working at Gambi's. Redd went to Joe and Ralph and said, "Well, hey, you got to get this guy." I'll never forget it—they called those brothers who owned the Baby Grand. I was supposed to be going in there for a week—I stayed over two months in the Baby Grand. The first night I was in there I saw this little guy sitting back there and I happened to notice the canes—somebody else is using those canes, I thought, well he ain't using them, this guy ain't using them, he's just sitting there, just looking. And all of a sudden, after the show (Nipsy Russell was emcee) everybody else is going out of the room. Doc is sitting there, legs stretched out, but the way he was sitting I couldn't actually detect at first. I went downstairs, got my coat and everything, came back up. Doc says, "Jimmy, I want to talk to you." I said, "Me?" I got to talking with him and everything and all of a sudden I noticed he got those canes, put them up around his arms, and stood up. I can't believe this. This cat is going. Where's he going? It just never dawned on me that, see—all his life he'd had this control, this determination . . . this was a determined young guy. You know, a lot of people in the condition that Doc was in, they were pitiful. They pitied themselves. This man would steady go here. Now he had done told me, "Man, I'll be by the hotel, I'll pick you up." Now I know nothing about New York. I knew nothing about New York at all. This man took me all over New York. Everything I had learned about I learned from Doc Pomus. While I was there at the Baby Grand.

JWC: I'll bet he took you all around Brooklyn.

JS: All through Brooklyn, all through the Bronx. Doc was a helluva blues singer himself. I mean he was a real soulful blues singer in his own right, not only being a person who—I know you know—created all these tunes for many of these artists—The Drifters, Coasters, all those kids . . . that's where they got their music from, from Doc Pomus. Doc Pomus created music that made them hits. Okay, it's just the little cat was frightened. But he could sing those things better than some of them cats he made the hits for. He was working clubs all around the place.

JWC: Did you see him singing in the clubs?

JS: Sure, we had a jam night at the Baby Grand; many times Doc got up and sang. We'd hang out at different places. And you know, everything was so together then and the relationships amongst people were so different than what we're dealing with today. When you'd go in a place, well, the people that were playing would say, hey, here's Jimmy Scott in the house, here's Doc Pomus in the house, come on up, and everybody pitched in. If you're hanging out over here, you got up many nights. Doc sang. Many nights we got up different places, and him and I took to running together. It was the craziest thing. If it was too late, he'd say, c'mon, let's get a cab, man, and we'd hop a cab. Did he ever tell you about the time I got drunk, and I was going to whip all the big cats? He had to rush me out of there. Here my buddy is on crutches and I'm going to beat up these big dudes. "Not these cats," he said. "C'mon get in the cab." He got me in that cab and we cut out of there. Many nights like that.

JWC: Now were you about 19 or 20?

JS: Him and I were exactly the same age. Well, I was about 19 or 20. Both of us were Cancers . . . For a while there we didn't go anywhere without each other.

JWC: Did you tell me that story about Charlie Parker? When somebody tried to kick Parker out of a club and it was Doc who rushed to his aid. Were you there?

JS: No, I wasn't there. But we knew about it. The funniest thing about entertainers is how they communicated then. You see, a cat would get on the phone, and if he were having a problem he would call somebody. Now, Parker had tried to call somebody to help, but he couldn't reach anybody. That night Doc jumped in and said, "No, hey man, you can't do this." Many times. And not only for Bird. Many times we'd been up and down Broadway late at night after the clubs had closed—once we saw Sonny, picked him up, got him off the street.

JWC: Sonny Stitt?

JS: Yeah.

JWC: What part of Broadway? Are we talking 40s and 50s?

JS: Well, that was in the area of 52nd, because I remember Dempsey's was along Broadway then. The Turf was at the corner of 49th, and above the Turf at that time, there was BeBop City.

It was a club. And 52nd Birdland was down there. And the Ebony was down a little further, going east on 52nd. The Ebony had moved in where Birdland was to be, that's what it was, and then the Ebony went out and Birdland came in.

JWC: And the same night you would hang at the Grand and go back and forth?

JS: Right.

JWC: And this was like the early forties?

JS: Mid. Say the mid.

JWC: After the war?

JS: Yeah, after the war. Around '48, something like that, because Doc started writing songs around the early fifties, like for Joe Turner, Laverne Baker. He wrote "Lonely Avenue" for Ray Charles. Doc, we'd talk about different songs, we'd talk about different entertainers, and he'd tell me about, well, you know, I'm writing a tune and I'm going to get it to Ahmet Ertegan. Doc was Ahmet's first writer. It was when Atlantic was in the Jefferson Hotel on 57th Street. Doc was the first songwriter signed. And I want to tell you who flipped over when I told him about being at Doc's funeral. Little Anthony.

JWC: He knew him?

JS: Yeah, because Doc would be out in the streets with the Crowns [later the Drifters] and in the clubs with other groups. It wasn't like he sat back and waited for groups to pop up. He was out there amongst them and a part of whatever they were doing. Yeah.

JWC: Ben E. King sang lead when the Drifters were with Doc. After Clyde McPhatter. Right?

JS: I think Ben E.'s lost the power of his voice now.

JWC: As Doc would say, he should change the key because he is singing in the original key.

JS: Honey, all of them. There's so many of them that I used to say—Doc would say the same thing—man, they need to come off the falsetto. See people do not realize that when you are growing your voice is changing, and if you're not singing at a natural level, you lose it.

JWC: Have you had to modulate your level at all?

JS: No. Because I sang high a lot of people thought it was like I was singing falsetto, but I wasn't. It was always my natural voice. My natural speaking tone of voice. Now it's gotten stronger, yes, over the years, you know, the muscles expand, vocal output, it's gotten stronger. That's the growth in my voice—that's the change in my voice. Because see I'm doing what I was doing then, only it's a little more powerful in expression, see.

JWC: I remember Doc used to say, Jimmy's singing as well as he ever sang, if not better. And he wouldn't say that about too many people; but he was quick to say who'd lost it.

JS: Well, he knew, babe. It's a funny thing about the old-timers. Him, myself, and everybody else, you knew from the education you got being a part of business, you knew in a moment if the expression was worth the output that the person was giving, or if it was a valuable expression coming from that person. You instantly knew, cause many times we'd sit there and say, "After this next one let's split." You know. Things like that because the song wasn't projecting. Doc would look at me and say, "Jimmy, there's no need to go on." Then we'd go and listen to more people. You see, then it wasn't a thing of like trying to outdo anybody. It was like appreciating the good things about the different artists. That's what it was with us. And Doc—it was just natural with him—if he liked what a cat was putting out, he'd be thinking about what he could do to enhance what he was doing.

JWC: You were away from the music for a taste in the seventies. Were those difficult times for you?

JS: Yeah, definitely, because, hey, this was all my life. Well, I mean it's your life in the sense that it's your survival. It's the possibility of your survival as well as a joy, and entertainment and show business is one of the businesses that had a predominant spiritual atmosphere. Always has.

JWC: In what ways?

JS: Because number one, it's one of the most creative. This is something you don't go to school for. Being an entertainer, you don't go to school for that. If it's in you, it's a natural thing with you. That's what I always thought about Doc.

Doc had a spiritual side. He found release in being an entertainer and a creative musician. Doc found it. He knew. He built from it. It's an education that unless you are a part of it, no one can understand. You see, this is something you just don't write down in books and learn to manipulate from technical angles or anything. It's inspiration.

JWC: He'd seen a lot of pain, the way other great singers and performers had.

JS: He did. And he also had a lot of emotion about the harm that came to other entertainers, especially if it was somebody he knew and liked; he felt bad about the things that were happening to them. You see, he played a big part in the change of Lou Reed and the change in Lou's attitude. When Doc passed we realized that Lou relied on Doc a lot.

JWC: That was a new friendship, too. He didn't go back that many years with Lou.

JS: Even though, to show you what effect the friendship had on a man's life. Lou poured his heart out to me after knowing that I knew Doc, he just poured his heart out to me and I knew that what Doc had been portraying to him or saying to him was affecting him like that. And Lou was struggling with himself with this message that he got from Doc—it was like bringing Lou to himself. And that's why he dedicated *Power and Glory, Magic and Loss* to Doc. This was revealed to me in conversations.

JWC: In what ways do you experience that spiritual thing?

JS: Well, it's very hard. I can express an idea of how profound it is in a person's life. But it has to do with creativeness in your work. You know, and the surrendering to that element of your life, the spiritual side of your life, and dealing with it in a positive way. There's nothing like it. See, so many people blaspheme in the expression of the spiritual element of life. For an example, these preachers that have lately been found to be blasphemers. Then there are other people that can accept the spiritual side of life, live with it and enjoy it, and reap the benefits or submit to the power of it. It's nothing but the reality of our existence. That's the real part of your existence, that spiritual self within you. In my belief and my understanding, it is the most powerful part. It is for anybody, not just myself or Doc—being able to learn to submit to it and realize the good that comes from it. A person that sincerely accepts it, they're not out to abuse you, they're not out to step on you. Everyone knows the stuff that Doc put into his work, and the things he did for people. He wasn't stepping on people. He was successful by his own right. By his own talent he was successful. He wasn't successful by dogging somebody's else's life, or by taking from somebody. He gave. He gave to the careers of people.

JWC: It was around the time of Doc's illness and death that you returned to the New York scene?

JS: Right before the seriousness of his illness, but we'd been in touch for quite a few years before that.

JWC: So when you sang at his funeral, what was that like? Being such good friends.

JS: Well, I said, "you [Doc] peeped my hole card." In my own way. I said you peeped my hole card, because actually I knew the song I sang ("Someone to Watch Over Me") was one of the things he liked for me to sing. And then his daughter Sharyn [Felder] had told me that was what she wanted me to sing, and it was great. It was kind of eerie.

JWC: So do you sort of feel that in his death Doc helped you get your next album together? I mean, didn't Seymour Stein, president of Sire Records, sign you after seeing you sing at Doc's funeral?

JS: Yes. Definitely. And the producers say . . . they'd say, here's a cat that Doc reached to out of his grave and put him in help's way. So in a sense, looking at it from the side that I do, the spiritual side, yeah, he was the great motivator of the whole thing—he had preached before he had passed about the importance of my being recorded.

Doc was one of those rare few that you would meet in life. He was just a rarity. I ain't never heard nothing bad from nobody about that boy. Never heard nothing bad from nobody about that boy.

VI

RACHEL FELDER

The Girls in the Band: A Profile of Women in Alternative Music

"Feminist" is a loaded label. For a generation of kids whose parents smoked pot and went to Woodstock, it brings up images of burnt bras and unshaved armpits. For this age bracket, the equality of women is a given. Women simply are equal, and don't have to fight for that equality: they can have high-powered jobs and be on the pill and get respect in a skirt and high heels without even trying. Frequently, the word "post-feminism" has cropped up to describe the attitudes of this generation's women.

Some of the clearest examples of post-feminism at work exist in alternative music. The women in bands like PJ Harvey, Bettie Serveert, Come, and Sonic Youth reject the *Ms.* magazine image of the feminist as an almost militant fighter as much as they reject the musical norm. These women—namely, Polly Jean Harvey, Carol van Dijk, Thalia Zedek, and Kim Gordon—dress the way they want, say what they want, are "tough broads," but are also provocative, *feminine* women as well. But they still belt with the strength, passion, and sexual oomph of a Mick Jagger or vintage Rod Stewart.

When PJ Harvey, the British band named after its female front-person, released its debut single in England in the fall of 1991 (on the small independent label Too Pure), the British press went wild. And no wonder: its lead track, "Dress," is a hyper-intense shriek of realistic frenzy. The song's lyrical content—if I wear the right dress, maybe you'll take it off—is filled with strength and almost confessional calculation. It's coy but plotting; it's an expression of a woman making a choice to put herself in power. But what really expresses this woman's power is her voice: darting and building and sometimes nearly yelling to command an audience. The bottom line is that you've got to listen. And so a simple story of getting dressed to be attractive turns from a submissive tale to an ode to who's in charge. And as Polly Jean Harvey rips her hands down her gleaming red Gretsch guitar, that guitar seems more like a battle weapon than a strummy instrument. As confessional as her lyrics may get, Joni Mitchell she ain't.

On her debut album, *Dry,* which came out in 1992, she pairs almost confrontational sexual imagery with that same rip-through-you yelp and revved-up guitar. "Sheela-Na-Gig," to pull an example, is a song named after a medieval symbol of a woman with her hands opening her vagina, smiling with a grin that is equal parts invitation and menace. Its lyrics twist listeners' expectations in precisely the same way that the band's music—hell, all alternative music—does. "I'm gonna wash that man right out of my hair," she pounds. "I'm gonna take my hips to a man who cares." The music's clearest statement is one of strength.

Other tracks, like "Plants and Rags" and "Oh My Lover," are similarly powerful. What Polly Harvey tells her fans, without ever spelling it out, is that strength and femininity can easily go hand in hand. And, although there are moments of seeming vulnerability in some of these tracks (like "Plants and Rags") and some of Harvey's vocal style (like the whine of "Fountain"), "seeming" is the operative word: the singer is always in control. PJ Harvey—a band of three, featuring two men—is named after and focused around Ms. P.J. Harvey.

On her second album, *Rid of Me,* Harvey uses similar themes and techniques. Again, the music confronts its audience; the album, produced by Steve Albini with his trademark low-frills sound, is raw as an open wound. Which is exactly in sync with its lyrics, as the mere title of one track, "Rub 'Til It Bleeds," shows. On this LP, Harvey is tougher than the guys she's paired with. In the title track, she and her guitar yell, side by side, that "you're not rid of me," with threatening venom. On "Man-Size," she adopts a male persona and taunts the cliched role of a man on a date "Got my girl, she's a wow," she deadpans. In "Me-Jane" she becomes Jane (as in Tarzan-and) and shrieks, "Tarzan why can't you stop your fucking screaming." Always in control, she puts men in what she sees as their place, which is often subordinate to hers. To cut one down, she bluntly sings "you leave me dry."

The point of both the sound and lyrical content of Harvey's music is that women can be sexual *and* powerful. For post-feminists, equal treatment does not mean suppressing, say, the lipstick Harvey features inside the cover of *Dry.* Harvey's look in photographs, both on the albums and in the press, is definitely tough, featuring Doctor Marten big bulky boots, little make-up, and severe thick eyebrows. But it always features lighter, more traditionally feminine touches, like hoop earrings or hair in a bun or a feather boa. Sometimes she's topless, but the message is never frilly sex but blunt shock value. Which is the way the sexuality in her lyrics works as well: as an expression of force instead of a mini-skirted plea to be swept away by a man.

Carol van Dijk, the lead singer of the Dutch band Bettie Serveert, also uses sexuality without submission. Her band's music is more subtle, more Neil Young-style guitar wash and less bluesy roar, and her voice has a softer tone which sometimes sounds flirty even when it's not trying to. But on its debut album, *Palomine,* van Dijk has as much strength as the powerful male players in her band. There's an almost effortless but unavoidable presence to her voice, which bounds over layers of guitars like, well, another layer of guitars. Instead of confronting the audience like PJ Harvey does, van Dijk writes lyrics which are opaque and somewhat unreadable, filled with mystery and depth, as the line from one song, "Down under lock and key there is a brain-tag to every secret," shows. But there is sexuality to her voice along the lines of a singer like The Pretenders' Chrissie Hynde. Without ever trying, or falling into a purring, cliched, sound-of-sex tone, she simply includes a sexual presence in the work. And so, when the lyrics do put their object on the line—as in *Leg's* "You don't worry/I can take care of myself somehow"—they do so with the sexual bravado of Harvey's.

It's noteworthy that, although van Dijk's voice has that commanding presence, Bettie Serveert is very much a band. While PJ Harvey feels like Polly and her two anonymous backing musicians, Bettie is a sum of four players, one of whom happens to be female and uses her voice in addition to a guitar. In photos and onstage, van Dijk wears jeans and T-shirts; she's simply one of the band. And so she tells fans that to be a woman in a band you don't have to wear fishnet stockings and look like the Go-Gos. The look—the post-feminist look—is about reality: fashions and attitudes which work in the real world. And van Dijk's look is one of equality.

The same could be said of Come lead singer Thalia Zedek's look and stance. Although her voice—a mottled yelp somewhere between that of Marianne Faithfull, a Delta bluesman, and a punk rock singer circa 1977—is at the front of the band's music, she's an equal quarter of her band. Unlike Harvey and van Dijk, however, she is openly gay. The difference between feminism and post-feminism is that the latter says "we are equal, period—we don't need to make a fuss about it," and Zedek's lesbianism expresses a similarly matter-of-fact approach to sexuality. Certainly, if she didn't discuss it in interviews, many listeners would be unaware of her sexual preference. Frankly, I mention it only because, like Harvey, Zedek's vocals pound in a way that is, by society's definition, traditionally male: they are forceful, almost violent. More than being torchy, the vocals are growling yells of desperation. With its in-your-face force, the band's album, *Eleven: Eleven*, is not for the meek.

The label the band's music often gets is *blues*, which is correct only as it describes its hyperbolic intensity. Come are blues on heroin: wacked out, too emotional, dark and wild. And belting lyrics like "I don't remember being born" on "Fast Piss Blues" or the accusatory "don't treat me that way" story of "William," Zedek's voice booms with the nonstop need of either a Robert Johnson blues record or a drug trip.

Sonic Youth's Kim Gordon has equal force. Although she's not the lead singer of her band per se, since her husband Thurston Moore shares vocal duties, Gordon's voice craves the spotlight. It's a deadpan combination of attitude, confidence, and an "I dare you" mix of balls and femininity. It's not about conventional beauty, but more about power. As, incidentally, is Gordon's public persona: sexy clothes like short shorts and tight T-shirts are more about the freedom to wear whatever one wants and still be a tough player—regardless of sex—than sex appeal. But while the guitarists in a band like My Bloody Valentine are de-sexed, Gordon's sexuality is present—it's just something which she controls, consciously, as Madonna seems to control her public persona. And her sassy delivery of some of her lyrics ("Don't ever call me mom" on "JC"; "Don't touch my breast" and "I ain't giving you head" screamed on "Swimsuit Issue") reiterates that strength. Like a *Cosmo* girl from Hell, Gordon entices her audience visually and by means of that almost taunting speak/singing. As enticing as it may get, however, you never forget that she calls the shots.

Often, her tone is give-me-a-break cynical. It's reminiscent of some of the language word-heavy artists like Jenny Holzer and Barbara Kruger use. (In the former's work: "protect me from what I want," in the latter's: "We don't need another hero," "I shop therefore I am.") And it's more than just congruent in tone. On *Daydream Nation*'s "The Sprawl," she asks (almost dares) her listeners, "Does this sound simple? Fuck You. Is this for sale?" On *Dirty*'s "Drunken Butterfly," she repeats, like a sex addict's bible verse, "I love you—what's your name?" Many of the songs Gordon sings lead on deal with modern female problems, without ever holding back. On *Goo*'s "Tunic (Song For

Karen)" she examines Karen Carpenter's fatal anorexia. Another song off that album, "Swimsuit Issue," explores sexual harassment. Gordon's frankness in dealing with these issues is mirrored by films like *Thelma and Louise* and *Gas, Food, Lodging*: treated with neither fanfare nor restraint, women's issues are approached because they affect the lives of the writers of these texts and their audience.

A lot is made in the alternative world of the impact Gordon has had as a role model for other bands. In the wake of Sonic Youth, from the release of *Daydream Nation* (1988) through the early nineties, a slew of all-female, heavy alternative bands, sometimes called "foxcore" bands by the press, have popped up. These groups often go by names which deal with their Gordon-esque brand of post-feminist femininity with irony or double entendre: examples includes Babes in Toyland, Hole, L7, Lunachicks. These bands are important on a cultural level as they reject the stereotype of women as demure and innocent. Often dressed in little girls' dresses paired with "don't fuck with me" Doc Martens unisex boots, these guitar bands bolt with an intensity which never makes concessions to being female. They feature gory, loud guitars and emergencied vocals. Sometimes, as with Hole, those vocals are close to Gordon's nearspeak. Sometimes, as with a band like L7, they are more traditionally sung. And just as their look implies that a woman's reality is not all the sweet submissive sexuality of the top 40 pop queens, their lyrics are filled with gritty, sometimes painfully frank, but usually matter-of-fact details of the intimacies of modern female life. The Lunachicks have a song called "Plugg" about menstruation and their second album is called *Binge and Purge,* referring to eating disorders. L7's self-explanatory song titles include "Diet Pill" and "This Ain't Pleasure." Their almost brutal approach to real life, when compared to the cooing, soft vocals of Whitney Houston or Paula Abdul, who sing boy-meets-girl stories, is like the dichotomy between playing with Barbie and Ken dolls and having teenage sex with condoms to prevent contracting the AIDS virus.

Although many critics have lumped these bands in with the American grunge scene of heavy, all-male bands like Nirvana, Mudhoney, et al., I see them as having a stronger link to the hip, harsh but sexy femininity/feminism of Kim Gordon. Certainly, the overall sound and age of bands like L7 and Babes in Toyland is closer to Nirvana's, but if you're going to categorize these bands by their sex and their direct and semiotic approach to that sex, they belong clumped with Gordon. These younger women approach their sexuality in a way which parallels Gordon's stance; it's as if they're saying: "we're women and we can be sexy—but so what? we're also tougher than tough." For Gordon and the women who have followed in her path, that attitude is reflected in music, lyrics, and fashion sense.

They also belong alongside artists from Cindy Sherman, who comments on outdated ways of viewing women in her series of simulated B-movie stills, to Karen Finley, who criticizes the objectification of women in her performance pieces. But many women in alternative music comment through more than just their music. Babes in Toyland lead singer Kat Bjelland and Hole lead singer Courtney Love regularly wear near-Victorian, three-sizes-too-small baby doll dresses, big boots, and too, too much red lipstick: the look is somewhere between punk rock Betty Boop and a rag doll on LSD. Love even writes provocative slogans—like "mother" when she was pregnant with her first child—on her skin in lipstick, like a post-feminist tattoo. But as powerful, commanding women, appropriating clothing which typically represents demure, soft-and-sweet femininity—but twisting it so they control it instead of it defining them—these singers are not only declaring their strength but, hey, are doing exactly what their music does: taking a traditional form and bending/contorting/jolting it into a form which is relevant to them and their lives.

And although Kim Gordon is a contemporary influence for the so-called foxcore bands, there are certainly others. In the late seventies in New York City, Patti Smith and Blondie's Debbie Harry played with preconceived notions of femininity and sexiness and came out with their own proportions of both. In punk England, the Slits examined the same issues with an irony and attitude which would seem at home on a Lunachicks or L7 lyric sheet or album cover; in early eighties England, the Au Pairs and the Delta 5 featured too-tough women singers denying the validity of female stereotypes. All turned the image of the clean, glossy, neatly groomed and made-up woman pop star inside out. Sort of the Bangles-gone-grunge, bands like L7 and Babes in Toyland tip their hats to female stereotypes, and then aggressively (as is the post-modern way) refuse to buy into them.

A more recent school of bands, the Riot Grrrls, are clearly in debt to role models like Kim Gordon. A small movement of growling, almost whining young female-fronted bands, the Riot Grrrls are closer musically—not to mention in terms of images and fashion-sense—to bands like the Delta 5 and the late seventies British punk band X-Ray Spex, which featured the animalesque squawk and consumer-cynical lyrics of lead singer Poly Styrene. Riot Grrl bands have cynical, taunting names like Bikini Kill, Bratmobile, and Heavens To Betsy; they bask in a "don't fuck with me" attitude along the lines of Gordon's. With members' ages hovering around the twenty mark, they're equal parts *Ms.* and *Sassy.* Expressing their preachy, often lesbian-focused, nineties'- radical-feminist dialectic via fanzines, singles on indie labels, virtually exclusively college radio airplay, and small-club gigs, the Riot Grrrls (who have some British sister bands, like Huggy Bear and Mambo Taxi) exemplify alternative musical systems at work. Yet although their stance (and, more often than not, deadpan, anti-beautiful vocals) parallels Kim Gordon's, their music for the most part doesn't have the depth of Sonic Youth's. The Riot Grrls are more about youthful, angry energy than songwriting or record-it-for-posterity longevity.

But whether these bands are producing memorable listen-to-it-in-twenty-years music, like a PJ Harvey is, or energized rants with a limited shelf-life, like some of the Riot Grrrls are, the point is that alternative music affords women the freedom to be more than just ingenues. Just as these performers can reject the musical cliches of top 40 mainstream music, its women performers can reject the cliche of female frontperson as pin-up, dressed-up, made-up beauty queen. With those limited standards removed, these artists can use their lyrics to confront, question, and, in some cases, offend.

STEVE METCALF

Just Listening: A Musical Memoir of the Fifties

The first piece of music I can remember is Perry Como's "Don't Let the Stars Get in Your Eyes." It wasn't a great tune, but it had a run-on lyric that I thought was funny, like a tongue twister:

"Love blooms at night, in daylight it dies don't let the stars get in your eyes don't keep your heart from me for someday I'll return and you know you're the only one I'll ever love."

"Don't Let the Stars Get in Your Eyes" came out in 1952; I was four.

I know the memory is authentic because I can picture myself listening to the song in our family's little basement apartment in downtown Schenectady, New York. We moved to a house in the suburbs in 1953.

I was obsessive about music from the beginning, it seems—a moony little kid who would spend hours on end in his room, alone, just listening. Because of my early start, I can place myself among that dwindling group whose musical memory extends back to the time before rock 'n' roll, before "Heartbreak Hotel" and "Maybellene" changed everything. But just barely: my first musical stirrings came just as music was entering its last, sweet pre-electric days.

Besides Perry Como, the earliest voices I can remember belong to Frankie Laine singing "High Noon," to Les Paul and Mary Ford doing "Vaya Con Dios," to Ezio Pinza singing "This Nearly Was Mine," even to the Saturday afternoon Metropolitan Opera radio broadcasts, about which I mainly recall the grandfatherly announcer Milton Cross and his patient, amiable attempts to explain what was going on.

Music for me had two main sources. One was a red Philco table radio, about the size of a toaster. It was AM only, and it pulled in only three or four stations decently. An additional few stations, inexplicably and excitingly distant, came in at night.

The other source was a compact brown record player with a grainy fabric cover and sturdy handle that made it look like a miniature suitcase. Its turntable was covered in a fine dark fuzz, bits of which came off on your hand, and its bronze-colored tone arm was so heavy that after playing a record there would sometimes be a tiny black ball of wax on the needle. It played only 78s.

Both the radio and the record player resided in the bedroom I shared with my brother, five years older than I.

There is no TV in these early memories, my parents having taken a solemn stand against it. They caved in in 1955, but by this time my habit of listening—listening as a daily, ritualized communion with the outside world—was already established.

The early fifties, of course, are widely scorned today as a musical dry spell, an arid little bridge between the end of the swing era and the arrival of Elvis.

The period did produce its stinkers. And there may even be, as some claim, a distinctive early-Eisenhower blandness to such specimens as, say, Jo Stafford's "Shrimp Boats" or "The Naughty Lady of Shady Lane" by the Ames Brothers, or the Four Aces' adenoidal treatment of "Perfidia." (To give this last tune its due, it did teach me the meaning of the word "perfidious.")

But for a small boy devoted to listening, the era was golden.

One of Schenectady's radio stations had an early evening program that played tunes from the recently-departed big band era. I gratefully absorbed "Frenesi" and "Take the A Train" and "I've Got a Gal in Kalamazoo."

The Broadway musical, which had taken its modern form in 1943 with *Oklahoma*, was in full flower. Show tunes seemed just to be in the air, somehow—my kindergarten teacher taught the class "Getting to Know You" and "Dites Moi," but we already knew them anyway.

The last of the radio serials were still hanging on, and though I don't remember the stories, I remember the music: the portentous organ theme heralding "One Man's Family," the lonely clip-clop theme from "Gunsmoke."

And even the now-maligned mainstream pop music of the day— the square, safe music that a sheltered white kid huddled close to his table radio would routinely encounter—had something to say for itself.

I was haunted, for instance, by the song "I Worry and Wonder," the theme from the movie *Moulin Rouge*. The melody gave off exotic, worldly vibes, and the vocalist on Percy Faith's 1954 recording, a smoky-voiced mezzo named Felicia Sanders, awakened in me a complex web of feelings, only some of which were musical.

"Worry and Wonder," I learned from a book about composers, had been written by a Frenchman named Georges Auric, who had belonged to the Paris-based group known as Les Six. This was a pleasing thought: a serious composer writing a sexy hit song.

The Chordettes' version of "Mr. Sandman" made a deep impression. I can no longer summon exactly what it was that so thrilled me about these close-harmonizing women and their plea for companionship. I can remember that, in one of the verses, they put the melody in the middle of the chord, rather than on the top. Not that I, at age six, figured this out for myself—credit for the observation goes to Earl Pudney, one of the more esteemed of Schenectady's radio personalities. Pudney, who moonlighted as a lounge pianist, dispensed musical opinion and information on his radio show. It was Earl who pointed out the unusual major-minor relationships in "Let's Face the Music and Dance," and who ventured that "All the Things You Are," with its elegant cycle of falling-seventh chords, might be the most structurally sophisticated of all pop tunes.

The repertoire on Earl's station was quaintly inclusive. A show tune, say, "People Will Say We're in Love," might be followed by a light orchestral piece like Leroy Anderson's "Blue Tango," which might be followed, irritatingly, by a novelty number like "How Much Is That Doggie in the Window."

There were, to be sure, some elements missing from Earl's mix. Late at night, spinning the radio dial, I would sometimes be transfixed by a sound from some far-away city, a sound like Ivory Joe Hunter singing his "I Almost Lost My Mind," or Lloyd Price doing "Lawdy, Miss Clawdy." Black rhythm-and-blues artists had not yet broken into the Schenectady playlist.

The late-night dial casting might also yield an occasional whiff of new jazz, of Miles Davis or Charlie Parker. These were rare moments, though. Jazz was already being pushed to the margins of radio and one result was that I never really formed a solid bond with it, to my embarrassment and regret.

Whatever music there was arrived in an undifferentiated mass. Before narrowly drawn "formats" carved radio into ever thinner slices, it all poured out as one. I have a friend who owns a jukebox, circa 1954, that used to stand in the corner of a Schenectady pizzeria. Among its tunes:

"Wish You Were Here," Eddie Fisher;
"Your Cheatin' Heart," Hank Williams and His Drifting Cowboys;
"Glow Worm," the Mills Brothers; and
"Stranger in Paradise," Tony Bennett.

Note the diversity: a middle-of-the-road crooner doing a Broadway tune; a country singer singing his own composition; a black family act then into its third decade in the business; a nightclub singer doing a song adapted, as was often done in the pre-rock era, from a classical piece, in this case Borodin's "Polovtsian Dances." In my zeal, I had these songs down cold before I could do long division.

If the red radio furnished a random survey course, the record player was a more purposeful thing.

This was still a time when a relationship with classical music was considered desirable among, to use my mother's well-intentioned term, "cultivated" people. Children of striving middle-class families were expected to have some "exposure" to "good" music, in the same way that they were expected to pick up the rudiments of ballroom dancing.

My own exposure—the crucial first taste—came from a series of records called *The Children's Treasury of Music,* put out by RCA Victor.

I still have them. The heavy old 78s, with their burnished maroon labels, are objects of hilarity to my three school-age daughters, each of whom, even the eight-year-old, has a Sony CD boombox in her room.

I have tried, on one or two shrill occasions, to convey to the girls the idea that these black discs, massive and fragile as dinner plates, were as magically transporting to me as their silvery digital wafers are to them. This is literally true, of course: Not once did it ever occur to me that the fidelity of my records was somehow inadequate. Who imagined they could be any better? In fact, as I talk to people who go back to the pre-hi-fi age, I become increasingly convinced that the sheer effort we all had to make to distill the music from the scratches and the clicks and oceans of distortion actually sharpened our receptive, pathetically forgiving ears.

The musical sections on the *Children's Treasury* were chosen by a panel of experts, headed by one George Marek, identified as holding the unstressful-sounding position of Music Editor of *Good Housekeeping* magazine. Marek concedes, in the lengthy liner notes, that the task of choosing classical music for children is "unscientific."

"In music, as well as in books or pictures, one child's sweet is another child's spinach," Marek writes. Nevertheless, he promises, the selections on these particular records "will be attractive to the modern child at first hearing."

He was only partly right.

Wagner's "Entrance of the Gods into Valhalla" from *Das Rheingold* was not attractive to this child at first or any subsequent hearing. I should be, but am not, ashamed to say that my unenthusiasm for Wagner extends to this day.

I didn't like the excerpt from Berlioz's *Damnation of Faust*, either.

On the other hand I fell heavily for "The Skater's Waltz" by Walteufel, the Barcarolle from Offenbach's *Tales of Hoffmann*, and the Overture to *The Barber of Seville* by Rossini.

And I formed a crazy, almost spiritual attachment to a little piece by Jaromir Weinberger, the jaunty Polka and Fugue from his opera *Schwanda*. Though the opera never got very popular outside Weinberger's native Czechoslovakia, this excerpt was once a fairly common item on light concert programs a generation or two ago. It now seems to have all but disappeared. In a lifetime of concert-going I have only heard it performed live once, about ten years ago, played by the Philadelphia Orchestra and conducted by Eugene Ormandy. Ormandy, then nearly at the end of his career, got lost in the fugue and the piece nearly broke down.

I played the Polka and Fugue incessantly on the brown record player. As the record spun, I would wonder about the composer Weinberger, about whom nobody seemed to know anything. I read many years later that he had moved to the United States and had settled in a suburb of St. Petersburg, Florida. As it happens, it was the same community that my maternal grandparents had retired to. During my childhood, we visited them down there a number of times. Is it possible that I might have seen Weinberger during one of these visits? Might I have passed him on the street, the composer of *Schwanda*, or seen him at the beach? Might he have been cheered by a visit from a music-struck, head-in-the-clouds kid telling him about his obsession with the Polka and Fugue? The thought tugs at me from time to time. The books tell us that Weinberger, despondent over the obscurity of his later years, committed suicide in 1967.

There were, strange to say, rather few actual children's records in my little collection.

I had some disks of songs from the movie *Hans Christian Andersen*, with Danny Kaye. Of these, the bouncy and ingenious "Wonderful Copenhagen" was the clear favorite.

This must have led to a request for more Danny Kaye material, because there appeared a few additional records. God knows what I made of lyrics like:

> I'm Anatole of Paris,
> I reek with chic,
> My hat of the week,
> Caused six divorces, three runaway horses . . .

And there was a Disney version of "The Grasshopper and the Ants." This was one of the early examples of the read-along-with-the-record combos, and I think about it every so often because it contained a much-loved song called, "The World Owes Me a Living." It was sung by the delinquent grasshopper as he watched the ants preparing for winter, and I believe the voice of the grasshopper belonged to the same person who did the voice of Goofy. But I can't be sure of this, and even the melody of the song is slipping away from me now because the record is long out of print and has never been reissued as far as I know. A song lost forever, I fear.

My little stack of records, along with the radio, had come to cast a comfortable kind of spell over my dreamy but unexceptional childhood.

In 1956, when I was eight, two things happened to break the spell.

First, one summer night, when I was doing my customary late-night spin of the radio dial, I landed on a song that stopped me cold, like it was from Mars. It felt like it was constructed entirely of rhythm. It was "Speedo," by the Cadillacs.

This song has, in the intervening decades, come to be seen as an endearing, defining specimen of the rock 'n' roll sub-genre called doo-wop; it's hard to imagine that it ever sounded revolutionary.

The song was not my first encounter with rock 'n' roll. I was aware of Elvis, and recall being especially impressed by "I Want You I Need

You I Love You." I know I had heard and admired "Eddie My Love" by the Teen Queens. Bill Haley's "Rock Around the Clock," for some reason, had made a negligible impression.

But "Speedo" somehow suggested a new definition of what music might be, and what it could do to you. For what it's worth, I didn't have the slightest idea that the Cadillacs were black.

The second thing happened a few months later at Christmas. My brother and I got, as a joint present, a new Zenith portable record player. It was a burnt-orange color with white trim, giving it, I thought, a sharp two-tone look like certain cars of the period.

Like those cars, the Zenith was hideous, and it was beautiful. The grille-cloth, a loud plaid flecked with shiny gold thread, concealed a five- or six-inch speaker that would furnish unheard-of sonic richness.

But the main thing about the Zenith, the crucial feature, was that it would play 45s.

Forty-fives had been in currency for three or four years, but frustratingly, had yet to make their appearance in our household. Most of my friends' households already had them. Forty-fives were what the new music was available on; 45s were the future.

Miraculously, they were also affordable—89 cents at Apex Music Korner, the crowded downtown Schenectady record store where you could listen to a record in a glass-walled booth before you bought.

With the arrival of the Zenith, I would at last be joining the company of record buyers, and as I saw it, of modern, with-it people generally.

Easing the Christmas ribbon off the Zenith's vinyl-covered lid, I felt, correctly as it turned out, that I was stepping into a new age.

INDIRA GANESAN

Musical Heroes: A Memoir

I listen to Tracey Chapman and am lost. At dusk, when I begin to turn on lights in the house and I face a meal alone, I turn to Tracey Chapman and am companioned. This singer, educated at Tufts and singing with an acoustic guitar, fills my room with sound. She sings about the police and domestic violence, shelters and poor people's revolutions, but she also sings about love. She uses words like *baby, baby,* and I am filled with longing. I light candles, set my place, eat and listen. I do the dishes. Of course I sing along:

> Careful of my heart
> This time, I'm going to be my own best friend
> But you can say, baby, can I hold you tonight?

There are other singers who serenade my heart with pure pop melodies. Joni Mitchell is a fine accompaniment to rain. Anita Baker. Joan Baez, who in my mind will always be in love with Bob Dylan who doesn't love her back. I sip my wine and ally myself with her and salute women the world over.

Other times require different music. There's the kind you need to shake your toes. I flip on MTV and see young girls in hip-hop clothing with delicious hair who clown around and ask the camera, "What about your friends?" There's Janet and Madonna and Salt n' Peppa chanting and chiding, saying, girl, wake up, join in the dance. Singers as teaches, as life promoters, who say, look I'll mouth these words and have some fun, and by all means, join in.

Heroes are a funny thing. Growing up Indian in a white society, an Asian in America, I remember liking Snow White because she had black hair. Black as ebony comforted me, despite the chants of "brownie" on the bus, and being asked, "Are you Jewish? Are you Catholic? Are you Puerto Rican?" At school, groups consulted one another on the TV shows watched last night, the records one bought. Forbidden by parents to watch "The Partridge Family" because there was too much kissing on the screen, I cut out Jackson Five discs from the back of cereal boxes and grooved to Motown. *LIFE* magazine published a picture of Michael, Marlon, Tito, Jermaine, and Jackie with their parents by their swimming pool and my parents approved.

Then I learned to close the door to my room and listen to the radio. I discovered the oldies station and the Beatles. I fell in love with George Harrison who fell in love with India, so in a sense, loved me. Searching for secrets in liner notes, reading *Rolling Stone,* deciphering lyrics, I tried to find out the clues to American life, the codes to dating and sex. My parents had emigrated to the States, thinking to take part in Kennedy's Camelot; instead, they found assassinations and social upheaval. Why can't I be like my friends, I wailed, wanting to hang out at the mall, at the movies? So I bought more records and listened to Alternative Rock on the radio. Denied the prom, I exchanged tapes with other dateless souls and dreamed of college.

My parents had other plans. Off I went to India with twelve TDK cassettes, determined not to lose touch with music. For a year, I listened to this prerecorded music, which included the soundtrack from *Hair,* and attempted to change the consciousness of my Indian friends who liked the Bee-Gees. Finally, I went to see *Saturday Night Fever,* a censored version, and became converted to disco. How was I to know that a continent away, punk and new wave were breaking down the barriers of old multi-layered rock and roll?

While in India, I began to question my own identity. Was it Indian or American? What group did I belong to? I began to listen to new music, trying on the new clothes of attitude. Like so many others, I began to wear black and listen to minimal sounds, the avant garde, while still sticking to the borders of pop music. I became a fan of The Talking Heads. I decided to become a writer while I secretly yearned to be a singer. I wanted to move audiences the way music moved me. While in college, I listened to a reading by Nikki Giovanni and was astonished to discover that her audience demanded she recite their favorite poems as if she were a rock and roll band.

Naturally, I became a DJ. From six to nine on Monday mornings I had a show on community radio on Cape Cod. At eight, after a few hours of lilting folk, I'd play Blondie, the B-52's, The Jacksons, Patti Smith. I'd play reggae and blues, even a little country, trying to forge a musical identity, a voice. I'd play sets of songs around a theme like my favorite DJs in the seventies had, I'd celebrate revolutions and love.

When a boyfriend unkindly dumped me, I played an entire set to describe my loss, words and sound meant for him alone. And still I wondered who I was. Was I white or black or brown, hetero or gay, cool or uncool? Should I stick to one kind of sound or embrace a world music eclecticism?

My brother, who is more hip than I'll ever be, these days describes himself as Indo-African. He tells me to listen to *Fear of a Black Planet* and listen to the words. I wonder, where is the melody? and retreat to my more familiar world of pop tunes, things recognizable. I don't ignore my own roots and listen to Revi Shankar and Zakir Huessein and popular Hindi film music when I'm feeling sentimental. We're living in a time when music is undergoing tremendous change and crossover. Music is funkier now than when I was growing up, and it's no longer a white man's world.

Recently I visited a Hindu temple in New Jersey with some Indian friends and family. After praying to the gods, we crowded into the gift shop to look at the CDs being offered for sale next to the bangles and miniature idols. My young friend Shuba, a college student who travels to India constantly to study classical dance, who wears a nosering, suggested some new names to me. Mandolin Srinivas, a child prodigy who makes sitar-like sounds out of an electric mandolin. He's performed at my cousin's wedding, and I can only imagine the scene. Later, we went to the local Sam Goody's and selected some Brazilian music to take home.

That weekend I watched *A Man and a Woman (Un Homme et une Femme)* on television, and listened again as a Frenchman praised the samba. Here was interculturalism, here was appropriation, here was a celebration of color, here was a proud and humble song thanking the makers of samba, saluting genius. These days, I am no longer a DJ but I still passionately listen to music. I switch songs to suit my mood and no longer worry about questions of identity. At least, not all the time. Music still comforts me and rallies my spirits. It always will.

JEANNE WILMOT CARTER

Dancing Lessons

When I see the young white girls jumping up and down like pogo sticks or slamming or moshing to Nirvana, I wonder about how they move with their boys. Alan Lomax said that cultures and peoples move differently—some one-dimensionally, others two, and yet others in full three dimension, capable of making movements with their head, neck, and shoulders simultaneous with, yet in opposite direction to, the motions of the rest of the body at that moment. I might have remained in the one-dimensional culture had I not witnessed Tina Turner early enough for imprinting. Growing up in Kansas City, I learned the true riff down on Paseo Boulevard and Troost where the clubs shrieked their blues and soul. We'd sneak out of our air-conditioned bedrooms, meet our boyfriends two streets over so our parents wouldn't hear their Porsches on the cool isolated suburban street, and make it to the club where Betty Carter or Miles or Bobby Blue Bland or even James and Maceo were playing.

Never having been initiated into the rhythms of the tribe on my mother's back in the bleating Mesopotamian sun as she rhythmically planted rows of cassava root or vegetable tubers, nor having lived early years as a papoose, all I could do as a girlchild was to watch, like a duck, those women around me for cues, while flexing the rhythm in my pelvis secretly. I learned about passion and romance in front of my father's state-of-the-art high fidelity unit where nightly I would belt out "Tu, che di gel sei cinta" with Maria Callas. In my life, the physical was separated from the soul—not an uncommon condition in Anglo-Saxon culture—until I was about nine, when I first saw Tina "shake a tail feather." My soul had finally found a physical form and I learned as best I could. *Listen*, Tina said. *There's this sound and if you were Sound, this would be yours.* Its soft excitement is reminiscent of hot weather, summer nights. A girl swaying, hips one way, arms the other, to this sound, on a stoop up on St. Nicholas, say, around 143rd. It's a city sound, it's dancing subway-close, balanced shoulders high and subtle as the rhythm comes from the radio, Smokey or Curtis, maybe even Clyde in the old days. Or it grinds like the moving knees and groins of one against an-other, one life against another's, somebody else's blues causing yours. Solomon Burke or Ike with Earl "Two Bugs and a Roach" Hooker on a three-chord pump. Or it's screamed country-style, with Etta James or Big Maybelle crying, "Tell mama."

From that moment onward, as I stood alone in the center of my darkened bedroom listening to Patti Labelle and the Blue Bells singing "I Sold My Heart To The Junkman" or the beloved Annie Mae Bul-lock née Tina Turner roaring "When I was just a little girl...," I would just disappear into the Sound and Tina's dance, and be only the movement in her hips, following the Sound through the bodies of all the Ikettes.

It is rock 'n' roll that makes America America. Plenty of people live this fact but aren't even conscious of it. Jazz is our classical music. It's just about the only art form America has given to the rest of the world that is intrinsic to our folks—which is to say, those of our folks who are black folks. From gospel came the blues and jazz and rhythm and blues and rock 'n' roll. Through music that permeated the national consciousness by periodic and perceptible alteration so that every cul-ture in America openly embraced it, came the contemporary culture of the latter half of the twentieth century—the first world culture. We were all defined by its language, its dress, its expectations—and yes, its sexu-ality. And with a history like that of early American, filled with witch-hunts and Calvinists and the puritanical approach to sexuality, we white folks didn't have the romantic tradition of the Romans or the pru-rient tradition of the French or the passionate tradition of the Spanish passion. So while black Americans created role models for themselves, since they knew white America in ways that white America did not know itself, Chuck Berry and Tina Turner and Darlene Love and the Crystals and the Ronettes and later Marvin Gaye and others did it for white folks, too. Tina donned a straight-hair wig, the Ikettes followed suit, and they instructed us girls to bend over and shake a tail feather, and then they showed us all how to do it. They shared their passion and artistry with us, yet tragically we did not share the income stream from their music with them. We had no soul.

Some of us were given a second chance on that score nonetheless. Back in my darkened bedroom, I leaned over and turned my hips in a way that had not occurred to me before seeing Tina. And it worked. They could move like Tina's. In fact I seemed to work just like Tina did. The magic was in the desire to do it that way, not just the ability.

Maybe that desire was a kind of "soul." I switched on my turntable, walked to the center of the room and stood, back held straight with slightly elevated shoulders. And I spread my legs and placed them firmly in the Tina-stance. I wore the squash heels of those days, not yet old enough to be allowed to purchase spikes—like Tina's. Once my legs were rooted—my feet not exactly parallel, but separated wide enough to intimate sensuality was soon to follow—my hips loosened as if the joints were unlocked, and my knees took up the slack by sliding into an ever-so-slightly-bent-knee attitude. I felt an opening in my body. It was natural—my body was opening in places that should never have been closed. My hips moved. They startled me at first because they moved so like Tina's. It was not like learning a complicated dance step. It was like being a gifted vocalist with the range of Ima Sumak; all I needed was the structure of the song for my voice to fall into—the gift could accomplish the rest. It was natural, with the slightest touch of guidance— as long as the urgency was there. And my hips quickened. With the rolling motion being controlled by a central metronome in my body which monitored direction and rhythm, I maintained the pace. I sped it up until I was rotating like a demon, sideways, to the front, around the world. Sophistication and age—that cool distance—would teach the proper pace. I could be an expert in no time. I would be a certain kind of woman—I knew it then. I would feel at home in my body's dailiness, in all of its intents. Like a professional athlete, I would be a professional woman. It felt good.

I learned every move Tina had done the first night I saw her playing in that club in Kansas City. And I taught all my friends. Then we got her to play at one of the junior dances or proms at our school—a small private girls' school with a large budget for its students—which gave me the chance to dance for Tina, to show her what she'd given me.

I still dance to Tina—often late at night in the darkened living room of my home, alone—but now with a baby in my belly. As I wait for my little girl to be born, I dance tough—to Tina and Patti and the Pointers, to Gloria and Janet and Darlene. My girl's not going to wait till she's the age I was when I first learned to move to Tina's Sound. She's coming out dancing like Tina. I feel my strength when I dance, like the strength I had when I was a teenager, that terrible hardness that promises us immortality, not like Scriabin's where the Mysterium would swoop us up and make us all one, but like Tina's, where our individual experiences are so vividly a part of reality that time has become irrelevant.

VII

FEDERICO GARCÍA LORCA

TRANSLATED BY CHRISTOPHER MAURER

Cante Jondo

February 19, 1922

You have gathered tonight in the salon of the Centro Artístico de Granada to hear my humble but sincere word, and I would like to be so luminous and profound as to convince you of the marvelous artistic truth to be found in the primitive Andalusian music called *cante jondo*.

The intellectuals and enthusiastic friends who are backing the idea of this reunion are sounding an alarm. Gentlemen, the musical soul of our people is in great danger! The artistic treasure of an entire race is passing into oblivion. Each day another leaf falls from the admirable tree of Andalusian lyrics, old men carry off to the grave the priceless treasures of past generations, and a gross, stupid avalanche of cheap music clouds the clear folk atmosphere of all Spain.

We are trying to do something worthy and patriotic—a labor of salvation, friendship, and love.

You have all heard speak of *cante jondo* and surely you all have some idea what it is. But to all of you who are not aware of its historical and artistic transcendence, it almost certainly evokes immoral things, the tavern, rowdy parties, the café dance floor, and all that is "typically Spanish." We must guard against this, for the sake of Andalusia, our millennial spirit, and each of our own hearts.

It does not seem possible that the most emotional, the deepest songs of our mysterious soul should be maligned as being debauched and dirty; that people should insist upon consigning to the drunken brawl this art that ties us to the impenetrable Orient; that they should pour the wine of the professional pimp onto the most diamantine part of our song.

And so the time has come for Spanish musicians, composers, poets, and artists to unite their voices in an instinct of conservation, in order to define and exalt the limpid beauty and suggestiveness of these songs.

To confuse the patriotic and artistic ideals of this undertaking with the lamentable, familiar vision of the *cantaor* [singer] with his little tapstick and his vulgar wailing about cemeteries would show a total lack of understanding of what has been planned. On reading the announcements for this festival, every sensible man who is uninformed about the matter will say to himself: "What is *cante jondo?*"

Before going ahead we ought to make a special distinction between *cante jondo* and Flamenco song—an essential distinction based on their relative antiquity, structure, and spirit.

The name *cante jondo* is given to a group of Andalusian songs whose genuine, perfect prototype is the Gypsy *siguiriya* [seguidilla], from which are derived other songs still conserved by the people—*polos, martinetes, carceleras,* and *soleares.* The songs called *malagueñas, granadinas, rondeñas, peteneras,* etc. must be considered only as offshoots of the songs cited above, for they differ both in architecture and rhythm. These latter songs constitute the so-called Flamenco repertory.

The great maestro Manuel de Falla, a true glory of Spain and the soul of this undertaking, believes that in their primitive style the *caña* and the *playera* (today almost nonexistent) have the same composition as the *siguiriya* and its related forms, and that not too long ago they were its simple variants. Estebanez Calderón, in his lovely *Escenas Andaluces,* notes that the *caña* is the primitive trunk of the songs of Arab and Moorish filiation, and he observes with characteristic keen-sightedness that the word *caña* much resembles the word *rhounia,* which is Arabic for "song."

The essential difference between *cante jondo* and Flamenco is that the origins of the former must be sought in the primitive musical systems of India—in the very first manifestations of song—while Flamenco (a consequence of *cante jondo*) did not acquire its definitive form until the eighteenth century.

Cante jondo is imbued with the mysterious color of primordial ages; Flamenco is relatively modern song, whose emotional interest fades before that of *cante jondo.* Local color versus spiritual color—this is the profound difference.

Like the primitive Indian musical systems, *cante jondo* is actually a stammering, a wavering emission of the voice, a wonderful buccal undulation that smashes the sonorous cells of our tempered scale, bypasses the cold, rigid staves of contemporary music, and makes the tightly shut flowers of the semitones open to reveal a thousand petals.

Flamenco does not proceed by undulation but by leaps. Its rhythm is as sure as that of our own music, and it was born centuries after Guido d'Arezzo had named the notes.

Cante jondo is akin to the trilling of birds, the song of the rooster, and the natural music of the forest and the fountain.

It is a very rare example of primitive song—the oldest example in all Europe, and its notes carry the naked, spine-tingling emotion of the first Oriental races.

Maestro Falla, who has made a profound study of the matter, on which I document my own work, affirms that the Gypsy *siguiriya* is the prototype of *cante jondo*, and he roundly declares that it is perhaps the only genre of song on our continent that has conserved in all its purity (both structurally and stylistically) the profoundest qualities of the primitive songs of Oriental peoples.

But even before I knew of the Maestro's opinion, *cante jondo* had always evoked (in me, the incurable lyric) and endless road, a road without crossroads, ending at the palpitating fountain of the childhood of poetry, the road where the first bird died and where the first arrow grew rusty.

The Gypsy *siguiriya* begins with a terrible cry that divides the landscape into two ideal hemispheres. It is the scream of dead generations, a poignant elegy for lost centuries, the pathetic evocation of love under other moons and other winds.

Afterwards the melodic phrase begins to pry open the mystery of the tones, and to extract from them the sob within, that audible tear falling onto the river of the voice. No Andalusian can help but shiver upon hearing that [initial] cry, nor can any regional song be compared to this in poetic greatness: seldom—very seldom—has the human spirit managed to create art of that sort.

Do not think that the *siguiriya* and its variants are simply songs transplanted from the Orient to the West. Rather, Falla says:

> It is a matter of graft or, better said, of a coincidence of origins, and certainly it was not revealed all at once, but grew from an accumulation of secular, historical events that developed on our peninsula. Thus it is that the song of Andalusia, though essentially like that of a people geographically remote from us, possesses its own intimate, unmistakable, national character.

The historical events which Falla says have influenced our songs are threefold: the Spanish Church's adoption of Byzantine liturgical chant, the Saracen invasion, and the arrival in Spain of numerous bands of Gypsies, the mysterious roving folk who gave *cante jondo* its definitive form.

The Gypsy influence is attested to by the denomination "Gypsy" *siguiriya*, and by the extraordinary number of Caló words in the texts of the songs.

Not that this chant is purely Gypsy: Gypsies live all over Europe as well as in other regions of the peninsula, but these songs are cultivated only by ours.

It is a purely Andalusian chant, which flourished in this region before the Gypsies came.

The maestro notes these similarities between the essential elements of *cante jondo* and those still extant in certain songs of India: enharmonic modulation, melody that is usually restricted to the compass of a sixth, and the reiterative, almost obsessive use of one same note, a procedure proper to certain formulas of incantation, including recited ones we might call prehistoric and which have made some people suppose that song is older than language. In this way, *cante jondo*, especially the *siguiriya*, gives the impression of being sung prose, all sense of metric rhythm destroyed, though in fact its literary texts are assonant tercets or quatrains.

According to Falla:

> Though gypsy melody is rich in ornamental turns, in it—as in the primitive Oriental songs—they are used only at certain moments, like expansions or sudden gusts of expression suggested by the emotive strength of the poem, and we must think of them more as ample vocal inflexions than as ornamental turns, though they resemble the latter on being translated into the geometric intervals of the tempered scale.

One can say with certainty that in *cante jondo*, just as in the songs of the heart of Asia, the musical gamut is a direct consequence of what we might call the oral gamut.

Many authors suppose that word and song were once the same thing, and Louis Lucas, in his *Acoustique nouvelle* (Paris, 1840) says, while treating of the excellence of the enharmonic genre, "it is the first which appears in Nature, through the imitation of birdsong, the cries of animals, and the infinite sounds of matter."

Hugo Riemann, in his *Musical Aesthetics*, affirms that the song of birds is close to being true music and cannot be treated differently than the song of men, insofar as both are the expression of sensibilities.

The great maestro Felipe Pedrell, one of the first Spaniards to study folklore scientifically, writes in his magnificent *Cancionero Popular Español:*

> Musical orientalism persists in various popular Spanish songs and is deeply rooted in our nation owing to the influence of the ancient Byzantine civilization upon the ritual formulas of the Spanish Church. This influence persisted from the conversion of our country to Christianity until the eleventh century, when the Roman liturgy . . . was introduced.

Falla adds to what his old teacher has said, ascertaining that the elements of Byzantine chant also present in the *siguiriya* consist of: the tonal modes of primitive systems (not to be confused with the so-called Greek ones); the enharmonism inherent in those modes; and the melodic line's lack of metric rhythm.

These properties also characterize certain Andalusian songs whose origin was much later than the Spanish Church's adoption of Byzantine liturgical music, and which are closely akin to the music that in Morocco, Algeria, and Tunisia is still called (this will move all true Granadans) "music of the Moors of Granada."

With his solid musical knowledge and exquisite intuition, Manuel de Falla has found in the *siguiriya* "certain forms and characteristics" uninfluenced by sacred chant or by the "music of the Moors." That is, having examined the strange melody of *cante jondo*, Falla has detected an extraordinary agglutinative Gypsy element. He accepts the historical thesis that gives the Gypsies an Indic origin; and that thesis seems marvelously to fit the results of his fascinating research.

According to the thesis, in the year 1400 of our era, the Gypsies, pursued by the 100,000 horsemen of the great Tamerlane, fled from India.

Twenty years later these tribes appear in different cities of Europe and enter Spain with the Saracen armies then periodically arriving (from Egypt and Arabia) on our coasts.

On arriving in Andalusia, these Gypsies combined ancient indigenous elements with what they themselves brought, and gave what we now call *cante jondo* its definitive form.

So it is to them we owe the creation of these songs, soul of our soul.

We owe the Gypsies the building of these lyric channels through which all the pain, all the ritual gestures of the race can escape.

And these are the songs, gentlemen, that for over fifty years Spaniards have wanted to confine to fetid taverns and brothels. The incredulous, terrible epoch of the Spanish zarzuela, the epoch of Grilo and of historical paintings, is to blame. While Russia burned with love for folklore—the one source, as Robert Schumann once said, of all true, characteristic art—and while the gilded wave of Impressionism trembled in France, in Spain (a country almost unique in her tradition of popular beauty) the guitar and *cante jondo* were scorned.

The prejudice has become so widespread that we must now raise our voices in defense of these songs so pure and so true.

This is the way the spiritual youth of Spain understands it.

Cultivated since time immemorial, the *cante jondo*'s profound psalmody has moved every illustrious traveler who ever ventured across our varied, strange landscapes. From the peaks of the Sierra Nevada to the thirsty olive groves of Córdoba—from the Sierra de Cazorla to the fair delta of the Guadalquivir, *cante jondo* has traversed and defined our unique, complicated land of Andalusia.

From the time when Jovellanos called attention to the lovely, incoherent *danza prima* of Asturias till the time of the formidable Menendez Pelayo, much progress was made in understanding folklore. Isolated artists, minor poets have studied folkloric questions from different points of view until at last they have managed to get under way a useful, patriotic compilation of poems and songs. Evidence of this are the Songbook of Burgos, by Federico Olmeda; the Songbook of Salamanca, of Damaso Ledesma; and Eduardo Martinez Torner's Songbook of Asturias, generously financed by the respective provincial governments.

But the way we can really gauge the importance of *cante jondo* is by its almost decisive influence on the formation of the modern Russian school, and by the high esteem in which it was held by Claude Debussy, that lyric argonaut, discoverer of a new musical world.

In 1845 Mikhail Ivanovich Glinka came to Granada. He had been in Berlin studying composition with Siegfried Dehn and had observed the musical patriotism of Weber struggling against the pernicious influence of the Italian composers in Germany. Glinka was much impressed with the songs of Russia, immense Russia, and he dreamed of a natural music, a national music which would convey the sensation of her grandeur.

The visit to our city of the father and founder of the Slavic-Orientalist school is most curious.

He made friends with a celebrated guitarist of those days, Francisco Rodriguez Murciano, from whom, for hours on end, he heard the variations and *falsetas* of our songs, and amid the eternal rhythm of our city's waters he conceived the magnificent idea of creating his school, and found the courage to use, for the first time, the whole-tone scale.

On returning to his people he announced the good news, explained the peculiarities of our songs, and studied and employed them in his music.

Music changes direction: the composer has at last discovered its true source!

Glinka's friends and disciples turn to folklore and seek structures for their creations not only in Russia but in the south of Spain.

Proof of this are Glinka's "Souvenirs d'une nuit d'été à Madrid" and parts of the "Scheherezade" and the "Capriccio Espagnol" of Nikolai Rimski-Korsakov, pieces you know.

Thus the sad modulations and sober orientalism of our chant reached from Granada to Moscow, and the melancholy of the Vela is recaptured by the Kremlin's mysterious bells.

At the Spanish pavilion of the great Paris Exhibition of 1900, a group of Gypsies sang the *cante jondo* in all its purity. They startled the whole city, but especially a young composer who was then engaged in the terrible fight we young artists must all carry on—the struggle for what is new and unforeseen, the treasure hunt, in the sea of thought, for untouched emotion.

Day after day that young man went to hear the Andalusian *cantaores,* and he whose soul was wide open to the four winds of the spirit was soon made pregnant by the ancient Orient of our melodies. He was Claude Debussy.

With the passage of time he was to formulate the new theories and become the high point of European musical culture.

Sure enough, from his compositions rise the subtlest evocations of Spain, above all of Granada, a city he knew for what it really is—paradise.

Claude Debussy, composer of fragrance and sensation, reaches his highest creative pitch in the poem "Ibéria," a truly genial work in which float, as through a dream, essences and suggestions of Andalusia.

But where he most exactly reveals how much he was influenced by *cante jondo* is in the marvelous prelude titled "La Puerta del Vino" and in the vague, tender "Soirée en Grenade" where, I think, one finds all the emotional themes of the Granadan night—the blue remoteness of the Vela, the sierra greeting the tremulous Mediterranean, the enormous barbs of the clouds sunk into the distance, the admirable rubato of the city, the fascinating play of its subterranean waters.

And the most remarkable thing about all this is that Debussy, though he seriously studied our song, never saw Granada. It is a stupendous case of artistic divination, of profound and brilliant intuition, which I mention in eulogy of the great composer and to the honor of our people.

It reminds me of the great mystic Swedenborg when, from London, he saw the burning of Stockholm; and of the profound prophecies of the saints of antiquity.

In Spain *cante jondo* has undeniably influenced all the best composers, from Albéniz through Granados to Falla. Felipe Pedrell had already used popular songs in his magnificent opera *La Celestina* (to our shame never performed in Spain), thus indicating the direction in which we were headed. But the master stroke was left to Isaac Albéniz, who used in his work the lyric depths of Andalusian song. Years later, Manuel de Falla fills his music with our motifs, beautiful and pure in their faraway spectral form. The latest generation of Spanish composers, like Adolfo Salazar, Roberto Gerard, Federico Mompou, and our Angel Barrios, enthusiastic organizers of this conference, are turning their attention to the pure revivifying font of *cante jondo* and to the delicious songs of Granada, songs that might well be called Castilian-Andalusian.

Notice, gentlemen, the transcendence of *cante jondo,* and how rightly our people named it "deep." It is deep, truly deep, deeper than all the wells and seas which surround the world, much deeper than the present-day heart that creates it or the voice that sings it, because it is almost infinite. It comes from distant races, reaching across the cemetery of the years and beyond the tips of the dry wind. It comes from the first sob, the first kiss.

One of the marvels of *cante jondo* (apart from its melody) consists in the choice of words for its texts.

We poets who in some degree are concerned with pruning and caring for the over-luxuriant lyric tree left to us by the Romantics and post-Romantics are astonished by these poems.

The finest gradations of sorrow and pain, in the service of the purest, most exact expression, pulse inside the tercets and quatrains of the *siguiriya* and its derivatives.

There is nothing, absolutely nothing in Spain to equal the *siguiriya* in style, atmosphere, and emotional rightness.

The metaphors that people the Andalusian songbook are almost always within the *siguiriya*'s orbit. The spiritual members of its verses are uniformly excellent, and take peremptory possession of our hearts.

It is marvelous and strange how the anonymous poet of the people can extract, in three or four lines, all the complexity of the deepest sentimental moments in a man's life. There are poems where the lyric tremor reaches a point inaccessible to any but a few a poets:

Cerco tiene la luna,
mi amor ha muerto.

The moon has a halo,
my love has died.

There is much more mystery in those two lines than in all the plays of Maeterlinck. Simple genuine mystery, clean and sound without dark forests or unpiloted ships. It is the living, eternal enigma of death:

The moon has a halo,
my love has died.

Whether they come from the heart of the sierra, the orange groves of Seville, or from the tranquil shores of the Mediterranean, the songs have common roots: love and death. But love and death as seen by the Sibyl, that most Oriental personage, the true sphinx of Andalusia.

At the bottom of all these poems lurks a terrible question that has no answer. Our people stretch out their hands in prayer, look at the stars, and vainly await a sign of salvation. The gesture is pathetic but true. And the poem either poses a deep emotional question that cannot be answered or solves it with death, which itself is the question of questions.

The greater part of the poems of Andalusia, except for certain of those born in Seville, possess those characteristics. We are a sad, static people.

As Ivan Turgenev saw his countrymen—Russian blood and marrow turned to sphinx—so do I see many poems of our regional folk poetry.

Sphinx of the Andalusians!

A mi puerta has de llamar,
no te he de salir a abrir
y me has de sentir llorar.

You will have to knock at the door,
there is no way I will answer.
and you will have to hear me crying.

Asleep behind an impenetrable veil, those lines await an Oedipus to come by to awaken and decipher them, and return them to silence. . . .

One of the most notable characteristics of the poems of *cante jondo* is their almost complete lack of a tone of moderation.

In the songs of Asturias, as in those of Castile, Catalonia, the Basque country, and Galicia, there is a certain emotional equilibrium, a lyrical meditation which lends itself to the expression of simple states of mind and ingenuous feeling, an equilibrium that is almost totally lacking in the Andalusian songs.

We Andalusians hardly ever use a moderate tone. The Andalusian is either shouting at the stars or kissing the red dust of the road. If there is a middle tone, he sleeps right through it. And when, uncharacteristically, he uses it, he says:

A mí se me importa poco
que un pájaro en la "alamea"
se pase un árbol a otro.

It hardly matters to *me*
that a bird in the poplar grove
hops from tree to tree.

—albeit, in this song, on account of its sentiment rather than its architecture, I detect Andalusian lineage. At any rate, patheticism is the strongest characteristic of *cante jondo*.

And so while many of the songs of our peninsula can make us see the landscapes where they are sun, *cante jondo* sings like a nightingale without eyes; it sings blind, and both its words and its ancient melodies are most beautifully set in the night—the blue night of our countryside.

The capacity for plastic evocation, shared among many popular Spanish songs, keeps them from the intimacy and profundity that characterize *cante jondo*.

One song in particular, among a thousand in the Asturian musical tradition, seems to typify that sort of evocation:

Ay de mí, perdí el camino
en esta triste montaña.
ay de mí, perdí el camino,
déxame meté l'rebañu
por Dios en la tu cabaña.
Entre la espesa flubina,
ay de mí, perdí el camino.
Déxame pasar la noche
en la cabaña contigo.
Perdí el camino
entre la niebla del monte,
ay de mí, perdí el camino.

Ay, I have lost the road
on this sad mountain.
Ay, I have lost the road,
let me bring the flock
for God's sake, into your cabin.
In the thick clouds
Alas, I have lost the road.
Let me spend the night
in the cabin with you.
I have lost the road
in the mist on the mountain.
Ay, I have lost the road.

It is so marvelous, this evocation of a mountain with the wind moving in its pine trees; so exact the sensation of the road climbing to the peaks where the snow is asleep; so true the sight of the mist coming up out of the abyss to blur the moist rocks in innumerable tones of gray—it is so marvelous that one forgets all about the "honest shepherd" who, like a child, asks shelter of the poem's unknown shepherd girl. One forgets the essence of the poem. The melody of this Asturian song, with its monotonous green-gray rhythm of misty landscapes, is an extraordinary help toward its visual evocation.

In contrast, *cante jondo* always sings in the night. It knows neither morning nor evening, neither mountains nor plains. It has nothing but the night, a wide night steeped in stars. Nothing else matters.

It is song without landscape, withdrawn into itself, terrible in the dark. *Cante jondo* shoots its golden arrows straight into our hearts. In the darkness it is a terrifying blue archer whose quiver is never empty.

The questions everybody asks—who made these poems? what anonymous poet tossed them onto the rude, popular stage?—these questions really have no answers.

In his book *Les origines de la poésie lyrique en France,* Jeanroy writes that "Popular art is not only an impersonal, vague, unconscious creation, it is also the 'personal' creation that the people take up and adapt to their own sensibility." Jeanroy is in part correct, but one need not be very perceptive to discover such [personal] creation in hiding, however savage the colors that camouflage it. Our people sing poems of Melchor del Palau, of Manuel Machado, of Salvador Rueda, Ventura Ruiz Aguilera and others, but what a difference between the verse of these poets and the poems the people created themselves. It is like the difference between a paper rose and a real one!

The poets who compose "popular" songs cloud the clear lymph of the true heart; how one notices, in their poems, the confident, ugly rhythm of the man who knows grammar!

Nothing more than the quintessence and this or that triplet for its coloristic effect should be taken directly from the people. We should never want to copy their ineffable modulations—we can do nothing but smear them. Simply because of education.

The true poems of *cante jondo* belong to no one—they float in the wind like golden thistledown, and each generation dresses them in a different color and abandons them to the next.

The true poems of *cante jondo* are, in substance, atop an ideal weathervane changing direction with the wind of Time.

They are born because they are born—one more tree in the landscape, one more rivulet in the poplar grove.

Woman, heart of the world and immortal keeper of the "rose, the lyre, and the harmonious science," looms on the infinite horizons of these poems. The woman of *cante jondo* is called sorrow.

It is admirable how sentiment begins to acquire form in lyrical constructions, quickening into an almost material thing. This is the case with sorrow.

In these poems grief is made flesh, takes human form and shows her profile; she is a dark woman wanting to catch birds in nets of wind.

The poems of *cante jondo* are magnificently pantheistic about the wind, the earth, the sea and moon, and things so simple as a violet, a fish, a bird. All exterior objects assume striking personality and even play active roles in the lyric action:

En mitá der "ma"
había una piedra
y se sentaba mi compañerita
a contarle sus penas.

Tan solamente a la Tierra
le cuento lo que me pasa
porque en el mundo no encuentro
persona e mi confianza.

Todas las mañanas voy
a preguntarle al romero
si el mal de amor tiene cura
porque yo me estoy muriendo.

In the middle of the sea
was a stone,
and my friend sat down
to tell it her troubles.

To the Earth alone
do I tell what has happened;
for in the world I find
no one I can trust.

Each morning I go
to ask the pilot-fish
if I can be cured of love,
for I am dying fast.

The Andalusian, with profoundest spiritual feeling, entrusts to Nature his entire intimate treasure, completely confident of being heard.

One feature of *cante jondo*, one admirable poetic reality, is the way the wind materializes in many of these songs.

The wind is a character who emerges in the ultimate, most emotional moments. He comes into sight like a giant absorbed in pulling down stars and scattering nebulae; and in no popular poetry but ours have I seen him talk and console:

Subí a la muralla;
me respondió el viento:
¿para qué tantos suspiritos
si ya no hay remedio?

El aire lloró
al ver las "duquitas" tan grandes
e mi corazón.

Yo me enamoré del aire,
del aire de una mujer,
como la mujer es aire,
en el aire me quedé.

Tengo celos del aire
que da en tu cara,
si el aire fuera hombre
yo lo matara.

Yo no le temo a remar,
que yo remar remaría,
yo solo temo al viento
que sale de tu bahía.

I climbed up the wall
and the wind answered
"why so many little sighs
if now there is no hope?"

The wind cried to see
the huge little pains
of my heart.

I fell in love with the air,
the air of a woman,
and since a woman is air
in the air did I stay.

I am jealous of the air
that touches your face,
and were it a man
I would kill him.

I'm not afraid to row.
If I had to row I would do it.
I'm only afraid of the air
that comes out of your bay.

It is a delicious peculiarity of these poems that they are tangled in
the immobile helix of the mariner's compass.

Another very special theme, one repeated in most of these songs, is
that of weeping.

In the Gypsy *siguiriya,* the perfect poem of tears, the melody sobs as
does the poetry. There are lost bells in the depths, windows wide open
to the dawn:

De noche me sargo ar patio,
y me jarto de llomá.
en ver que te quiero tanto
y tú no me quieres ná

Llorar, llorar, ojos míos,
llorar si tenéis por qué,
que no es verguenza en un hombre
llorar por una mujer.

Cuando me veas llorar
no me quites el pañuelo,
que mis penitas son grandes
y llorando me consuelo.

At night I go out in the courtyard
and have my fill of tears
to see that I love you so
and you love me not at all.

Cry, keep crying, eyes,
cry if you have cause;
it is no shame to a man
to cry about a woman.

When you see me crying
don't take away my handkerchief
my little pains are huge;
my crying consoles me.

And this last one, very Andalusian and very Gypsy:

Si mi corazón tuviera
birieritas e cristar,
te asomaras y lo vieras
gotas de sangre llorar.

If my heart had
little windowpanes of glass
you'd look in and see it
weeping drops of blood.

These songs have an unmistakably popular air and are, in my judgment, the ones best suited to the pathetic melancholy of *cante jondo*.

Their sadness is so irresistible, their emotive force so keen that they cause all true Andalusians to weep inwardly, with tears that wash the spirit and carry it away to the shining lemon grove of Love.

Nothing can compare with these songs in delicacy and tenderness, and I insist again that it is infamy simply to forget them or to impute to them base, sensual intentions or gross caricature. But that only happens in cities. Fortunately for the virgin whose name is Poetry and for all poets, there still exist sailors who sing at sea, women who rock their children to sleep in the shade of grapevines, churlish shepherds on mountain paths. The passionate wind of poetry will throw fuel on the vanishing fire, livening its flames, and these people will go on singing— the women in the shade of the grapevine, the shepherds on their rough paths, the sailors on the fecund rhythm of the sea.

Just as in the *siguiriya* and in its daughter-genres are to be found the most ancient Oriental elements, so in many poems of *cante jondo* there is an affinity to the oldest Oriental verse.

When our songs reach the extremes of pain and love they come very close in expression to the magnificent verses of Arab and Persian poets.

The truth is that in the air of Córdoba and Granada one still finds gestures and traces of remote Arabia, and that from the turbid palimpsest of the Albaicín arise memories of lost cities.

One finds the same themes of sacrifice, wine, and undying love expressed in the same spirit, as in the works of the Asiatic poets.

Siraj ed Din al Uarraq, an Egyptian poet, says:

The turtledove that, with her complaints,
keeps me from sleeping
has a breast like mine—
burning with living fire.

Ibn Zenati, another Arab poet, upon the death of his mistress, writes the same elegy that an Andalusian would have written:

To console me, my friends say,
"Visit your mistress' tomb."
"Has she a tomb," I answer,
"Other than in my breast?"

But where the resemblance is most striking of all is in the sublime amorous *ghazals* of Hafiz, national poet of Persia, who sang of wine, beautiful women, mysterious stones, and the infinite blue night of Shiraz.

In his *ghazals,* Hafiz displays various poetic obsessions, among them a preoccupation with the lock of hair:

Even if she did not love me
I would trade the whole orb of the earth
for one single hair from her tresses.

And he writes later:

My heart has been ensnared in your black tresses since childhood.
Not until death will a bond so wonderful be undone, nor effaced.

The same obsession with tresses is found in many examples of our singular *cante jondo*—poems full of allusions to locks of hair preserved in reliquaries and the curl on the forehead capable of provoking a whole tragedy.

This example, among many, demonstrates it. It is a *siguiriya:*

If I should happen to die, I order you,
tie up my hands
with the tresses of your black hair.

There is nothing more profoundly poetic than those three lines with their sad, aristocratic amorousness.

When Hafiz takes up the theme of weeping he uses the same expressions as our poet of the people, using the same spectral construction, and based on the same sentiments:

I weep endlessly, you are gone.
But what use is all my longing
if the wind will not carry my sighs to your ears?

is the same as:

Yo doy suspiros al aire,
¡ay pobrecito do mi!
y no los recoge nadie

I give my sighs to the wind
alas for me!
and nobody takes them.

Hafiz says:

Since you stopped listening to the echo of my voice,
my heart has been plunged in pain. It sends
burning jets of blood to my eyes.

And our poet:

Cada vez que miro el sitio
donde te he solido hablar,
comienzan mis pobres ojos
gotas de sangre a llorar.

Whenever I look at the place
where I used to talk to you
my poor eyes begin
weeping drops of blood.

Or this terrible poem, a *siguiriya*:

De aquellos quereres
no quiero acordarme
porque me llora mi corazoncito
gotas de sangre.

It was a love
I must not recall
or my little heart will weep
drops of blood.

In the 27th *ghazal*, the man of Shiraz sings:

> In the end my bones
> will be dust in the grave,
> but the soul will never be able
> to wipe away such a strong love.

which is exactly the same solution struck by countless poems of *cante jondo:* love is stronger than death.

And so I was deeply moved when I read these Asiatic poems (translated into Spanish by don Gaspar María de Nava and published in Paris in 1838) for they reminded me immediately of our own "deepest" poems.

Then too, the Andalusian singers of *siguiriyas* and the Oriental poets both praise wine. They praise the clear, relaxing wine that reminds one of women's lips—happy wine, quite unlike the frightening Baudelairian stuff. I will cite one song (I think it is a *martinete*) which is sung by a character who tells his Christian name and surname (a rare occurrence), and in whom I see the personification of all true Andalusian poets:

> *Yo me llamo Curro Pulla*
> *por la tierra y por el mar,*
> *y en la puerta de la tasca*
> *la piedra fundamental.*

> My name is Curro Pulla
> on the land and on the sea
> and I am the bottom stone in
> the portal of the tavern.

This is the greatest eulogy of wine in any of Curro Pulla's songs. Like the marvelous Omar Khayyám, he knew that

> My love will end,
> my grief will end,
> my tears will end,
> and all will end.

Crowning himself with the roses of the moment, he stares into a glass of nectar and sees a falling star. Like the grandiose bard of Nishapur, he perceives life to be a chessboard.

Gentlemen, *cante jondo*, both because of its melody and its poems, is one of the strongest popular creations in the world. In your hands is the task of conserving it and dignifying it, for the sake of Andalusia and her people.

Before bringing this poor, badly designed lecture to a close, I want to remember the marvelous singers thanks to whom *cante jondo* has come down to our day.

The figure of the *cantaor* is found between two great lines—the arc of the sky on the outside, and on the inside the zigzag that wanders snakelike through his soul.

When the *cantaor* sings he is celebrating a solemn ritual, as he rouses ancient forces from their sleep, wraps them in his voice, and flings them to the wind. His sense of song is a profoundly religious one. He sings at the most dramatic moments, never to amuse himself, as in the capework of the bullfight, but rather to fly, to evade, to suffer, to endow everyday existence with a supreme aesthetic atmosphere.

Through these singers the race releases its suffering and its true history. They are like mediums, or like the crest-feathers of our lyrical heritage.

They sing hallucinated by a brilliant point trembling on the horizon. They are strange, simple folk.

The women have sung *soleares*, a melancholy, human genre within easy reach of the heart; but the men have cultivated by preference the portentous Gypsy *siguiriya*, and almost all of them have been martyrized by an irresistible passion for *cante jondo*. The *siguiriya* is like a cauter that burns the heart, throat, and lips of those who sing it. One must beware of the fire, sing it just at the right moment.

I should like to call to mind some of the great singers of *soleares:* Romerillo, Mateo the ghostly maniac, Antonia (of San Roque), Dolores la Parrala, Anita (the one form Ronda), and Juan Breva, with the body of a giant and the voice of a small girl. And the masters of the *siguiriya:* Curro Pablos, Paquirri, El Curro, Manuel Torres, Pastora Pavon, and the marvelous Silverio Franconetti, inventor of several styles and *cante jondo*'s last pope, who sang the song of songs like no other man, and whose opening cry often shattered the mirrors. Almost all of them died of heart attacks, which is to say that they exploded like enormous cicadas after having peopled our atmosphere with their perfect rhythms.

Ladies and gentlemen, all you who have been moved by the distant song approaching along the road; all whose mature hearts have been pinched by the white dove of Love; all who love the tradition that is strung (as beads are strung) upon the future; you who study books, and you who plow the earth: I appeal respectfully to all of you not to let the precious, living jewels of a race—the immense, thousand-year-old treasure covering the spiritual surface of Andalusia—not to let that die. I hope you will mediate, beneath this Granadan night, on the patriotic transcendence of the project which a few Spanish artists have come here to present.

ALMA GUILLERMOPRIETO

Samba

SAMBA: *A musical composition based on a two-by-four beat.*

SAMBA: *Dance(s) the samba (second and third person singular present of the verb sambar).*

SAMBA: *A gathering that takes place specifically to dance the samba.*

When I first arrived in Rio de Janeiro several years ago, I rented an apartment in Ipanema, a pleasant middle-class district, and along with the refrigerator and the bed and a couple of chests of drawers I inherited a maid: a stocky, very black woman in her fifties whom my landlady insisted she loved as one of the family. Nieta was nice, the landlady then warned me, but she had a tendency to steal little things, and it was important that as a foreigner I start off by imposing my authority, otherwise Nieta would, as maids do, start to get "uppity" on me. My secretary issued the same warning, and so did almost everyone else I met at the time. "Don't let her take advantage of you or you're in for trouble," they said urgently, as if the entire Brazilian social order were at stake. I liked Nieta enormously, but I was on the lookout for insubordination.

"*Ciao!*" she would say in the mornings, sending me off to work with a smile, one hand on hip, the other waving gracefully in a pose learned from television. In my own country, Mexico, maids were not supposed to be so casual or say sophisticated things like "*Ciao.*" Was this a sign of uppitiness? She had been trained to stand whenever she was in her employer's presence, but I had not been trained to provide a television for the tiny room off the kitchen where she lived. Consequently, when I came in late and found her watching television in the study she would stand up and I would sit down and we would watch television together. I encouraged her to sit, but I worried. Was I asking for trouble?

Despite the awkwardness of the situation, I enjoyed watching television with her: She was hip, in the way Cariocas—the people of Rio de Janeiro—are, and she had excellent information on the singers who appeared on the screen: which ones were fakes, which ones had spoiled their talent by going commercial, which were involved with the underworld. She filled me in on the background of the prime-time soap opera. The one then playing was set in nineteenth-century Brazil, and Nieta didn't think much of one of the actresses. "That woman has no originality, her body isn't expressive," she commented. And another night, as we watched the heroine being waited on by her favorite house slave: "Whites adore soap operas set in the old times. They really love to look at the slaves."

The first time we went to the market together I asked her why she was calling the elevator at the back of the hall. She rode down with me in the front elevator. We did this a second time, and then the third time she refused, saying a neighbor had seen us and complained to the doorman. "We're not supposed to ride the front elevator," she said then, for the first time, and I was too confused to ask her if the "we" referred to blacks or maids. In theory, Rio de Janeiro city codes prohibit servants, delivery people, and tenants in bathing suits from using the front elevators. In practice, the regulation ends up discriminating mostly against blacks.

Nieta went home on weekends and invariably came back edgy. Sometimes her problems had to do with the complicated lives of her two adult daughters, but more often it was a question of money. Refrigerator door off the hinge. Rains caving in one of the two rooms in her house. She lived about two hours away by bus, and when I suggested that she (that is, I) might prefer day work only, it was clear she had no appetite for the daily commute or the unrelieved contact with her own misery. Instead she said that some weekend she would like to invite me out to her neighborhood for a meal at home. But before I could make the trip—only a few weeks after she had begun working for me—I became convinced that she *was* stealing things like sugar and helping herself liberally to my makeup and perfume, and the loose change. I agonized over the unfairness of her situation: Perhaps the level of stealing she indulged in was normal and expected from underpaid servants in Brazil. Perhaps the sugar bowl and the small-change drawer were producing evidence of nothing but my own paranoia, fueled by a landlady's slander. Perhaps I had taken at face value a warning that she had intended not against Nieta but against the entire black race, meaning, "You've got to watch these people; they're unreliable." Perhaps it wasn't Nieta's fault that I couldn't trust her. But I couldn't, and I fired her.

I missed her very much after she wished me "everything good" at the kitchen door and waved "*Ciao!*" for the last time. For one thing, she was the only person who had—or could invent—answers for the growing pool of questions in my mind. The odd situation of blacks in Rio provoked my curiosity much more forcefully than the free-wheeling culture of beer and chatter common to white Cariocas of my income level, but I realized only after Nieta left that she was my single contact with the culture of a race that constitutes nearly half the Brazilian population. The new maid, a shy white woman from the Minas Gerais countryside who had converted to evangelism, certainly could not provide the answers Nieta could have come up with. Why aren't there any black waiters? Where can I find black music? Who is the black woman with blue eyes and a metal gag whose plaster image appears in all the religious-supplies stores? Just what, exactly, is a samba school? Why is it that at sunset, when the beaches in Ipanema are emptying, black women will sometimes approach the waves and toss white flowers into the foam?

The heat bloomed in December as the carnival season kicked into gear, Nearly helpless with sun and glare, I avoided Rio's brilliant sidewalks and glittering beaches, panting in dark corners and waiting out the inverted southern summer. Nevertheless, certain rhythms, an unmistakable urgency in the air got through to me. Although there were still three months left to the carnival celebrations that would close down Rio for nearly a week in March, the momentum was already building. The groups of men who normally gathered for coffee or beer in front of the tiny grocery stores that dot Rio were now adding a percussion backup to their usual excited conversation. They beat a drum, clapped their hands in counterpoint; and toyed with a stray verse of song before letting the rhythm die out again. There was a faster, more imposing beat to the sambas on the radio. I made tentative inquiries: Carnival? Boring. Vulgar. Noisy, some people said, and recommended that I leave town for that horrible weekend. Samba schools? Tacky, some said. Highly original, said others, and volunteered that the "schools" were in reality organizations that compete on carnival weekend with floats and songs and extravagant costumes, each group dressed entirely in its official colors. But was it true that carnival was something that happened principally in the slums? Why? There were shrugs, raised eyebrows. Who knows. Opium of the people. Blacks are like that. We Brazilians are like that. You know: On the day of the coup, back in 1964, people were happy because it meant they had the day off and could go to the beach. I recalled the way Nieta's gestures became expansive when she mentioned carnival. Opium, yes, probably. But surely it was fun? In March, I ended up with a ticket for the first of two all-night samba school parades.

In the official parade grounds—the Sambadrome—I though the silence eerie until I realized it was in fact a solid wall of sound, a percussive din that did not sound like music and advanced gradually toward the spectators on an elaborate loudspeaker system set up on either side of the central "avenue," or parade space. At the head of the noise was a gigantic waggling lion's head that floated down the avenue and overtook us, giving way to dazzling hordes in red and gold. A marmalade-thick river of people swept past; outlandish dancers in feathers and capes, ball gowns and G-strings, hundreds of drummers, thousands of leaping princes singing at the top of their lungs. Drowning in red and gold, I struggled to focus. In the ocean of feathers and banners faces emerged: brown, white, pink, tan, olive. Young black men bopping in sweat-drenched suits; old women in cascades of flounces whirling ecstatically; middle-aged men and women with paunches and eyeglasses bouncing happily in their headdresses and bikinis. How much money did they make? How much had their costumes cost? Why, in Brazil's pervasively segregated society, had all the colors decided to mix? Four Styrofoam elephants trundled past on golden platforms, followed by gigantic Balinese dancers in red and gold. There were acrobatic dancers with tambourines; more spinning old women; a flag-bearing couple, who should have been paralyzed by the weight of their glittering costumes, twirling and curtsying instead through a dance that looked like a samba-minuet. Nothing was familiar or logical, and I was reduced to the most simple questions. How could that large woman over there in the sequined bikini be so unconcerned about her cellulite? Why was everyone singing a song about the Mexican chicle tree, and who had come up with this idea? Why were a spectacularly beautiful woman dressed only in a few feathers and a little boy in a formal suit pretending to have sex with each other for the audience's benefit, and why was everyone involved so cheerful? Were all these people from the slums? And if they were, how could they look so happy when their lives were so awful?

It was well after dawn when I left the crowd of ever more enthusiastic spectators, as the seventh samba school was about to begin its slow progress. Beyond the Sambadrome were the squalid last alley-ways of a moribund red-light district, and beyond that the favelas—the slums, perched on their outcrops of rock. Back home, the Ipanema universe of orderly tree-lined streets and air-conditioned buildings seemed remote and barren when compared to the favelas I knew only from Nieta's descriptions, now suddenly come alive in my mind as the magical enclaves where carnival could be imagined and then made flesh. The peopled hills were everywhere—there was one only three blocks from my apartment building—and I spent months staring at the jumble of shacks pitched so artlessly across the steep slopes, imagining the hot, crazy life within. But it was a long time before I could find an excuse to get close.

I went to a North Zone favela for my first visit to a samba school. It was springtime in Brazil, when the weather in Rio is loveliest: washed clear of rains, the sky turns a cool and peaceful blue. The nights too are soothing, spattered with clean bright stars and edged with promise. Spring signals the beginning of the carnival season, which starts up in September with nightlong rehearsals designed to set the festive sap running for the real event. Year-round planning for the parade also shifts into full gear with weekly meetings at which samba school directorates define their strategies and assign tasks.

The taxi crossed the tunnel under Corcovado hill, which links Ipanema and Copacabana to the North Zone; skimmed past the massive shadow of Maracanã Stadium and the concrete wastelands of the state university; and stopped at the edge of a favela that channels precipitously from one particularly tall hill right down to the pavement itself. This was Mangueira.

The directors of the First Station of Mangueira Recreational Association and Samba School were holding one of their weekly planning meetings, chaired by the school president, Carlos Dória. With the other school directors—mostly black, mostly middle-aged to old—Dória discussed the coming parade, which was to commemorate the hundredth anniversary of the decree that abolished slavery, signed by the Brazilian Crown in 1888.

Like the other schools, Mangueira had already begun its samba harvest—a process of winnowing out competing sambas composed around the official parade theme, until one is selected to be sung in the Sambadrome by the school's five thousand members. There was general enthusiasm for the theme, and agreement that the competing sambas offered a rich crop, but some members of the directorate were unsatisfied with the costumes and the floats: They were too frilly, and they did not convey enough about the present situation of blacks in Brazil or about their past hardships.

I hung around the edges of the meeting and at the end spoke briefly with Dória, a burly man in his mid-forties with a paunch, thick gold jewelry, a moustache, and an unfriendly air. I told him I was a reporter and said I would like to follow Mangueira through its process of making carnival. Roughly, he told me I was wasting my time. I was persistent, but he was mean; he was a member of the state military police, and the hostility in his manner was both professional and frightening.

After we had reached an impasse, a young woman listening to our conversation interceded and took me aside. Nilsemar was very pretty, with the modest, precise gestures of a skillful nurse. She had been sitting at the directorate table with other women to whom she now introduced me: her grandmother, Dona Zica, widow of Cartola, one of the founders and outstanding composers of the Mangueira samba school; her friend Marilia, a white sociologist; Dona Neuma, daughter of a founder of Mangueira and an all-time sambista; and Neuma's daughter, Guezinha. The women were as friendly as Dória was brusque. They listened to me questions and invited me to attend the harvest dance the following Saturday. "Don't worry," Nilsemar said softly, when I said Dória might not approve of my presence. "He's gruff, but we'll convince him to let you see what you want to see."

The turnstiles were green, the rest of the façade glaring pink. A man in a pink T-shirt waved me through the turnstile of Mangueira's Palacio do Samba into the bright pink and green space beyond. It was shortly before midnight, and the harvest was not scheduled to start until one. The huge central dance space was empty and only a few of the red folding tables around it were occupied. A man in a pink and green crocheted muscle shirt, another in a pink felt hat, women in pink shirts and green dresses leaned casually against the green and pink walls. Banners hanging from the metal roof structure advertised the support of Xerox and Ypiranga Paints for the Mangueira cause. Ypiranga's contribution was evident: Other than the metal tables emblazoned with the Coca-Cola logo, not an inch of space was painted any other color than the two Mangueira favorites.

At the opposite end of the central area a few children were scrambling onto a green platform twelve feet high. When they reached the top, others handed them sticks, drums as tall as they, smaller metal objects that jangled. Soon the platform was full: some twenty small boys and their director, a wiry young white man in a Hawaiian shirt. It was 11:58. The boys, skinny and solemn-faced, fidgeted, fiddled, adjusted their shoulder straps, their shirts, their faded baggy shorts, and hit the drums. The sound wave began.

It was what one tied to the railroad tracks might hear as a train hurtles immediately overhead: a vast, rolling, marching, overpowering wave of sound set up by the *surdos de marcação*—bass drums about two feet in diameter in charge of carrying the underlying beat. Gradually a ripple set in, laid over the basic rhythm by smaller drums. Then the *cuica:* a subversive, humorous squeak, dirty and enticing, produced by rubbing a stick inserted into the middle of a drumskin. The *cuica* is like an itch, and the only way to scratch it is to dance. Already, people were wiggling in place to the beat, not yet dancing, building up the rhythm inside their bodies, waiting for some releasing command of the drums. Gradually, as the children drummed on with all the solemnity of a funeral band, husky morose men climbed the platform, hoisted their instruments, and joined in. There were more *surdos,* another *cuica,* a clackety metal *agogô,* a tambourine, and something that looked like a Christmas tree and sounded like a shiver—the *chocalho.*

For long minutes the wave rolled over us, a formal presentation of the *bateria,* the rhythm section that forms a school's core. Without a *bateria,* no school can parade, no school can exist. These percussionists are recognized as the hardest-working members of the samba world. While everyone else is having a good time, they are raising bloody welts on their shoulders from the drums' heavy straps, tearing the calloused skin on their hands with their ceaseless beating and rubbing of the metal instruments. Others enter and leave rehearsals as they wish; the drummers anchor a samba from the beginning. They are a paradoxical aristocracy, sweat-drenched princes who are among the poorest members of the school. By inheritance and tradition, most of the *bateria* make their living as day laborers in the Rio dockyards. They never smile.

The *bateria* director brought his arms down sharply. With a final shudder and slam the wave came to a halt. The samba harvest was open.

The *quadra*—or samba building—had filled up quickly. About five hundred people were now milling about, lining up for beer, occupying the tables or marking off private spaces for themselves along the edges of the *quadra* by setting their beer bottles in the center of where they intended to dance. There were groups of middle-aged women out for a night on the town, and whole families sitting at tables crowded with beer, soda pop and, here and there, sandwiches brought from home. A birthday party was in progress at one end of the *quadra*. Lounging at the opposite end were a handful of young men in slouchy felt hats, long T-shirts, Bermudas, and hightops. I spotted Guezinha and the sociologist, Marilia, at one of the front-row tables, and then, as I stood in line for a soft drink, Carlos Dória. I smiled in greeting and he turned away. Shortly afterward, he left.

The dance space itself remained empty, separated from the tables by metal parade barriers. Eventually two older men strolled into the inviolate space, slowly and with authority. One was short, stocky, heavily moustached and slightly stooped. He wore an assortment of whistles around his neck and something of the tired, impatient air of a boxing referee. The other was improbably tall, with a hatchet face crowned by a narrow-brimmed straw hat. He was as long-legged and deliberate as a praying mantis, and as brightly colored in his grass-green suit. His head rotated on an axis as he paused for a moment and inspected the *quadra*, chewing on a piece of gum with toothless jaws. Slowly his head returned to center and he resumed his crossing. As if the two men's presence were a command, several other men climbed onto a singers' tower placed at right angles to the drummers' platform, on which they were soon joined by Beto End-of-the-Night. Beto Fim da Noite, energetic, bald, and very black, announced the evening's events over a foggy microphone that stirred his words into the general soup of noise and confusion and only sporadically let some meaning through: "The harvest now commences . . . best team win . . . great Mangueira nation . . . this night memorable . . . end of the evening three finalists . . . competing for the glory of carrying our school to victory at carnival . . . now sing the Mangueira anthem . . . "

The drums slammed into action, there was a piercing short whistle, and as if released from coils the dancers bounced into the air. At the center of the dance space stood Alberto Pontes, the heavy-shouldered man with the whistles, looking now more like a gladiator ready to take on all the Colosseum's lions. He crouched menacingly and blew sharp commands on his whistle, and as a stream of hyperkinetic women charged onto the dance floor he growled, gestured, stamped his foot, and pushed the herd away from the center of the floor and back toward the barriers. Unheeding, the women jumped and swayed and broke into frenzied little circles of movement, hips and jewelry flying in every direction; they surged forward and grabbed all the available space while Pontes cursed and ordered them back again with a righteous forefinger, Moses compelling the waters to retract, God expelling a thousand Eves. The samba pounded on and the women multiplied, but Pontes did not interrupt his labors.

"The shepherdesses," Marilia shouted over the commotion when I sought her out in the crowd. "They're called *pastôras,*" she repeated. "By tradition, only women are allowed to dance in the central space during real rehearsals." But in fact it was Pontes who seemed more like their sheepdog, herding his flock away from their Dionysian instincts and back to a world of order and sobriety.

A skinny little man approached the central space, giddily drunk and full of gay mannerisms, dance bursting out of him. Swiftly he was scooped up by two youths in pink "Mangueira Security" T-shirts. It was not time for him to dance yet. It would not be time until the end of the harvest, when Mangueira began its more commercial round of "rehearsals" designed to fill the school's coffers. Then the dance floor would be open to all.

Meanwhile the men danced on the edges of the *quadra,* between the beer counter and the tables. The real bambas danced in all-male groups, whipping their legs in circular movements over the beer bottles set on the floor, knifing out with one leg to upset the balance of another male dancer, shifting from high to low movements and from sitting to standing to spinning positions like break-dancers.

Couples danced too, provocatively. A teenage girl sheathed in a tight white strapless dress circled her hips slowly to the floor in front of her enthusiastic middle-aged partner and then slid straight up again, her pubic bone pressed into the man's thigh. Eventually the man offered his place to a little boy who had been practicing samba off in a corner on his own. The boy kept his distance from the girl for a few seconds with elaborate dips and bops, a little out of breath with shyness. He stood still, hesitating, before diving into the space between her thighs. Chest level to her hips, he grinned awkwardly while she pulsated against him. Then he leapt away, laughing and proud and cheered on by a circle of observers.

A chunky gray-haired woman in a plain cotton shift and slippers stood at the center of a group of teenagers. Too old to jump or spin, she faced her adolescent partner and wiggled as hard as she could, bursting into great roars of laughter every time she managed to set her entire body shaking. "Vovó," the kids called her, "Granny." But she explained that she had no children of her own, and that the teenager who had brought her here were children she had helped raise in her suburban favela.

Through the mad crowd that had formed at the center of the rehearsal space a serene dancer emerged. The flag-bearer and the major-domo, a royal pair, head the dancing section of every parade, and a candidate to the flag-bearing position was now just beginning her practice. She was very young, shy and hesitant. For a second she seemed to be floating alone, but out of the crowd her partner appeared, scything the air with his long bones, folding his limbs at the joints and then stretching them out again to full, preposterous length: Delegado, the green-and-brown praying mantis. Together they dipped and spun and circled for a few seconds, and then Delegado turned the flag-bearer over to her teenage coapprentice. The women marched behind, tirelessly, over and over, while the sound wave broke and shattered against the wall.

By now it was almost one in the morning. The song we had been listening to, someone said, was the samba from the previous carnival parade, in which Mangueira had won first prize. The contest for this season's samba had in fact not yet begun, but now that the song had come to its abrupt end the composers and singers on the tower shifted and cleared their throats and consulted. There was a great flurry of activity down in the table area, where Marilia and Guezinha and several other members of the directorate were sitting. A hopped-up, nervous young man named Rody came up and with a superb smile handed me a slip of pink paper with the mimeographed lyrics of his samba, a heavy crowd favorite. He had written it together with Verinha—a woman composer—and Bus-Stop Bira; the three made up a team that had written the previous year's winning samba. He shook hands earnestly with everyone in sight. "Give me a little strength," he asked Marilia, but I knew his fate was sealed. "We in the directorate are rooting for Helinho's samba," the women had said on the night I met them.

This is what Rody's song said:

The black race came to this country,
Bringing their strong arms and their roots.
They planted their culture here,
Yoruba, Gêgê and Nagô.
In the refineries, mines and fields,

Blacks were always oppressed,
And in the rebel enclave of Palmares
Zumbi our leader fought for freedom.

(Chorus)
Finally light dawned,
Reason prevailed,
and Princess Isabel
Abolished slavery.
Or did she?
Is it true, is it a lie?
Because to be born with a black skin
Has not given us the right to freedom.
One hundred years of liberty:
Is this reality or illusion?
Let's all wave our white handkerchiefs
And with Mangueira ask
For an end to discrimination.

(Chorus)
Throw off the ties that bind!
Please give people their freedom!

Rody's song ended, another samba began. A messenger broke through the dancing crowd, breathless and tragic. The music stopped, there was a moment of silence, and the singer at the microphone announced that Carlos Dória had just been murdered.

The news sent people whirling centrifugally toward the exit doors, concentrically into each other's arms. Mangueira emptied out. I stood on the stairs leading to the mezzanine and the directorate offices and watched Dona Zica being carried out in a half-faint. Marilia gathered her ten-year-old daughter and her friends off the dance floor and headed down the road for Dona Neuma's house. The school's vice-president staggered by, clutching at his chest with one hand. A large, fortyish woman, considerably drunk, screamed *"Meu presidente! Meu president!"* and flung herself repeatedly against a standing column at the foot of the stairs. A man climbed up to the directorate offices—slender as a knife, of indeterminate age, wearing a bright pink leather jacket and pitch-dark glasses at four in the morning, surrounded by bodyguards. He emerged again, sliced his way through the clots of hysterical bystanders on the stairway, paused at the landing to announce, "A lot of blood will run for this," and was gone. The last stragglers left. The *quadra* shut down.

Dória had been sitting in his car a short drive north from the *quadra*, waiting for the garage door in his apartment building to open, when someone came up and shot him four times through the head and chest. His murder was never solved. The few Mangueirenses I had met were not forthcoming on the possible causes or culprits, and I had to rely on the Rio papers, where the murder made the front page and then filled the crime section for almost a week with the latest speculations on the assassins' motives: that Dória had been involved with a drug group and was killed by a rival gang; that the entrenched leadership of Rio's League of Samba Schools had had him murdered after he threatened to set up an independent association. This last became the official Mangueira version, volunteered to all and just as vigorously denied by League leaders. In any event Mangueira never resigned from the League, nor did the school or Dória's relatives ever press charges. Over the months, as carnival activity spread beyond the favelas and took hold of the entire city, the case faded from public attention.

In the wake of the murder Mangueira's carnival prospects were assumed to be nil. The samba harvest was suspended for two weeks. There was a funeral and then, eight days after the murder, a mass for the resurrection of the soul of Carlinhos Dória.

There were few tears during the resurrection mass for Dória. The young foreign priest from the church down the road set up an improvised altar in a corner of the nearly empty *quadra*, led his uncertain parishioners through the church rituals, and spoke about crime and the difference between forgiveness and justice, hinting broadly that those who knew who had killed Dória might absolve the culprits in their hearts but let the criminal justice system know exactly who it was they had forgiven all the same. The priest seemed realistic about the limits of his moral influence and kept the sermon brief. Shortly after he finished folding the altar cloth he was out the door.

The sambistas lingered in the drafty *quadra* until well after nightfall. There were people here who did not meet in the course of daily life except at rehearsal time, when the din of the *bateria* made real conversation impossible; but on this chilly evening, made nostalgic and vulnerable by the presence of death, they clustered together for comfort and in the congenial silence soon found themselves laughing at old stories, singing forgotten samba verses quietly to each other as they remembered this or that carnival or party. They talked about Dória and his brief tenure as Mangueira president, about his violent temper and his devotion to the school, and because the future was looming in the shape of an upcoming carnival with no president to lead it, they talked about the past, with special emphasis on the moments of glory.

"Mangueira was, after all, the first of all the schools to come out with a story samba," a trim old man said, to murmurs of agreement. "Other schools keep claiming that honor, but they know the truth." The speaker, Carlos Cachaça, was the last surviving founder of the Mangueira school, having outlived almost every other bamba of the period when samba first became popular and led indirectly to the invention of the samba schools. "Story samba" is the proper name for the song that sets forth the theme of a school parade, easily distinguishable through its speed and emphatic marching beat from song samba, counterpoint samba (known outside Brazil as "bossa nova") and the earliest form of the genre, call-and-response samba. Cachaça liked to remind people of Mangueira's historical if much-disputed claim to leadership in the field of story sambas because, as it happened, he had invented the subcategory himself back in 1933, when samba—the whole broad genre of highly ornamented two-by-four rhythms—was just establishing itself as Brazil's national music. Cachaça was in his early thirties then, Mangueira was a miserable stop on the suburban rail line, and Brazilian carnival was about to witness its great flowering, brought about by the fusion of black and white carnival cultures in the crucible of the newly created samba schools.

Brazilian whites today readily admit that carnival would not have amounted to much had it remained in their hands. The Portuguese colonizers' idea of enjoyment during the week before Lent was to spray each other with syringes filled with water, foul-smelling liquids, or worse. In the mid-nineteenth century someone came up with the only slightly better idea of beating a very large drum while a crowd followed him around the neighborhood. Carnival life began to improve only toward the end of Emperor Pedro II's progressive regime, when a restless new urban elite championed the abolition of slavery, which the emperor also favored; republicanism, which the emperor, understandably, was against; and a more sophisticated, "European" form of carnival to which Dom Pedro, as far as the evidence shows, did not object.

Patterned on the elegant celebrations of Paris and Venice, elaborate costume balls quickly became the rage. "Carnival societies" were formed to parade through the main streets of the city dressed in complicated allegorical costumes, often designed to satirize the old regime and promote the liberal agenda. This was the carnival that blacks would imitate and preserve long after the tradition had died out among whites: a daydream vision of European elegance, of white aristocrats at their dazzling play.

It was getting late. The mass had ended hours before, and someone in the control room flashed the *quadra*'s lights off and on impatiently. A voluble conversationalist with an Assyrian profile and a sculpted beard to match was still eagerly talking to his friend Marilia, the Mangueira sociologist, about the political aspects of samba. Djalma belonged to the much younger samba school of Vila Isabel, and had come to Dória's mass to pay the respects due a school considered by many the last holdout against encroaching commercialization. "Because look here, the schools are dying: Do you know what some big companies are trying to do? They want the float-pushers—the only school members who are not in costume—to wear T-shirts with the company logo on their backs. The day is coming, I want you to know, when one school will belong to Coca-Cola and another to a supermarket chain. It's the same thing that happened to the soccer clubs, and I want no part of it. I live and die for my school, but for me the schools are the people on the hills, and watch out; the day the companies take over, I'm out of here." He had much more to say about the current state of samba, and the other groups of stragglers were also in no mood to end the evening. Someone suggested the party move down the road to Dona Neuma's house, whose doors remained open at all hours of the day and night. She had not attended the mass, and Djalma thought it would be a good idea to stop and pay his respects to her as well.

Dona Neuma was the daughter of a school founder who had died of tuberculosis and poverty many years before. Her husband had worked as a carpenter until his death, and for most of their lives Dona Neuma and her family had lived in a brick-and-wood shack on the same spot where their house now stood. One of the daughters, Chininha, had married well, to an airline attendant. Another, Ceci, had a government job with which to support herself, her daughter, and granddaughter, while Guezinha, married to a car salesman, also worked off and on at a store or at other clerical jobs. The family's combined incomes and a little money from carnival-related activities had built the house, which was magnificent by hill standards. Half a dozen people sprawled on a frayed living room set, watching television. New family members constantly emerged from a set of back bedrooms and joined the others on the couch. Someone made coffee. Beers were poured. Guezinha stored the week's shopping—beans, rice, macaroni, detergent, toilet paper, and gallons of cooking oil—in a carved wood highboy that formed part of a fancy uncomfortable dining room set. I fidgeted, feeling both out of place and eager to linger in the household's chaotic warmth. Guezinha gave me an amused look. "You're here to learn, aren't you? Come here, I'll show you something." She led me to the huge kitchen, where an excited group of women was studying a sketch of a svelte creature in a feather-topped turban, sequined bra, and ankle-length, below-the-navel skirt, seductively draped and slit thigh-high up the front. The outfit looked like something the chorus girls at the Crazy Horse in Paris might wear for their presentation walk-on, but Guezinha said it was supposed to be a parade costume representing an *orixá*, or African goddess. Looking at the sketch I understood why the Portuguese word for costume is *fantasia*—"fantasy": all my life, I had wanted to look like that, if only for a few minutes, a few seconds.

"It's for my wing," Guezinha explained. "I have an all-woman wing, fifty of us, and this is the costume we'll wear. Do you like it?" I said I did. She gave me a sidelong glance, then looked around at the other women. "Well, how would you like to join my wing and parade with us at carnival time?" I said I would like that very much indeed. "But first," Guezinha said, with hardly the shadow of a smile, "you have to learn to samba."

One of the subtler forms of amusement for blacks at carnival time is watching whites try to samba. White people have had nearly the whole century to work it out, and most of them still can't quite get it right. It's not that blacks mind; that whites look clumsy while they're trying to have fun is a misfortune too great to be compounded by mockery, but it's also a fact that can't be denied. Whites are certainly given points for trying, though, and in the Samba Palace the ones who got up to dance seemed to be much more warmly regarded than those who tried to maintain their dignity. But I was terrified of what I might look like, and in the weeks before carnival, after lurking in the corners of the *quadra* at almost every rehearsal, I went home and practiced samba grimly and in secret.

How to Samba (Women's Version)

1. Start before a mirror, with no music. You may prefer to practice with a pair of very high heels. Though samba is a dance that started out barefoot, and can still be danced that way, high heels will throw your spinal column out of whack and give your pelvis the appearance of greater flexibility. Platform shoes with relatively wide heels provide the best combination of stability and shock absorption.

2. Stand with feet parallel, close together. Step and hop in place on your right foot as you brush your left foot quickly across. Step in quick succession onto your left, then your right foot. Although your hips will swivel to the right as far as possible for this sequence, your head and shoulders should remain strictly forward. Otherwise you'll start looking like you're doing the *hora*. Practice this sequence right and left until you can do it without counting.

3. Test yourself: Are your lips moving? Are your shoulders scrunched? No? Are you able to manage one complete left-right sequence per second? Good! Now that you've mastered the basic samba step, you're ready to add music. Choose Zeca Pagodinho, Jovelina the Black Pearl, Neguinho of the Hummingbird or any other sambista you like and start practicing. The key thing at this stage is speed: When you are up to two complete sequences per second you are well on your way to samba. Aim for four.

4. A samba secret: Add hips. They're probably moving already, but if you are trying to hit required minimum speed they may be a little out of control. You want to move them, but purposefully. When you step on your right foot your hips switch left-right. When you step on your left they switch again, right-left. Two hip beats per foot beat, or about twelve beats per second, if you can manage.

5. Stop hopping! Keep your shoulders down! Face front! The magic of samba lies in the illusion that somebody is going like crazy from the waist down while an entirely different person is observing the proceedings from the waist up. Keep your torso detached from your hips and facing where you're looking, and practice with a book on your head until you can stay level at full speed.

You've mastered the mechanics of samba. Now you're ready to start dancing. If the following essentials seem a little daunting, don't be discouraged. Remember, you've come a long way from your beginning days. Dress appropriately for this next stage. Preferably something that emphasizes the waist, so that hip movement is maximized. Go for shine. Twelve hip beats per second will look like a hundred if you're wearing sequins.

Arms: If you are up to two to four sequences per second with a book on your head and your hips swiveling at least forty-five degrees in each direction away from the wall you're facing, you're ready to ornament your dance by holding your arms out and ruffling your shoulders as you move. Think of a fine-plumed bird rearranging its wings. Keep the movement flexible and easy. Reach out with your fingertips. If you can't shimmy without looking scrunched or panicky, drop it.

Smile: The key rule is, don't make it sexy. You will look arch, coy or, if you are working really hard, terribly American. Your smile should be the full-tilt cheer of someone watching her favorite team hit a home run. Or it should imitate the serene curve of a Hindu deity's. The other key rule: There is no point to samba if it doesn't make you smile.

Sweat: Obviously, you will produce lots of it. You will soon discover that it looks wrong when it is dripping off the tip of your nose. Don't let this upset you. Perseverance and practice have got you this far; keep at it. Practice. When you find that your body is moving below you in a whirlpool frenzy and your mind is floating above it all in benign accompaniment; when your torso grows curiously light and your legs feel like carving little arabesques in the air on their own for the sheer fun of it; when everything around you seems too slow for the rush that's carrying you through the music, you'll probably discover that sweat is clothing your body in one glorious, uniform, scintillating sheet, flying around you in a magic halo of drops, and you'll know that you have arrived at samba.

Two weeks after Dória's death, on a wet, cold Friday evening, the Mangueira samba harvest resumed with the selection of the story-samba semifinalists. Dória's murder had had a number of devastating consequences, not the least of which was a nearly empty *quadra* that mid-October night. Bereft of crowds, the Samba Palace looked garish and lonely in the late-winter drizzle. Garbage overflowed a dumpster between the *quadra* and Dona Neuma's house, and pigs and dogs rooted about in the soggy mess. The few hundred people from the hill who did show up looked chilled and uncomfortable among the puddles in the dance space. The sound system ground the music into mush, the singers repeatedly wavered off key and the *bateria* did the worst thing possible: It lost contact with the singers and went off the beat. When this happens during a parade the result is unsalvageable ruin; caught between the competing rhythms of the marching drummers and the singers, who travel separately on a sound track, school members wander off on their own, and the parade's tight ranks soon dissolve into chaos. When this "crossing up" occurs in the course of a rehearsal, the result is simply to make the music unbearable.

Sometime around two in the morning I stopped by the table where Guezinha was sitting with a few of her sisters and friends, looking close to tears and very slightly drunk. We stared for a while at the dance space, where the shepherdess-herder Alberto Pontes was halfheartedly chivying a handful of women. "The samba is really hot tonight, isn't it?" Guezinha said, smiling at me like a television announcer. I said that it certainly was, and we sat together wordlessly for a while, listening to the *bateria*'s excruciating hammer. Guezinha pushed back her chair. "I'm going to bed," she announced, and went home.

The school's situation was no better in the daytime. When Mangueira was mentioned in the press, it was in the context of police interrogations and speculations on Dória off-duty life: Had he participated in a death squad? Was he involved in the drug trade? Dona Neuma and Dona Zica, the two "First Ladies" of Mangueira, were interviewed by the press not on the usual colorful subject of carnival's early days but on the question of who had murdered their president. "If I knew, I would have chased the culprit all the way to Japan," Dona Neuma avowed, and tried unsuccessfully to get her questioners interested in the wonderful theme for the coming carnival.

Comment on the misfortune was generally avoided around the samba school, as if reference to it might attract additional bad luck. "Dória is dead but the school lives on," was one standard answer to questions about the current adversity. And it was a sign of how bad things were that the most devastating consequence of Dória's murder was the one that was never mentioned. Mangueira had won first place in the carnival for the previous two years running. With a striking theme and a first-rate story samba this year, there had been little doubt in the community's mind that the school could win a third time in the upcoming carnival, an achievement only two other schools could boast of and that was permanently associated with their names. That Mangueira, bereft of leadership, was no longer in the running for a triple championship was the great unstated fact casting its miserable spell on the harvest evening that followed Dória's murder. "Mangueira is going to have to parade any old way," Vila Isabel's Djalma had commented sorrowfully on the night of the resurrection mass. "And I, for one, am not looking forward to watching what will happen. It's going to be a very sad thing." The disastrous semifinal rehearsal was evidence of the school's depression and disarray. Now, less than twelve hours later, the *finalissima,* or final contest night, loomed ahead.

When I walked in at midnight, the Samba Palace was unrecognizable. The walls looked scrubbed and the floor was dry and spotless. Every table in the house had been set out and all were full. A huge crowd threaded its way among them, dodging radio reporters and school members busing trays of fancy appetizers to a section of tables that had been cordoned off for VIPs. The master sambista Delegado had clothed his long body in a hot-pink suit. Pontes the shepherdess-herder had an extraordinary array of whistles bouncing off his chest. There was a phalanx of standard-bearers: old ones, new ones, apprenticing adolescents. Guezinha, a woman I associated with hard work and practical clothes, stood smiling at the center of the dance area, enclosed in the halo of her own sexuality, dressed in a strapless sheath someone must have stitched directly onto her body, exhaling perfume with every movement, unapproachable as a shrine. "What happened?" I asked, bewildered. The goddess, remote and knowing, only smiled.

"What happened?" I asked another member of the directorate. He smiled too. That morning, he said, people had recognized that things looked bad and that a final harvest session like the previous night's would be fatal. A cleanup brigade was organized. Emissaries were sent to the radio stations with pleas for a little promotional help to get Mangueira back on its feet. The hill membership was asked to turn out in force. Dona Neuma and her family brigade worded overtime cooking up platters of special tidbits for the press and the VIPs. In short, Mangueira drew on the habits, discipline, infrastructure, and reflexes that wealthier and younger schools covet and cannot reproduce. After all, what sambistas call tradition is often simply the training provided by years of endurance.

The walls were aglow with paper banners in magenta and green for Helinho Turco's team—the school directorate's favorite—and green and yellow, the Brazilian national colors, for the other finalists. This was the team made up of the composers Ivo, Otacilio, and Sinval, and their song was a favorite with the *bateria,* especially because it included a catchy little drum riff in the middle. A huge white banner hanging from the metal rafters depicted this team's logo; a bare-chested black man with arms open in a victory sign. The directorate had in fact settled on the samba they preferred practically at the beginning of the harvest, but the teams whose songs were popular with the audience had continued lobbying among school members, hoping to overturn the decision with a display of enthusiasm on the dance floor. They had a lot at stake. The display of flags, the photocopied handouts of each samba's lyrics, the singers hired for the night to present the song, all cost money—perhaps as much as two or three thousand dollars in the course of the season. The school contributed some of the funds, but a composer who believed his samba was likely to win would invest as much as he could rummage, because the royalties for a winning samba would solve his financial worries for a healthy period of time. Now, caught up in the excitement, the claques for the two finalist teams shuttled between tables, egging their supporters on, flashing victory signs at each other, handing out bags of confetti to be thrown into the air at the appropriate moment. Even the sound was clean, and as the loudspeakers broadcast recorded sambas from the current hit parade the crowd was on its feet and dancing, wired so tightly to the music they seemed to anticipate and create every riff and flourish. Friends called greetings to each other across tables. The slouching young men in Bermudas looked alert and bright-eyed. On the mezzanine, the VIP balconies filled with men in white linen suits and women in skintight halter tops and miniskirts. Through the gap between the *quadra* walls and the corrugated metal roof suspended high overhead, the favela was visible, and in the houses that bordered directly on the Samba Palace spectators hung out of windows for the best view of the action below.

At a table near the VIP section an old woman who had been sitting with a group of young white men got up and began to dance. She was tall and ruined by age. Her hair was pulled back in a scrawny ponytail, and her generous grin showed few teeth. She wore thick glasses and a faded T-shirt over a pair of patched, much-washed blue jeans, but when she rose from her chair, the groups at the surrounding tables turned to her expectantly. Leisurely, she began her dance: shuffle to the left, shuffle to the right, circle all around and wiggle on down. Shuffle again, do it one more time, put your hands on your hips and shake them down the line. . . . The men at her table were grinning with her, waiting, clapping in time, egging her on as she smiled down on them. Standing in place, immobile, she began a shiver that climbed slowly from her heels to her calves, crawled up her thighs and settled in her haunches, dividing the samba rhythm into a hundred faster particles without ever losing a beat. Then, with her hips trembling in isolation from the rest of her body, she produced her pièce de résistance: bunching up her fingers, she blew a bouquet of kisses on each one and bestowed them on her admirable behind, first on her tremulous left buttock and then, with a second appreciative smile, on her right. Her audience went wild, and the woman, delighted, doubled over with laughter. When she saw me staring in captivated amazement, she performed the routine all over again and raised her bottle of beer at the end in a mischievous toast.

"That," said Marilia, "was Dona Nininha Xoxoba, one of the great Mangueira flag-bearers."

A burst of rockets interrupted her explanation. In the great open space between the *quadra* walls and the roof, the view of the favela was momentarily erased by a curtain of fireworks, exploding in constellations of silver, green, and gold. The *bateria* rammed its sound wave into the night, a huge cheer went up, and on the singers' tower Ivo, Otacilio, and Sinval's team raced into its samba, pursued by the drums. "Black men are outcasts,—But they're the kings of the parade!" they sang, and later, Helinho Turco's team answered, "They are the kings, pink and green, of all Mangueira!" And, "Has freedom really dawned / Or was it all an illusion?" To which Ivo's team answered, "It's going to change, or isn't it? / It's going to change, or isn't it? Who knows. . . . " The dance space filled to overflowing for both teams, the women sweating and pushing the samba on. Nininha stood up once again to dance. Guezinha made her way onto the dance floor, and Dona Zica, in her granny glasses and white hair, led the river of women, escorted by the preening Delegado. Both sambas were hot, the drums were brilliant, confetti filled the air, there was no stopping the dancers.

Beto End-of-the-Night announced the winner at dawn, and as light filled the *quadra*, a hoarse white man, Percy Pires, acting as rehearsal coordinator, evoked Dória's name and Mangueira's past and assured the happy, sweaty crowd that another school victory was on its way. His speech did not sound hollow. As the Mangueirenses streamed out through the turnstiles into a hazy, unclouded day, someone ventured a timid cheer: "Mangueira Triple Crown!"

BRIAN CULLMAN

Cheb Khaled & the Politics of Pleasure

Whenever things would get too quiet backstage, the dwarf would start to dance. It was a harsh, unlovely dance, frightening in its power and disdain; his large head thrown back, eyes narrowed to slits, tongue hanging out of his pink, wet mouth, the tiny body surging and gyrating in a mockery of a belly-dancer's dark and passionate rhythms, his hands describing small concentric circles in the air.

On the couch, Cheb Khaled sat drinking and laughing, checking his watch to see how long before the concert hall would clear so that we could unload and head back to the hotel; scattered about the room, half a dozen band members ignored the dwarf and went about packing their instruments, changing their shirts, and kibbitzing about the night's show. Someone picked up a clay drum from the corner and began playing along to the dance, working up a slow, Arabic groove. The dwarf stopped, kicked the drum viciously, upsetting a tray of beers, and spat on the floor.

"Turds," he sneered. "Assholes. Musicians." The last insult delivered with an air of unspeakable contempt and finality. There was a knock, and a man with a raincoat, a pencil-thin mustache, and the saddest expression in the world entered the room.

"I'm not supposed to be here. I talked my way in," he said to no one in particular and then turned his attention to Khaled.

"You," he said. "I knew you in Oran when you were a boy. And now I'm going to kill you." Reaching into his coat, he pulled out a bottle of J&B Scotch, Khaled's drink of choice.

"Back in Algeria, we were always getting into trouble," he mused, nodding at Khaled, but addressing his whiskey. "One time, we'd been up for three, maybe four days, drinking and carousing and carrying on, breaking windows, whatever. Up to no good.

"Finally," he shrugged, pulling on his mustache, "we were arrested. What else could they do? But when the chief of police saw Khaled being led into court in handcuffs, he was furious; he leaped over the desk and knocked the arresting officer down to the ground and let us go. He even told Khaled that it was okay, he could kick the policeman if he wanted to, if it would make him feel better."

Did he?

"Khaled? No, no, he's a poet, he wants peace and happiness, he wouldn't do something like that. But me . . ." he shrugged, "me, I'm not so nice."

The next night, driving back to Paris from Barcelona, I ask Khaled about the story.

"Yes, of course," Khaled shrugs, as if stating the obvious. "But that was a long time ago. Anyway, that's not the funny part."

The funny part?

"Yes, you know that skinny guy you were talking to? He's a good friend and a big fan of rai—that and whiskey, they're everything to him. Anyway, he's in jail someplace in Algeria, for what, I don't know, there's always something. Whenever he hears that I'm playing a concert somewhere in Spain, he breaks out of jail and sneaks across the border—he doesn't have a passport, of course, he's not that type—hitchhikes to the town I'm playing in and talks his way in. He hears the music, we drink a few bottles, and the next day he sneaks back across the border, gives himself up, and goes back to jail.

"Only last night, he got the times wrong. He broke out of jail, came all the way to Barcelona, and he missed the whole fucking show!" Khaled throws his head back and laughs, beating his hands against the steering wheel and speeding up. We're already going 180 kilometers an hour; accelerating, it feels like we're driving straight into the night sky.

This is the world of *rai*, the Algerian music that has swept North Africa, the Middle East, and now Europe. With its surging rhythms, melding the sultry trance feel of an Oriental belly dance with Latin trumpet, the electronic pulse of hip-hop, and funky, propulsive bass lines, rai may be the most exciting music being made on the planet right now and is the first international sound to develop and take hold since the emergence of reggae over twenty years ago. With wars, emigration, and a constantly declining infant mortality rate creating a population curve, over 60 percent of the people in North Africa and in much of the Middle East are under twenty-five years of age, and rai is their beat, their music, the sound of young Islam getting down to a serious groove. And Cheb (or "young") Khaled, the charismatic architect of modern rai, is their Elvis, their Beatles, and their Sex Pistols rolled into one.

"He represents what rock 'n' roll is really about," says Don Was, the producer of Bonnie Raitt and the B-52's, and the Was part of Was/Not Was, who recently produced tracks for Khaled's first major Western release. "Just like you have to leave Hollywood to make a real movie these days, now it seems like you have to leave America to really find that spirit, that attitude in music. I haven't heard anything this exciting in years."

Given the Gulf War and the recent bombing of the World Trade Center ("Muslims," they said. "Those Muslims."), it's understandable that rai hasn't been given a lot of radio play in America; but all through the Middle East as well, Islamic fundamentalists have gone out of their way to suppress and ban it, and for them Khaled may just be the devil within, their worst nightmare: a passionate and articulate man with an enormous and enthusiastic audience who is preaching the politics of pleasure, the joys of drinking and dancing and making love, having a good time now, on this earth, as opposed to after you're dead. Bad enough that that philosophy is espoused in the West, with its Madonnas and Princes and transsexual madmen luring their youth to hell and beyond; but when the messages comes in their own language, from within their own ranks, that's surely more than they can bear.

"I travelled to Egypt and Tunisia last fall," says Martin Meissonier, the French world music entrepreneur who co-produced *Kutche*, Khaled's last release, "and everywhere I went, Khaled was number one, the most popular album in Morocco, Tunisia, Egypt, Syria. Of course," he sighs, "it was never actually *released* in any of those countries."

Not very long ago, in Algeria's port town of Oran, a man driving through town in a convertible, listening to a tape of Khaled, was dragged out of his car and beaten to death by fundamentalists. Small wonder Khaled has made his home in Marseilles for the last five years, where, among France's three to four million resident Arabs, he is regarded as a king in exile.

Khaled seems an unlikely figure to have caused so much trouble and stirred so much anger; saddled with a reputation as rai's bad boy and known for his excesses with alcohol and women, Khaled comes across as neither a brooding rebel nor a spoiled pop star, but as that rarest of commodities, a genuinely happy man on whom both talent and fortune have smiled. With dark good looks, almond eyes, and thick black hair and mustache, he resembles a handsome Richard Pryor, with a mouth that is sensual and slightly over-indulged, but saved by a warm and easy smile. In performance, it's the laugh you notice first, and it's no accident that all of his concert posters show him laughing, head thrown back in absolute abandon. Surrounded by his band on stage, he seems oblivious to everything but the music; he sings and is clearly delighted by the sound of his voice (a rich, unmistakable baritone that mixes the wail of a muezzin's call to prayer with the sassy bravado of a Wilson Pickett); by the arc of the melody; and by the way the sound swirls around him in spirals of interconnecting rhythms. He stands there locked inside a happiness as serious as a child's, as if pleasure itself were a prayer, and this were the only way to heaven.

In concert, Khaled seems like a character from *The Thousand and One Nights,* an ordinary man who, through chance or luck or by catching an enchanted fish, has suddenly and inexplicably been made king or vizier... and who, just as inexplicably, turns out to be a splendid ruler. In front of his six-piece band, a crack outfit that seems able to read his every gesture, Khaled looks uncontrollably happy, as if he can't believe his good fortune in having this band and this audience, in being able to live this moment. He watches the band proudly: the drummer and percussionist trade patterns, creating a circular rhythm; the bass and guitar player groove, finding a place somewhere between reggae and latin funk; the keyboard keens a high, Oriental melody; and the trumpet player fills in the spaces, a tiny red sports car weaving in and out of traffic.

And then he starts to sing, and the band members take turns grinning at each other, shaking their heads, digging just a little deeper into the beat. Those are the sort of looks people in Jimi Hendrix's band or Charlie Parker's group must have exchanged when Hendrix or Parker started to play and the heavens opened up. You know the look or you can imagine it, the look that says, "We're here, we've found it, that place at the center of the world, that tick at the center of the clock. We're fucking here!" And of course they're right.

The word *"rai"* means "opinion" in Arabic, and like Greek rebetika music or American blues, country, or rap, it's always been based on a straight-talking look at life as it's actually lived, detailing in raw and graphic terms the pain and humiliation of the daily grind while acknowledging the occasional consolations of whiskey and sex.

"In rai, you sing your true feelings," says Khaled. "The lyrics come straight from your life, from your heart. It's about real life, not life as it's supposed to be or as it's shown on TV."

"There is a certain roughness to rai, the same as there's a roughness to blues," explains Cheb Sahroui, a singer and composer, who, with his wife Chaba Fadela, has recorded some of rai's most successful songs. "In some ways it's a reaction to all of the flowery Arabic songs we grew up with, all the flowers in the misty pool and the young gazelle whose heart quickens in the forest of night. I've never seen a gazelle, have you? That's not what our lives are about, those of us who live in cities, those of us who've come to Paris or Marseilles looking for more out of life.

"Rai is about our past as well as our present, it's where we come from as well as where we think we're going. It's about love and money and security. And it's about their absence, their lack.

"I remember a session from a few years ago in Oran, when a singer came in to record a new song. The producer started the tape, and the singer began this really passionate, really gritty piece . . . something like:

> Late tonight
> when the moon is full and golden
> I will fuck you on the floor
> of the dirtiest hotel in town
> and the moon will shine on your ass.

And the producer went *stop!* You can't sing that! You have to tone this down or no one will ever play the record. So the singer took a walk for an hour or so, had a drink, and when he came back, he said, I know how to fix it, no problem, start the tape. And he sang:

> Late tonight
> when the moon is full and golden
> I will fuck you on the floor
> of the most expensive hotel in town."

"Rai really started in the 1920s in Oran," Khaled explains. "The music in the rest of Algeria and in Morocco was different; being a port, Oran had the most nightclubs and bars and bordellos, and it had the most trade, the most travel. The city was open to a real mix of cultures—

Spanish, French, Moroccan, even American, and that mix found its way into the music."

Accompanied by *darbukas* (clay drums) and homemade flutes, local singers would improvise songs about the hardships of life, while listeners would exhort them with shouts of "ya-rai" (roughly, "Tell it like it is," or "Tell me about it!"). Slowly, the rougher qualities of rai were smoothed out, violins and guitars and accordions found their way into the music, and the grit and fire of the lyrics gave way to flowery words and sentiments (even as a more risque form began to thrive underground in bars and back rooms and "whiskey parlors" based around the provocative and sexually charged performances of Cheikha Rimitti).

By the fifties, the coming of television helped soften what was already a watered-down sound, and, with the exception of Messaoud Bellemou (a trumpet player and bandleader who helped electrify and resurrect the spirit of the music) and a few others, rai had drifted into a musical and cultural dead end.

"When I was young," says Khaled, "rai wasn't something that kids would listen to or relate to. It was for old men. They would go off in the evenings and leave their women at home and just sit somewhere with a bottle and listen to rai. It was nightclub music, cabaret music."

Khaled was born Khaled Hadjbrahim on Leap Year—February 29, 1960—in Oran, Algeria, the son of a sometime policeman and his young wife. Fixated on music, by the age of nine or ten, he had learned to play harmonica, bass, guitar, accordion, and anything else he could get his hands on, playing traditional music as well as imitating the pop music from the West that filled the streets and the airwaves.

"We'd listen to the Beatles, James Brown, Johnny Hallyday, all sorts of dance music," Khaled recalls. "No one knew what the words meant, but we'd imitate them anyway. I'd go up to my father and start singing 'Sex Machine,' and he'd just be there smiling. He didn't know what I was singing about. And actually I didn't know what I was singing about!

"We all tried to imitate James Dean, Johnny Hallyday, Gene Vincent, Elvis Presley, trying to find the right look, the right style. My uncle used to go to the barbershop and get what was called a Marlon Brando cut; you had to have a good 'look' if you wanted to pick up girls."

Asked if there weren't Algerian or Arab stars or role models, Khaled is momentarily puzzled, as if the idea itself were odd.

"No, no, no. We had singers, we had musicians, but *the look, the style,* that all came from over there," he says, tilting his head toward an imagined America.

In Oran, as a teenager in the 1970s, Khaled began singing at weddings and was soon noticed and given a chance to cut a single. Released in 1974, when Khaled was fourteen, the song was a sensation. Despite the fact that it was ignored by radio and TV, it was heard all over the streets, in clubs and cabarets and blasting from tape stalls in the markets.

"When we finished the record, the old guy who produced it asked what name I wanted to use; in our culture, entertainers always changed their names. I wanted my own name, so he said, right, you're young, in Arabic that's cheb, so we'll call you Cheb Khaled."

From then on, virtually every artist working in rai has taken on the monicker of Cheb (Chebba for women), not only in emulation of Khaled, but in recognition of Algeria's burgeoning youth culture. Most singers before were older and took on the title Cheikh or Cheikha, a mark of respect (like Master or Sir) but also of age and experience. The title "cheb" not only implied youth, but a certain pride and cockiness in being young, and it had a streetwise edge to it, like DJ or MC.

Khaled's music grew with his career, and as he electrified his sound, adding drum machines and synths and electric guitars, his tapes were labelled "Pop-Rai" to differentiate them from the more traditional and acoustic music of the past. From a dark, spare sound, as raw and powerful as country blues, Khaled's music grew into a dense electric sprawl, rich and entwined as the rhythms of P-Funk or Prince, unbelievably soulful, yet always ethereal (based partly on the fact that unlike most Western funk and dance music that emphasizes the backbeat, the constant 2 and 4, rai puts its emphasis on the one, giving the music an emotional lift). The end result often sounds like reggae that's been sped up and dragged through the casbah.

"That's Moroccan music you're hearing, not reggae," Khaled insists. "I've heard records made from before I was born of Gnawa music that has the same groove as reggae, the same root in the bass, the same rhythm you hear in Bob Marley."

Like Marley in reggae, Khaled has become the central, fixed point in the world of rai, the singer against whom every other singer is measured, the one who is defining the boundaries of the music and, in the process, the boundaries of Algerian culture. By the early eighties, the "Pop-Rai" tag was quietly dropped; Khaled's success was so pervasive that when people talked about rai, nine times out of ten they were talking about him.

For all the acclaim, money was never plentiful. Rai artists were treated much the way blues musicians were in the thirties and forties in America; i.e., publishing and royalties for sales didn't exist, and an artist was simply handed a wad of money (in Khaled's case, usually about $2,000) for each album they recorded. That was all they'd ever earn for that record, and it led to artists rerecording the same songs (with slight variations) for as many labels as possible.

"The people who put out my tapes all have diamond rings and beautiful cars, beautiful women, fine houses, so I know those tapes sold well," Khaled shrugs. "You can find tapes of mine all through the Arab world and all through Europe, but I don't know numbers, I don't really know how many are out there."

Throughout the Arab world, music is sold on cassette, and popular cassettes are easily and frequently bootlegged. There are no pop charts, no *Billboard* top ten lists, and it's convenient for everyone but the artist to be vague about sales figures. According to what passes for reliable information, Khaled sells upwards of two hundred thousand "official" copies of his releases and maybe another million or so in bootlegs in Algeria alone; given his popularity in North Africa and the Middle East, you should probably start multiplying, though whatever number you multiply by, Khaled was still left with the same flat fee of $2,000. To supplement his income Khaled performed at weddings; smuggled cars and motorcycles into Algeria from Morocco; and started to seriously look West.

"I first heard tapes of Khaled in the mid-eighties, and I flipped," says Martin Meissonier. "I went to Algeria to find him and see about making a record, but I found he already had two different 'exclusive' contracts within Algeria alone; putting something together just wasn't possible."

A year later, Meissonier finally got a chance to work with Khaled through the intervention of Safy Boutella, a wealthy young Algerian who had studied music at the Berklee School in Boston and who had government connections; and through Hocine Snoussi, a colonel in the Algerian army who was able to get Khaled a visa and who helped finance a state-of-the-art album recorded in Paris. The record (*Kutche*) has a dedication to Colonel Snoussi, thanking him for "the greatness of his heart." Future pressings may also want to mention the greatness of his bank account; Khaled has yet to receive any royalties from the album, probably his most popular and fully produced work up to now.

"It was a trade," sighs Djellali Ahmed Ourak, Khaled's manager. "Khaled never received a cent from that record, but he got his papers and his freedom. He's been here for five years, and he hasn't been back to Algeria since. At least," he lowers his voice, "not officially."

Never having completed his military service, if he returns, Khaled would be subject to the draft, as well as to the wrath of the fundamentalists, not a cheery prospect in even the best of times. And these are not the best of times.

"Ever since I was young, I've always said what I thought," says Khaled. "There's no anger in it, it's just who I am. The people who like me and my music love that about me, they know I tell the truth; at least my truth. But those who don't like me get furious when they hear my songs because they're about change, and change is dangerous to Islam. Islam doesn't take well to change."

When the weather grows warmer, Khaled gives a free concert on the outskirts of Paris, near Mairie D'Ivry. Khaled and I drive down together, along with Khaled's cousin, a hefty man with a thick black mustache who runs a nearby café.

"In Paris they stop me," his cousin complains, shaking his head as a police car drives past. "They see an Arab in an expensive car and phhht . . . they pull me over. So I go out to L.A. and what happens? They still pull me over, only *there* they think I'm Mexican. And over there I *want* to look Arab. What do I do?"

"Easy," I explain. "Wear a turban and carry a bomb. Works every time."

Humor does not always translate well. Khaled and his cousin stare at me for a moment and then drive on in silence.

"America," Khaled says after a while, shaking his head.

"America," his cousin agrees.

Fortunately, we get lost, which changes the subject. We think we're looking for a concert hall and drive around in circles until a local points out the actual venue: a beautiful sixteenth-century farmyard, enclosed by barns and fences, a stage set up just in front of a chicken coop filled with hens and ducks and turkeys and geese, all of whom stare warily at the throngs of young Algerians pouring into the yard, hoping they're not hungry.

Khaled and his band take the stage late in the afternoon, and even before they begin, the young Arab girls move up front and start to dance, moving to a still-unheard pulse, getting ready, adjusting their rhythms to fit the beat as the music starts; closing their eyes, they lift their arms to just above their heads, their fingers weaving tiny patterns in the air, their hips moving at half the speed of their hands; and then the pattern is reversed and their hips are flying, their hands in slow motion. The men stand back a few paces, drinking beer, watching the women and trying half-heartedly to avoid being pulled into the ring. Dancing, the men seem shy and slightly demure, looking over at their friends as if asking for help, never quite sure what to do with their beers, where to put their feet, while the women luxuriate in the music, at one with the beat, until it seems as if the rhythm is actually coming from their hips, fed to the drummer and the darbuka player by a wild and invisible current.

In the middle of a song, two young girls run onto the stage, and then three more, and then more still, until Khaled is surrounded by sixteen, seventeen, eighteen of them, all embracing him and touching him. And, as the security guard stands momentarily baffled, Khaled simply throws his arms around as many as he can hold, delighted by the scene, carried away by the music, and by all the different pleasures of his life. The moon is just coming up, the air is still, and there is a faint smell of honeysuckle and of fresh-baked bread. And, lost in a sea of girls, surrounded on stage, Khaled simply throws his head back and laughs.

CONTRIBUTORS

ARISTOTLE's "A Music Theory" is taken from *Politics,* Book 8.

W.H. AUDEN's *The Prolific and the Devourer* will be published as a book by The Ecco Press this fall.

AMIRI BARAKA, a poet and playwright, has been awarded a Whiting Fellowship, a Guggenheim Fellowship, and grants for the Rockefeller Foundation and the National Endowment for the Arts among other honors. Recently, *The LeRoi Jones/Amiri Baraka Reader* was published by Thunder's Mouth Press.

WILLIAM BRATTON is the Director of Stazybo and Pomus Music.

HAYDEN CARRUTH's most recent book, *Collected Shorter Poems, 1946–1991,* won the 1993 National Book Award. His other prizes include the Lenore Marshall/*Nation* Poetry Prize, the Ruth Lilly Poetry Prize, and the Governor's Medal from the State of Vermont.

JEANNE WILMOT CARTER is a former book review editor for *Soul Magazine.* Ms. Carter, an attorney practicing in New York, has recently completed her first collection of stories.

ALFRED CORN's sixth book of poetry, *Autobiographies,* was published in 1992 by Viking Penguin.

BRIAN CULLMAN is a writer and composer who lives in New York and in Paris. In 1994, Atlantic Monthly Press will publish his first book, *Opportunity House.*

RACHEL FELDER was Managing Editor of *Alternative Press,* and Director of East Coast A & R for Morgan Creek Records. Ms. Felder currently runs a managing company, Salient, specializing in alternative music. Her book on alternative music, *Manic Pop Thrill,* will be published by The Ecco Press this fall.

INDIRA GANESAN was born in Srirangam, India, and educated largely in the United States. She attended the University of Madras, Vassar College, and the University of Iowa. Her first novel, *The Journey*, was published in 1990 by Alfred A. Knopf. She has won fellowships to the Fine Arts Work Center in Provincetown and the MacDowell Colony.

WILLIAM GASS is the Director of the International Writers Center at Washington University in St. Louis. His novel *The Tunnel* is scheduled for publication by Ticknor & Fields in spring 1994.

BABS GONZALEZ was a jazz pianist, best known for his bop hits, including Oop-Pop-A-Da. He toured extensively in the United States and Europe during the 1940s, '50s, and '60s.

EDWARD GOREY lives on the Massachusettes Cape. A frequent contributor to *The New Yorker,* he has just completed his ninetieth novel.

ALMA GUILLERMOPRIETO is a former South American bureau chief for *Newsweek.* Her book, *Sadness Is Over,* was published by Alfred A. Knopf in 1990.

ELIZABETH HARDWICK is a founder and advisory editor of *The New York Review of Books.* Her many books include *The Ghostly Lover, The Simple Truth,* and *A View of My Own* all published by The Ecco Press. Her most recent book is *Sleepless Nights* (1979).

KEITH JARRETT is a highly acclaimed pianist and composer who works concurrently in jazz, classical, and improvisational music. In 1970–71, he spent one year as a member of the late Miles Davis's group. His most recent recording, *Bye, Bye, Blackbird,* is an homage to Miles.

FEDERICO GARCÍA LORCA, Spain's best-known modern poet, was born in Granada in 1889. He began the study of law but soon abandoned it for the literary life in Madrid. He was murdered by Franco's soldiers in 1936. A bilingual edition of his *Collected Poems* was published by Farrar, Straus and Giroux in 1991. "Cante Jondo" is published by permission of New Directions, Agents for the estate of Federico García Lorca.

WILLIAM MATTHEWS is the author of several books of poetry including, most recently, *New & Selected Poems,* published by Houghton Mifflin & Co.

J.D. McCLATCHY, poet and critic, has written opera libretti for four composers. He is the editor of *The Yale Review.*

STEVEN METCALF is music critic for *The Hartford Courant.*

HOWARD MOSS's "Johann Sebastian Bach" and "Frederic Chopin" first appeared, along with the illustrations by Edward Gorey, in the Ecco Press book, *Instant Lives & More.* Mr. Moss was a National Book Award–winning poet, and poetry editor for *The New Yorker.*

DOC POMUS was inducted into both The Rock and Roll Hall of Fame and The Songwriters' Hall of Fame in 1992. During his long and prolific career he wrote such songs as "Little Sister" and "Viva Las Vegas" for Elvis Presley, "Young Blood" for the Coasters, and "Lonely Avenue" for Ray Charles. Doc Pomus died in 1991. The many journals from which the selections here were culled, are from a book in progress by Sharyn Felder and Peter Giralnick.

NED ROREM is a Pulitzer Prize–winner in musical composition, and the author of twelve books, including *Paris & New York Diaries* and *Settling the Score.* This excerpt is from his forthcoming memoir *Knowing When to Stop.*

MAY SARTON is the author of numerous novels, volumes of poetry, and journals. She lives in York, Maine.

JIMMY SCOTT, born in 1925, is a jazz singer and Sire recording artist of whom Ray Charles has said, "Jimmy Scott had soul when people weren't using the word." This year Mr. Scott was nominated for a Grammy Award for his album *All the Way.* A new album, *Lost and Found,* of material recorded in the 1970s but not released, has recently appeared.

CHARLES SIMIC is the author of sixteen collections of poetry, including the 1990 Pulitzer Prize–winning *The World Doesn't End.* His book of prose meditations on Joseph Cornell, *Dime-Store Alchemy*, was published by Ecco in 1992.

PHIL SPECTOR, the creator of the highly influential "Wall of Sound," is a songwriter and producer who has worked with such groups as the Beatles, the Righteous Brothers, and Ike and Tina Turner.

VIRGIL THOMSON's books include *Music with Words: A Composer's View* and *A Virgil Thompson Reader*. He was the grandfather of us all.

KIMIHIKO YAMASHITA was born in Osaka, Japan in 1957. He has been the editor of *Rockin' f*, *Keyboard Special*, and *Jazz Life*. The interview with Keith Jarrett is from his book of interviews with Keith Jarrett, *Keith Jarrett: Inner Views*. He is currently working on the companion volume to his book on Ryuchi Sakamoto.

AL YOUNG is the author of numerous screenplays, novels, poetry collections, and books of essays on music, including *Things Ain't What They Used to Be*, and *Mingus Mingus: Two Memoirs* (with Janet Coleman). *Heaven: Collected Poems 1956–1990* was recently published by Creative Arts Book Co.

ACKNOWLEDGMENTS

"Notes on Music and Opera" from *The Dyer's Hand and Other Essays* by W.H. Auden. Copyright © 1948, 1950, 1952, 1953, 1954, 1956, 1957, 1958, 1960, 1962 by W.H. Auden. Reprinted by permission of Random House, Inc.

"Paying Dues" excerpted from *I, Paid My Dues*, pages 30–49. Reprinted by permission of Expubidence Publishing Company.

Unterberg Poetry Center

OF THE 92ND STREET Y

Authors reading this season include —
(in order of appearance)

- American Writers
Joyce Carol Oates, Louis Auchincloss, Edmund White, Michael Dorris, Louise Erdrich, James Merrill, Stephen Dobyns, Rosanna Warren, Diane Ackerman, Tracy Kidder, Thulani Davis, Amy Clampitt, Debora Greger, Alice McDermott, Craig Lucas, Terrence McNally, Galway Kinnell, T. Coraghessan Boyle, Max Apple, Cynthia Ozick, Gwendolyn Brooks

- International Writers
Czeslaw Milosz, Mavis Gallant, David Malouf, Ida Fink, Amos Oz, Breyten Breytenbach, Ben Okri, Margaret Atwood, Mario Vargas Llosa, Chinua Achebe, Maryse Condé, Eavan Boland, Andrew Motion, John McGahern, Yves Bonnefoy, Penelope Lively, Caryl Phillips, Leon Rooke

Other Special Programs include —
- Two evenings celebrating the epic poem:
- Derek Walcott's *The Odyssey: A Stage Version*
- Robert Fagles and David Ferry read from their translations of the *Iliad* and *Gilgamesh*.

Derek Walcott

Margaret Atwood

Mario Vargas Llosa

- *The Paris Review*: A 40th Anniversary Reading with Francine du Plessix Gray, Donald Hall, Peter Matthiessen, George Plimpton and Mona Simpson

- The Republic of Verse: A Marathon of 19th Century American Poetry and Song, with twenty writers including Harold Bloom, Allan Gurganus, Anthony Hecht, John Hollander, Maureen Howard, X.J. Kennedy, Ann Lauterbach, J.D. McClatchy, James Merrill, N. Scott Momaday, Thylias Moss, Cynthia Ozick, Robert Pinsky, Calvin Trillin and others

- A Tribute to Zbigniew Herbert with Stanislaw Baranczak, Joseph Brodsky, Daniel Halpern, Susan Sontag and Mark Strand

- An Evening of German Romantic Literature with Irene Worth.

At $125, a Poetry Center Membership entitles you to attend all these events, running September through May, and much more. The Unterberg Poetry Center also offers an extensive Writing Program and a Sunday lecture series, "Biographers and Brunch."

Call **996-1100** for a brochure or to order your tickets.

The Unterberg Poetry Center of the 92nd Street Y
1395 Lexington Ave NYC 10128
An agency of UJA-Federation.   PT502

Amid the cinnamon and tobacco, amid the sounds of singing and berimbou drums, the festival begins and a miracle occurs. It's a time when stone warms to flesh, when a young girl and the city of Bahia change, as a saint walks the earth once again.

"Amado is Brazil's most illustrious and venerable novelist."
—*The New York Times*

"Amado has profound things to say."
—*The New Yorker*

JORGE AMADO
TRANSLATED BY GREGORY RABASSA

"One of the greatest writers alive, he's also one of the most entertaining! His novels display his artistic mastery."
— Mario Vargas Llosa

THE WAR OF THE SAINTS

THE
NATIONAL
POETRY SERIES

ANNOUNCING THE 1994 COMPETITION
BOOK PUBLICATION & $1,000 AWARDS

The National Poetry Series was established in 1978 to recognize and promote excellence in contemporary poetry by ensuring the publication of five books of poetry each year through a series of participating publishers. This year, five distinguished poets will each select one winning manuscript for publication from entries to the Open Competition. Each winner will also receive a $1,000 Award.

Recent Judges: Charles Simic, C.K. Williams, W.S. Merwin, Denise Levertov, Sharon Olds, Margaret Atwood, James Merrill, Seamus Heaney, Louise Glück, Carolyn Forché, and Robert Hass.

Entry Period: January 1 - February 15, 1994.

Entry Requirements: Previously unpublished book-length manuscripts of poetry accompanied by a $25.00 entrance fee. You must be an American citizen to participate. Due to the large volume of submissions received, manuscripts cannot be returned.

FOR A COPY OF THE COMPLETE GUIDELINES,
PLEASE SEND A STAMPED, SELF-ADDRESSED ENVELOPE TO:

THE NATIONAL POETRY SERIES
P.O. BOX G
HOPEWELL, NJ 08525

THE
FOLGER
POETRY
SERIES

25th ANNIVERSARY

**CALENDAR
OF READINGS
1993-1994**

JOHN FREDERICK NIMS
Winner of the O.B. Hardison Jr. Poetry Prize
October 21, 8 p.m.

KENNETH CARROLL & WANDA COLEMAN
November 16, 8 p.m.

FRANK BIDART
Emily Dickinson Birthday Reading
December 9, 8 p.m.

RITA DOVE
January 20, 8 p.m.

GALWAY KINNELL
February 8, 8 p.m.

AGHA SHAHID ALI & KILLARNEY CLARY
March 3, 8 p.m.

CZESLAW MILOSZ & ROBERT HASS
Folger Poetry Board Reading
April 8, 8 p.m.

LUCILLE CLIFTON
May 17, 8 p.m.

THE FOLGER SHAKESPEARE LIBRARY
201 E. Capitol St., S.E.
Washington, D.C. 20003

FOR INFORMATION CALL: (202) 544-7077